The demand for work-ready graduates who are familiar with organizational practices in the workplace is increasing, and so the need for greater work integrated learning is a growing concern for the education sector. With the globalization of higher education and the cultural and linguistic challenges this brings, work integrated learning has become a core strategic issue for many organizations. Examining work integrated learning as a process of integration between workplaces, higher education institutions, government, business and industry, this book includes:

- strategies for managing work integrated learning experiences;
- the what, when, where, why and who of work integrated learning across professions;
- advice on building relationships between higher education and the workplace;
- guidance on preparing learners effectively for work;
- practical case studies from first-hand experience;
- direct information and instruction on the use of work integrated learning.

Work Integrated Learning is a practical guide that can be used by the education sector and employers alike. An integrated resource, applicable to all involved in work integrated learning, it will also appeal to pro-vice-chancellors of teaching and learning, work integrated learning coordinators, careers services, and all those involved with standards and competency.

Lesley Cooper is Acting Principal and Vice-President at the Laurier Brantford Campus at Wilfred Laurier University, Canada, and Adjunct Professor of Social Work at Flinders University, Australia.

Janice Orrell is a Higher Education Consultant and Adjunct Associate Professor in the School of Education at Flinders University, Australia.

Margaret Bowden is a Research Assistant and Thesis Editing Consultant at Flinders University, Australia.

Work Integrated Learning

A guide to effective practice

Lesley Cooper, Janice Orrell and Margaret Bowden

Routledge
Taylor & Francis Group

LONDON AND NEW YORK

This first edition published 2010
by Routledge
2 Park Square, Milton Park, Abingdon, Oxon, OX14 4RN

Simultaneously published in the USA and Canada
by Routledge
270 Madison Avenue, New York, NY 10016

Routledge is an imprint of the Taylor & Francis Group, an informa business

© 2010 Lesley Cooper, Janice Orrell and Margaret Bowden

Typeset in Galliard by
Pindar NZ, Auckland, New Zealand
Printed and bound in Great Britain by
TJ International Ltd, Padstow, Cornwall

British Library Cataloguing in Publication Data
A catalogue record for this book is available from the British Library

Library of Congress Cataloging-in-Publication Data
Cooper, Lesley.
Work integrated learning : a guide to effective practice / Lesley
Cooper, Janice Orrell and Margaret Bowden. — 1st ed.
    p. cm.
  Includes bibliographical references.
  1. Career education. I. Orrell, Janice. II. Bowden, Margaret. III. Title.
  LC1037.C66 2010
    371.2'27—dc22   2009040602

ISBN10: 0-415-55676-7 (hbk)
ISBN10: 0-415-55677-5 (pbk)
ISBN10: 0-203-85450-0 (ebk)

ISBN13: 978-0-415-55676-7 (hbk)
ISBN13: 978-0-415-55677-4 (pbk)
ISBN13: 978-0-203-85450-1 (ebk)

Contents

Tables and Figures

Tables

Figures

Acknowledgements

This book has been enriched by the input of numerous people who have freely given their time and knowledge to the authors. These include work integrated learning curriculum designers, coordinators, supervisors, teachers, learning guides, students and placement providers who participated in interviews and focus groups, or provided us with written examples of issues that arise in work integrated learning and ways they deal with these. Thank you to the following people for sharing their experiences with us: Hannah Armitage, student, American Studies, Flinders University; Stacey Attril, Clinical Educator, Speech Pathology, Flinders University; Jan Baker, Work Integrated Learning Coordinator, Speech Pathology, Flinders University; Lesley Bastian, student, Nursing and Midwifery, Flinders University; Elaine Bourne, Placement Coordinator, Social Work, Flinders University; Heath Bowden, Accounting student, Flinders University and workplace learning guide; Michael Bull, Field Staff Supervisor, Social Work, Flinders University; Deidre Butler, Work Integrated Learning Supervisor, South Australian Department of Correctional Services; Luita Casey, Indigenous student, Health Sciences, Flinders University; Penny Clark, International Student Placement Liaison, Social Work, Flinders University; Giordana Cross, Nutrition and Dietetics, Work Integrated Learning Partnership model, Flinders University; Linda Cruickshank, Work Integrated Learning Supervisor, South Australian Department of Correctional Services; Glenn Dods, Sportsmed South Australia, previous work integrated learning experience provider; Kay Edgecombe, Dedicated Education Unit coordinator, Nursing and Midwifery, Flinders University; Chris Fanning, Work Integrated Learning Coordinator, Cultural Tourism, Flinders University; Helen Gooley, Work Integrated Learning Supervisor, South Australian Department of Correctional Services; John Grantley, Work Integrated Learning Coordinator, Disability Studies, Flinders University; John Harris, Manager, Practicum and Teaching Experience Programmes, Flinders University; Annie Jarvis, Work Integrated Learning Coordinator, Social Work, Flinders University; Helen Jones, Inspire Mentor Programme researcher, Flinders University; Verity Kingsmill, Graduate Skill Development Coordinator, Careers and Employment Liaison Centre, Flinders University; Katherine Koerner, Coordinator Inspire Mentor Programme, Flinders University; Gillian Lay, Manager, Equal Opportunity and Diversity Unit,

Flinders University; Maureen Lynch, Work Placement Coordinator, Bachelor of Business Information Systems, University of South Australia; Sue McAllister, Manager COMPASS project, Sydney and Newcastle Universities; Sue Maywald, Field Education Coordinator, Social Work, Flinders University; Ola Osthus, practitioner and work integrated learning international student, Social Work, Flinders University; Susan Owens, Steven Penley and Ollie Peters, Work Integrated Learning Supervisors, South Australian Department of Correctional Services; Cathy Pocknee, Curriculum Coordinator, Swinburne University of Technology; Lange Powell, Director, Community Corrections South Australia; Katie Priest, student, Social Work, Flinders University; Soon Lean Keng, international student, Nursing and Midwifery, Flinders University; Rachel Spencer, Director of Practical Legal Training, Flinders University; Kathleen Stalker, Coordinator of Interlink Programme, TAFE South Australia; Julia Stott, Graduate Recruitment Coordinator, Careers and Employer Liaison Centre, Flinders University; Heather Sutton, Nursing and Midwifery, Flinders University; Raylene Walker, Work Integrated Learning Supervisor, South Australian Department of Correctional Services. Their input was especially valuable in the writing of Chapters 3 and 7.

We are indebted to Richard Freeland for his tireless critical reading of chapters as they evolved and his humorous editorial comments that both lightened and enlightened the writing process.

It is with appreciation that we acknowledge those who have given us permission to quote or reproduce from their copyrighted material: John Biggs and the Higher Education Academy for use of Biggs' curriculum model; the National Commission for Cooperative Education for use of material from their website http://www.co-op.edu/aboutcoop.htm; e-Content Management for an excerpt from Grealish and Trevitt (2005); Flinders University Staff Development and Training Unit for reuse of material from *Working to Learn: Practicum Online* (Orrell, Cooper, Bridge and Bowden 2003) and *Workplace Learning Management Manual* (Cooper, Orrell and Bowden 2003); Jennifer Moon and the Higher Education Academy for an excerpt about reflection (Moon 2005); NCVER for use of factors identified as needed for learning guides to be successful learning facilitators (Smith and Blake 2005); Purich Publishing for use of excerpts from Battiste and Henderson's (2000) work on Indigenous knowledge; Sage Publications for use of Étienne Wenger's (2000) definition of 'communities of practice'; Victoria University Australia for material related to their 'Learning in the workplace and Community' initiative; John Wiley and Sons for Barbara Jacoby's (1996) definition of service-learning and excerpts from Merriam and Caffarella (1999); Lee Harvey for use of material from Harvey, Moon and Geall (1997) and Harvey, Geall and Moon (1998); Wolters Kluwer Health (*Academic Medicine* 65[Suppl]) for use of Miller's (1990) hierarchy of assessment model; and Professor Gordon Page for use of his adaptation of Miller's (1990) model (Waterman Oration 2000).

We also acknowledge the support of our families, in particular our respective partners Dick, Norman and Donald, who have sacrificed much personal time with us during the writing of this book.

Glossary

This glossary includes terms that are used interchangeably throughout the text, and those that are used in different contexts and so require definition.

Academics teachers and researchers in the higher education institution.

Academy formal higher education learning institution. Interchangeable with higher education institution, institution or university. Used particularly in sections of the book discussing cooperative learning models.

Assessment evaluation of student progress toward achieving the intended learning outcomes of work integrated learning.

Civic engagement university and student engagement with not-for-profit organizations; active student involvement in community problems; demonstration of values, knowledge, skills, efficacy and commitment (Eyler and Giles 1999: 157).

Civic responsibility understanding community needs and making active contributions towards those needs. Grows from civic engagement. One of the intended outcomes of service learning.

Classroom the formal teaching and learning context within the university.

Clients people to whom organizations or workplaces provide service and to whom they have a duty of care. In its broadest sense includes patients, consumers, community members and customers.

Communities of practice groups of people or communities with a shared knowledge, expectations, skills sets, understandings, products, ideas about the way things should be and aims for future action.

Consumers *see* clients, patients, customers.

Coordinators

1. Work integrated learning coordinators *in the university* whose role is to negotiate, coordinate and manage learning opportunities with workplaces, provide support to students and workplace supervisors during the work integrated learning programme, and resolve difficulties that may arise. They are normally employees of the university.

2. Workplace coordinators, otherwise known as workplace supervisors or mentors who support student learning *within the workplace* and liaise

with university coordinators. They are normally employees of the host organization.

Co-op   short term for cooperative education/cooperative learning.

Course of study   student's overall programme of study in the university which incorporates a work integrated learning component. Used interchangeably with programme of study.

Curriculum   all those elements that contribute to and influence students' learning experiences and outcomes. The broadest concept of curriculum includes the explicit and implicit learning agenda; students and their characteristics; the educational processes and activities (teaching, learning and assessment); and the learning environment.

Duty of care   legal and ethical requirement of ensuring as far as possible that no harm will come to any people involved in human transactions. In this case, it refers to the work integrated learning programme, involving transactions between all stakeholders, including the university, students, coordinators, workplaces and their clients.

Expert   a person in the workplace who possesses and generates advanced practice knowledge. Their practice is typified by automaticity grounded in wisdom of experience often referred to as 'expert intuition'. Expert also referred to as a 'professional practitioner'. Benner (1984) argues that development of expertise requires a minimum of ten years' continuous practice.

Higher education institution   *see* academy. Used interchangeably with university, academy and institution.

Host organization   organization with which the university has a work integrated learning partnership. Differentiated from 'workplace', since a single host organization may have several workplaces in which students undertake their work integrated learning experiences.

Industry   overarching term for a collective field of endeavour or enterprise.

Integration   the act or process of assimilating diverse elements to make whole or entire.

Learners   the students undertaking work integrated learning experiences. As students, they come to the workplace as learners. Used interchangeably with students.

Learning guides   teachers in the workplace who guide students in learning workplace practices. May also be called supervisors, coordinators or mentors, but here we differentiate between their role and that of the supervisor. Whilst supervisors are learning guides, they have greater managerial and administrative duties than other learning guides.

Mentors   *see* above concerning learning guides. Can be used interchangeably.

Parties   those directly involved in specific situations or actions in work integrated learning programmes, mainly in relation to difficult situations that arise and any legal or ethical implications. Differentiated from stakeholders, which refers to all those seeking benefit in work integrated learning programmes.

Partners   stakeholders involved in the work integrated learning partnerships between the higher education institution and host organization. Usually involves the institution, the host organization and sometimes the students.

Patients   people to whom health care providers have a duty of care. Like clients, patients expect certain standards of service and care.

Placement/work placement   another term for work integrated learning experience.

Professional practitioner   *see* expert.

Programme of study   the student's whole university course, not just the work integrated learning programme.

Real world   the world of work and community life in general in contrast to formal university classes.

Reciprocal learning   process of social and educational exchange in which the teacher and the student intentionally exchange learning and teaching roles.

Stakeholder   generic term for all parties involved in the work integrated learning process, including the university, university coordinator, student, workplace, workplace supervisor/coordinator, workplace learning guides, host organization and clients.

Stakeholder approach   rights and needs of all stakeholders are considered. Each stakeholder is inducted into their roles and responsibilities in preparation for work integrated learning.

Students   *see* learners. The term students is used interchangeably with learners as our focus is on the students as learners.

Supervisor/supervisory teacher   main person in the workplace who works with the student and the university coordinator to facilitate the student's learning in the workplace context. Sometimes called workplace coordinator or a mentor. Differentiated from 'learning guides' in the workplace who help the student learn workplace practice because the supervisor plays a greater role. Responsible for managing the student's learning in the workplace, communicating with the university coordinator and teaching the student how to reflect on their practice during supervision sessions.

Teachers   refers to the teachers in the university. We use the term 'learning guides' for teachers in the workplace, which is interchangeable with mentors.

University   *see* academy and higher education institution. Interchangeable.

Work integrated learning experience   time students spend learning in the workplace as part of the work integrated learning component of their formal programme of study. Also referred to as placement.

Work integrated learning   the intersection and engagement of theoretical and practice learning. The process of bringing together formal learning and productive work, or theory and practice. Constructing one system using available knowledge from several separate sources. Other terms used to describe work integrated learning include practicum, internships, fieldwork, cooperative education, field education, sandwich course, service learning, international service learning.

Work-based learning   term for learning programmes that are instigated by, and begin within a workplace. Industries and organizations negotiate with universities to accredit learning and accumulated expertise that has developed through practice within the workplace and professional development. This recognition of work-based learning is also enhanced with supplemental theoretical education provided by the universities. These programmes are driven by learning organizations that seek to enhance the capabilities of their existing workforce. Work integrated learning has broader goals – gaining a competitive edge in the student enrolment market, forging authentic, comprehensive industry and community partnerships, and producing work-ready graduates.

Workplace   the context in which students undertake the work integrated learning experiences that form part of their overall programme of study. May be an organization, a workplace that is part of an organization with many workplaces, or a private workplace run by its own management, policies and ways of working. The workplace is a learning environment within which two learning agendas are proactively managed so that students *work in order to learn* and at the same time *learn to work*. These two different but complementary learning agendas are recognized in terms of the instructional and supervisory arrangements, and legal, ethical and duty of care considerations.

Workplace learning   learning that happens in the workplace. Interchangeable with work integrated learning and learning in the workplace.

Workplace organization   the organization to which the workplace belongs. The organization would oversee policies, procedures and management structures in the workplace.

Introduction

This book provides a practical guide for designing and managing learning programmes that occur in the workplace. It focuses on workplace learning programmes that are implemented as a formal aspect of higher education curricula. The term growing in popularity for such programmes is *work integrated learning*. One of the major issues at the moment is the diverse range of programmes that fit this definition of this term and the variety of terms used to describe them. The programmes include cooperative education, collaborative education, learning in the workplace and the community, clinical education, field education, service learning and more. These terminologies are defined in the Glossary and the differences and similarities are described in Chapter 2. For the purposes of this book, what unites them is that they are an intentional aspect of a university curriculum whereby the learning is *situated* within the act of working, whether that work occurs within a recognizable workplace or a community. The term integration is significant because the principal purpose is the nexus of work and learning; each informs and critiques the other.

Another associated term is *work-based learning*. Some programmes that would fall under our definition of work integrated learning may use this term. However, we use the term work-based learning to signify another form of education in which the degree programme is based almost entirely in the workplace. This may result from a contract between an industry and a particular university whereby significant aspects of workplace activities of employees and their in-house professional development are accredited as parts of a degree (see Boud and Solomon 2001). This book does not address this type of programme.

Yet another commonly associated term is *work experience*. We reserve this term for the exploratory, observational programmes largely used by secondary education in which students are exposed to the world of work in order to gain some insight into potential life careers. This kind of experience does occur at the post-compulsory level of education, but it is largely a voluntary experience and notably is not an element of the formal curriculum.

The critical factor that distinguishes the focus of interest in this book is learning that is situated in the workplace or the community. It is a formal aspect of a university curriculum in which the learning is expected to entail an integration of theory and practice. Ideally the learning is intentional, guided by explicit objectives that have associated expected outcomes in terms of capacity to practise. This description is, of course, an ideal state. It is largely about students *working to learn*, while acknowledging that a major driver is often about students *learning to work*. The differences between these two conceptions will be described in Chapter 3.

Background to the book

The thinking and perspectives that foreground the concepts in this book are the result of 15 years of collaborative scholarship, research and development in universities by the authors, with regard to the design and management of workplace learning and its practice. Their collective viewpoints have been grounded in diverse stakeholder experiences including placements as students in professional education degree programmes, workplace supervision, as university supervisors and placement programme coordinators, as researchers of work integrated learning and as academic developers of work integrated learning in professional development in universities. The initial collaborations of the authors in the field of work integrated learning within social work, nursing and teacher education have broadened over time to include explorations of institutional, national and international perspectives. Especially important in their explorations was the identification of the ways that different disciplinary, professional, policy, cultural and legislative environments would impact on the management and design of workplace learning programmes. An element of the collaboration was to conduct a detailed institutional audit of the practice of learning in the workplace in their institution at the time (Flinders University, Adelaide, Australia). They found, as did other universities who followed suit, that there was no single database in the institution to indicate which degree programmes included workplace learning in the formal curriculum or to account for the numbers of students, staff and host organizations involved. Furthermore, unlike the emerging flexible/online education initiatives, there was no immediate line responsibility for the quality and conduct of work integrated learning in university education. Therefore, it remained largely invisible, without infrastructure or policies to support its practice.

As a result of this study, the senior leadership and wider Flinders University community were surprised to find that in any one year over one third of all students were learning out in workplaces. Large gaps in policy and infrastructure were found; inadequate processes for preparing students for placements and debriefing them were made apparent and large gaps in the quality assurance and student evaluation systems were identified. These findings mobilized institution-wide action. As other institutions became aware of the outcomes and impact of this audit and study, they too followed suit and their findings were not dissimilar. This was a watershed for this university and a number of others. Significant learning was also gained from collaborations involving bringing together academics and workplace supervisors from industry and government to identify and examine the range of issues that were important to them with regard to work placements.

An important feature of this study was that it was well funded both from within the university and from external sources (Committee for University Teaching and Staff Development (CUTSD)). It also had the support and engagement of all of the senior leadership of the institution. This support permeated down through faculties and departments to achieve a level of participation rarely experienced before. This enabled a high level of consultation and supported engagement of the university-based frontline practitioners. The study also engaged its stakeholders. Students were an important and valued voice. Government officers were interested in the outcomes and requested and funded additional work investigating the scope and requirements of rural placements. Finally, its findings were incrementally reported to, and discussed with, national teaching and learning networks, and the outputs were shared with other institutions which developed them further, thereby enhancing the innovation and its possibilities.

The situation today is vastly different from the conditions that motivated the study little more than a decade ago. Governments and universities are now deeply interested in the scope and quality of work integrated learning programmes, which have become a vital higher education enterprise. It is interesting to note that at the inception of the initial study there were very few institutional, national or international forums for sharing and developing knowledge and practice in this regard.

Today, 2010, the informal and formal networks in Australia and New Zealand have coalesced into national bodies such as the New Zealand Co-operative Network (NZACE) and the Australian Co-operative Network (ACEN), among others, which are formally aligned with an international body, the World Association of Cooperative Education (WACE). There is also the Canadian Co-operative Education Society, the United States of America has its National Commission for Cooperative Education and the United Kingdom has multiple Centres for Excellence that focus on professional and experiential learning (see for example SCEPTrE and The Institute for Work-Based Learning).These national and international networks have assisted in changing a field of academic work that was private and marginalized within institutions into a vibrant field of study that informs institutional development and plans, and encourages and disseminates the scholarship in the field. Its outputs can be readily observed in emerging, innovative institutional and government agendas and strategic plans. These are important factors to remember with the growth of the national and international movements to support and develop work integrated learning if systemic cultural change in this field is to become a reality. This issue will be addressed more fully in Chapter 1. The point to be made here is that the experiences of the authors as contributors to this emergent field of practice and scholarship have influenced significantly the content of this book.

Work integrated learning as an emerging higher education interest

Changing patterns of technology have altered the demand for particular occupations and skills, and require that employees' skill and knowledge level be developed continuously. This change has contributed to the new interest in work integrated learning. In addition, increased global competition amongst institutions for students has contributed significantly to the changed status of work integrated learning in higher education. There is considerable competition between universities to brand themselves in their competition for students. Many universities are now insisting that students combine work experience with academic work. Employers are also demanding these changes as they seek graduates who are work-ready and familiar with organizational practice. Universities are concerned that there is a move away from the liberal arts degree into more career-oriented courses. Work integrated learning provides a way for some universities to promote their institutional distinctiveness; to maintain students' interest in liberal arts while exposing them to both theory and practice; to contribute to the development of citizens with social responsibility; and to address the general concern that education has become too theorized. Work integrated learning, especially service learning, has been construed as an answer to the question: how do you produce a well-rounded person?

Work integrated learning is now seen as a strategy for developing knowledge workers for the knowledge economy who are competent not only in specific vocational skills, which increasingly include information technology skills, but also in understanding the interconnections between theoretical, practical and general life experience knowledge. The intention behind work integrated learning is to produce graduates who are able to integrate, adapt and apply this knowledge across diverse global contexts (Organisation for Economic Co-operation and Development 1996).

It is assumed that an emphasis on learning in the workplace will increase the innovative capacity within organizations. In the United Kingdom, employers anticipate that they will need job-related skills specific to their organization and to the industry more generally. This is in addition to core skills, including computing skills, communication and social skills, and problem-solving skills (Glass *et al.* 2002).

The partnerships between higher education institutions and work or community organizations are often based on goodwill alone. The new interest in work integrated learning is provoking universities to change their systems to find ways to engage in programmes and partnerships that are mutually beneficial. Despite this current emphasis on work integrated learning, in many instances there is no incentive for organizations to participate in the time- and resource-hungry practice of taking students under their wing and facilitating learning in real-world work contexts. So why is participation in work integrated learning programmes and partnerships increasing so rapidly?

If benefits are to accrue to those participating in work integrated learning enterprises, it is essential that the work integrated learning process is designed, implemented and continuously managed to meet as many needs as possible of the three major stakeholders: the higher education institution, the student and the host organization workplace, including the workplace staff who act as learning guides for students. We argue that those participating in work integrated learning programmes benefit from a four-way investment in their future:

- an investment in the organization's sustainability due to recruitment of future employees with the knowledge, skills and attributes to ensure the organization's ability to meet constantly changing demands;
- an investment in the student's professional, personal and civic educational development, and future employment and civic participation;
- an investment in sustainable higher education institution–organization partnerships and links with the institutions' local communities; and
- an investment in the future good of communities and society as a whole due to integration and sharing of theoretical, practical and life knowledge, and development of future generations of confident, competent, innovative, professional, civic-minded individuals equipped with the skills, knowledge and attitudes to lead in the face of ongoing change. This is the ideal outcome of work integrated learning.

The place of workplace learning programmes in university curricula

Despite a long history of workplace learning in both higher education and technical and further education, the nature of this learning has largely escaped the attention of traditional educational researchers who are only now producing important, extensive findings on the impact of partnerships between work, real-world learning and formal study (Billett 2001, 2002, 2004, 2006, 2009; Coll *et al.* 2009; and Eraut 2004, among others). This research has produced substantial evidence that there are considerable differences in the way learning occurs in actual real-world environments in contrast to how it occurs in university classrooms. Most importantly, there is evidence to demonstrate that real-world learning in the workplace has a positive impact on students' overall learning, and that motivation and engagement are also enhanced significantly. This positive outcome, however, does require considerable effort and resources. It comes at a significant cost to all stakeholders.

Unfortunately, within universities themselves, the two learning environments, namely the practicum and the theoreticum, are regarded as competing rather than complementary modes of learning. Learning in the workplace and community is often seen as a challenge to limited curriculum resources and time. The notions of synergy and integration between classroom, workplace and community-based learning cuts to the heart of contemporary concerns and will underpin much of the discussion in the following chapters. At its best, however, learning in the workplace and community can be a highly valuable, complementary part of a whole. This very positive impact rarely happens by accident but is reflected in careful, intentional curriculum planning, well-prepared students and authentic, constructive and mutually beneficial alliances between university disciplines and their related industries and community groups.

An issue that is sometimes forgotten when creating learning in the workplace partnerships is the recognition of, and agreement to work within, the differences between the university and host organization cultures. These differences are central to most rationales given to support the inclusion of work integrated learning programmes. The difference between workplaces and learning institutions is an important catalyst for learning, yet it can often be regarded as a barrier to learning. An essential requirement for effective workplace learning programmes is the establishment of partnerships to engender confidence and maintain respect for each other, and to foster collegiality that will ensure that experiences, knowledge, ideas and resources are shared. This can be accomplished through establishing initial and ongoing consultation and communication leading to continuous collaboration and cooperation. Honest feedback should be able to flow among partners to enable quality assurance and enhancement. Such relationships require a cultural shift in both universities and workplaces.

Professional development for participants

Professional development for the leaders and stakeholders is a critical element of effective programmes. We understand that in writing this guide we must allow for enormous diversity. There are major differences in the various disciplinary and professional approaches to learning in the workplace and in the community as an integral aspect of a university programme of study. In writing this book we are attempting to reflect upon and help you, the reader, understand the vast differences in approaches to designing and managing workplace learning programmes. Almost as vast is the diverse potential that, as yet, has not been tapped because so many programmes have been based on tradition, guided by routines and operated within silos, rather than engaging with their common concerns that occur in the all-too-evident differences in contexts, for example human services, health, science and technology, arts and research. Chapter 2 will begin the process of exposing this diversity.

Management of the proceses to support effective programmes

The management of work integrated learning programmes is a critical and essential role. We have found, however, that all too often this becomes a 'short straw job' or one reserved for entry academics. This is unfortunate and, as a result, the potential impact of many programmes is reduced. The development and management of workplace learning programmes is complex. Programme coordinators and managers need to become expert at devising effective strategies for:

- developing authentic and entrepreneurial partnerships;
- preparing students for the practicalities of the work environment;
- setting up efficient lines of communication with all involved;
- clearly identifying each other's expectations from work integrated learning;
- preparing workplaces as learning places;
- identifying and preparing the 'learning guides';
- seeking and allocating resources;
- working realistically within these resources;
- devising programmes for practical work-based experiences (may be structured or other);
- designing assessment – negotiating the authentic purpose of the assessment, what will be assessed, how it will be assessed, who will do it and how it will be interpreted and reported;
- establishing quality assurance and improvement processes, including making suggestions to policymakers.

Developing learning in the workplace programmes: A philosophy

This book is grounded in a philosophy that posits that workplace learning programmes are not new and that to be effective they have to be an integral part of university programmes. Furthermore, evidence makes it clear that effective learning in the workplace comes at a cost to all stakeholders. To warrant the attendant costs, therefore, the potential value and impact will depend primarily on grounding the programmes in clear intentions. There are quite diverse intentions that form the drivers of workplace learning programmes. The intentions underpinning each programme are often quite unique and localized to particular professional and disciplinary orientations, and to individual degree programmes. However, increasingly 'top-down' drivers have emerged from a new awareness and new motivations, and are observable in institutional strategic planning. Drivers for a particular programme might include a unique combination of the following:

- the *employability* of graduates, often codified as *work-ready graduates*;
- to provide opportunities for students' *civic engagement and service learning*;
- response to, or driven by, a need to generate *student interest*;
- requirements imposed by *professional/vocational registration/certification or professional statutory requirements*;
- to build on students' awareness of potential careers and *career development*;
- to develop students' dispositions with regard to *global citizenship*;
- to increase students' *workplace literacy* (educational);

- to enable and enhance *knowledge generation and transformation* (generic educational);
- *personal development* through enhancement of students' capacity for communication, negotiation, empathy and self-awareness;
- response to *consumer agency*;
- to enhance individual universities' *competitiveness and marketability*.

These drivers will be considered in depth in the following chapters, particularly in the comparison of the different models and modes of learning in the workplace and community in Chapter 2. Suffice to note that they are borne out in the explication of each programme's aims and expected learning outcomes.

Quality in workplace learning

Our collective experience, research and scholarship across two continents have led us to enumerate the following qualities of learning in the workplace programmes, which are supported by the conceptual work of Calway (2006).

Qualities of workplace learning programmes

1 The university programme is intentional, as is the engagement of the host organization.
2 All aspects of the programme are held to be an integral part of the institutional endeavour and, therefore, have the sponsorship of the university leadership.
3 The work integrated learning process has a set of core philosophical, educational, legal and ethical values that are common to all programmes in the institution.
4 The programme is integrated. This encompasses integration of work and learning and integration of workplace learning within the broader curriculum.
5 Practice is a core feature of the learning, but not at the expense of due regard to theory and research-generated evidence.
6 There is recognition and validation of the involvement of multiple stakeholders.
7 Programmes are designed to achieve mutual benefit and reciprocity for all stakeholders, and there are processes in place to ensure this occurs.
8 Assessment of the learning is an important factor and integral to the learning, because the assessment defines the concept of the work. The assessment of the student learning achievement is the ultimate responsibility of the university, but is informed by multiple stakeholders.
9 The programme is enhanced by authentic partnerships.
10 The programme is the fulcrum for engagement of the university and its community (a term used in its widest sense), and is visible in institutional infrastructure, policy and planning.

It can be noted from these statements that to assure and enhance the quality of workplace learning programmes, institutions will need to adopt a comprehensive approach to evaluation and enhancement, with a need for multiple points of evaluation from multiple sources. The evaluation cannot be focused on individual programmes but must recognize that they are situated in educational, industrial, economic and political contexts, all of which impact and inform any quality assurance process.

How to use this book

This book provides a hands-on approach to the everyday activities of work integrated learning, addressing issues that arise (presented as both direct instruction and case studies/scenarios derived from actual experience to encourage reader reflection), and providing strategies to simplify management of work integrated learning. It explores the what, when, where, why, who and how of work integrated learning. It addresses some of the hard issues that are often neglected, such as the difficulties that arise and the impact of the human factor on the real outcomes of work integrated learning.

How to read this book

There are three major sections in this book. The first encompasses Chapters 1 and 2 and explores aspects of leadership and vision (Chapter 1) as well as conceptually scoping the diverse dimensions of work integrated learning to discriminate between what it is and what it is not (Chapter 2). The second section focuses on the curriculum dimensions of work integrated learning in Chapters 3, 4, 5 and 6, and explores elements and issues of learning and learners (Chapter 3), teaching (Chapter 4), assessment (Chapter 5) and supervision (Chapter 6). The final section focuses on management concerns and explores the problematic nature of work integration and ways to mitigate against the inherent risks (Chapter 7). The book culminates in a detailed guide to the work integrated learning process; how to incorporate all the issues addressed in the preceding chapters to design a work integrated learning programme from the perspective of an institutional manager and leader, as well as from that of a programme coordinator (Chapter 8).

There is some repetition from chapter to chapter, but this is necessary so that each chapter can be read on its own, or in conjunction with the other chapters. Each chapter begins with an overview of its content and brief definitions or descriptions of its main focus. Tables of major points, key issues and strategies, diagrams of theoretical concepts and case studies/scenarios specific to the context intersperse the text. Each chapter provides a comprehensive exploration of its principal focus and can stand alone. The following is a detailed overview of each chapter.

Chapter 1, 'The New Higher Education Enterprise', provides a brief historical background to the current interpretation and forms of work integrated learning and its increasing value. It discusses the evolution of work integrated learning over the last two decades from a 'cottage industry' to the new paradigm, with recognition of its increased importance for students, higher education institutions and work organizations. Emphasis is placed on the higher education environment, quality leadership and management, new roles and tasks for institutional leaders, the imperative of building solid partnerships between higher education institutions, their communities and work organizations/industry, and the importance of evaluation of work integrated learning programmes to ensure sustainability.

Chapter 2, 'A Conceptual Framework for Work Integrated Learning', clarifies terminologies used for work integrated learning and makes distinctions between programmes that are or are not classified as 'work integrated learning'. Seven key dimensions in all work integrated learning programmes are identified and described: purpose; context; integration; curriculum; learning; partnerships; and support. Each subsequent chapter in the book focuses on one or more of these dimensions. The major focus of Chapter 2 is on the detailed description of three models of work integrated learning – professional internships, service learning and cooperative education models – and the distinctions and similarities between them.

The third chapter, 'Working to Learn, Learning to Work', focuses on the curriculum domain, which incorporates learning and the learning context. This chapter discusses pedagogies of learning and describes the learning agenda – the ideal for work integrated learning – the learners and the importance of understanding the impact of learner characteristics on their interactions with the work integrated learning environment.

Chapter 4, 'Teaching in Work Integrated Learning', is closely linked to Chapter 3. Its main focus is on the curriculum, context, integration and support domains. It describes the differences between teaching in the university and teaching in the workplace, responsibilities of university teachers in preparing students for learning and supporting them during learning, the task of workplaces to prepare students for learning in the workplace, and teaching strategies that will enable integrated learning to take place.

Chapter 5, 'Assessing Work Integrated Learning', discusses the curriculum and integration domains of the framework in relation to assessment. This chapter provides a set of guiding principles for work integrated learning assessment and examines the challenges inherent in assessing work integrated learning; the purposes of assessment; what is assessed, what can be assessed and how assessments might be conducted and interpreted; and how the resulting information is used. The chapter also provides strategies to aid institutional policymakers, curriculum designers, leaders and work integrated learning experience providers to meet these challenges.

Chapter 6, 'Supervision', addresses the domains of support and integration. The supervisory process is described in detail, with emphasis on the supervisory relationship between student and supervisor. Real-world examples are used to demonstrate situations that may arise during supervision and their impact on the student and supervisor, the university, workplace, host organization and possibly clients, consumers or patients. The priority for supervisors is maintaining professional standards and commitment to clients, while at the same time helping students develop professional identities through participation, open discussion during supervision sessions and reflection. Strategies to assist supervisors and students to accomplish this are provided.

Chapter 7, 'Managing Difficult Situations', addresses the difficulties that commonly arise but which are not so commonly spoken about. It includes real-life examples of difficult situations and stresses the need for sustained support for all parties involved. This chapter highlights the importance of understanding the legal frameworks within which work integrated learning programmes operate, and the necessity to undertake risk analysis. It also provides strategies to minimize risk as much as possible.

Chapter 8, 'The Work Integrated Learning Process', is the final chapter and incorporates the concerns raised in all of the preceding chapters. It outlines a five-step process for designing, setting up, implementing, managing and evaluating work integrated learning programmes, taking into consideration the issues and complexities discussed in the previous chapters. It addresses all seven domains of work integrated learning programmes. Consideration is given to issues such as timing of the programme, policy, partnerships, contracts, tasks and responsibilities of all stakeholders, budgeting, resources, management and evaluation.

In conclusion, this book aims to satisfy the need for a resource that can be used as a work integrated learning guide. With the growing focus on higher education programmes of study that incorporate work integrated learning, the complexities arising from managing large numbers of students before, during and after their work integrated learning experiences will require ongoing identification and research into best practice in this area of student education.

Conceptual map – where to go for what

Chapter	Dimension
Chapter 1: The New Higher Education Enterprise	Purpose Context Partnerships
Chapter 2: A Conceptual Framework for Work Integrated Learning	Purpose Context Integration Curriculum Learning Partnerships Support

Chapter 3:
Working to Learn, Learning to Work   Curriculum
                                                      Learning
                                                      Context

Chapter 4:
Teaching in Work Integrated Learning   Curriculum
                                                      Integration
                                                      Context
                                                      Support

Chapter 5:
Assessing Work Integrated Learning   Curriculum
                                                      Integration

Chapter 6:
Supervision   Support
                                                      Integration

Chapter 7:
Managing Difficult Situations   Context
                                                      Integration
                                                      Support

Chapter 8:
The Work Integrated Learning Process   All seven

Summary

This chapter has attempted to identify and briefly describe the contexts for writing this book and what might be tacitly understood to be the drivers for, and qualities of, workplace learning programmes, and why work integrated learning is important and what it can deliver. It has also explored the basic intersection of 'learning to work' in contrast to 'working to learn' and how these differ from 'learning at work'.

We have attempted to propose a common nomenclature to assist in the dialogue across different models of learning in the workplace and the community. To this end, this chapter has explored some of the origins of this terminology and why it has had to change from 'work-based learning' to 'work integrated learning'.

Based on the theory that learning is situated – that is, how, where and why students learn – we have defined work integrated learning as a complex integration of the learning that happens in the higher education and workplace contexts, not simply as a cross-fertilization or transfer of theory and practice, but as a whole learning experience that requires conscious planning and effort on the part of all involved, from university policymakers and host organization managers to professional accreditation bodies and students. Work integrated learning involves effective engagement of theory with practice – an integration of knowledge, skills, dispositions and actions that enables authentic learning experiences in different/ specific contexts and across contexts – to develop students' employability skills and attributes. This is based on an assumption that theory and practice are complementary parts of a whole. Each informs, challenges and shapes the other and without the other progress is limited. Without the integration of work and learning, theory and practice, there is NO work integrated learning! Without integration there is merely either work or a limited form of learning.

Section 1

The policy and conceptual framework

Chapter 1

The New Higher Education Enterprise

Introduction

This chapter focuses on the emergence of the work integrated learning agenda as a new enterprise in higher education. It describes the evolving higher education environment, institutional cultural change, the drivers for work integrated learning and the imperative for effective leadership and management. The argument is made for the necessity of establishing and maintaining strong partnerships between the learning institution, community and workplaces. Historically, notions of partnership between institutions and workplaces in relation to student learning have been unequal. This chapter makes a case for, and outlines, a potentially reciprocal relationship in which stakeholders work together to ensure (1) institutional involvement in, and contribution to, the wider community and (2) workplace involvement in, and contribution to, the development of relevant and dynamic curricula and graduate capabilities. Emergence of work integrated learning as a higher education endeavour has forged a new role for senior leadership and management in higher education institutions. This new role is to provide a vision for significant changes in workplace and community engagement with learning institutions to ensure the new agenda delivers full potential benefits to all stakeholders.

Changes brought about by the market-driven economy, coupled with an increased focus on community engagement, have generated an increased impetus for higher education institutions to work in partnership with government and non-government sector workplaces to ensure graduating students are 'work-ready'. These pressures have stimulated a need for institutions to be clearer and more purposeful in their approach to collaboration with workplaces and communities to increase opportunities to implement work integrated learning programmes. Communities and workplaces have also made their expectations clearer in relation to students who enter their spaces – expectations driven by social and legislative developments that seek to protect society and consumers from potential harm (Business Industry and Higher Education Collaboration Council 2007; Hesketh 2000; Nixon *et al.* 2006; Polyacskó 2009).

The higher education environment

In recent decades, higher education has changed rapidly from an elitist stance to a system of mass higher education. Changes since the 1960s and 1970s include major expansion of student places, introduction of programmes to improve equity, and greater accountability to society and governments for the impact of programmes on society, professional practice, skills shortages, graduate qualities and social, economic and environmental sustainability. For some time now, individual higher education institutions have revised their policies and programmes of study to demonstrate publicly that they are distinctive from all other institutions in terms of their specializations and engagement with, and responsiveness to, their local regional communities. Institutional policy and programme revisions also aim to demonstrate provision of high quality learning experiences for their students, equity in terms of student access and participation, and financial sustainability. Finally, these revisions aim to demonstrate that institutions produce research outputs that have a high impact on society generally and on their students' learning more specifically. Whilst these imperatives have significant implications for work integrated learning – the intersection and engagement of theoretical and workplace learning – some require greater attention than others.

Quality of teaching and learning is increasingly important. This is more of a challenge when teaching occurs outside the university in workplaces. The institutional culture in higher education generally has been slow to recognize its responsibility to understand and systematically address student needs while students are learning in the workplace and the community by providing safeguards to ensure appropriate duty of care. Similarly, academies have been slow to recognize the importance of understanding the needs of workplaces and communities as collaborative partners in educational provision. Much can be done to better prepare students for learning in the workplace, and to prepare workplaces for their educative contribution.

Institution policy, programmes and procedures need review to account for the very different circumstances of students' work integrated learning and the need for a high level of duty of care. Review of policy, programmes and procedures must take account of key factors that impact on planning and development of student learning. Some of these factors include increases in:

- number of students participating in higher education;
- international students;
- participation of equity groups attending higher education institutions;
- access for those disadvantaged by disability, regional distance and inaccessibility;
- students who study part time and simultaneously work or care for families;
- attention to graduate outcomes in terms of capabilities and standards of performance;
- attention to student satisfaction.

These significant changes to institutional student profiles impact on students' educational needs and experiences. They also impact on the nature of the institution's relationships with workplaces and the community. These developments require better management of work integrated learning, placing new demands on academics. The new focus on quality assurance in relation to the student learning experience also places new demands on supervisory teachers in workplaces and communities.

Governments around the world are increasingly concerned about returns on their investment in higher education. They want to know: What are graduates able to do when they finish a degree? How might this be measured? Government concern has promoted a burgeoning of interest in generic knowledge and skills that require interpretation and translation into discipline-specific learning outcomes through curriculum development and institution-wide assessment of graduate exit skills. Curriculum development is now underpinned by expectations that graduates will have multiple transferable skills for employment in the new, knowledge-based economy with its emphasis on knowledge and information production and distribution, and recognition of the necessity for practice-based learning in conjunction with 'formal education' (Organisation for Economic Co-operation and Development 1996: 14). Thus, in developing a work integrated learning curriculum, it is necessary to address some fundamental questions:

- What are students expected to learn?
- What outcomes are expected of students?
- What action is needed to provide this learning and these outcomes?
- How might the quality of these learning experiences be assured?

Leadership and management of effective learning and teaching systems has had to turn its attention to finding systematic ways of providing answers to the above questions. The institution, professions and discipline groups, and the workplace, all have distinct expectations about what students are to learn and how they can assist in preparing students for this learning. Integrating these expectations and managing them in curriculum development and improvement is a significant challenge to academic and institutional leadership.

The new higher education enterprise: work integrated learning

In this climate of change, there is a growing interest among higher education institutions, and the higher education sector as a whole, in the potential new directions and outcomes that invigorated and better aligned relationships between education and work might hold. Industries want to employ graduates who are already familiar with workplace culture and demands, and who understand the intersection of theory and practice. Students want to find everyday relevance and practical applications in their studies for their life after graduation. University leadership understands that this is what industry and potential students want.

As a result there have been institutional and sector-wide plans and projects that shift a significant portion of student learning experiences outside of classrooms and into actual, and sometimes virtual, workplace and community environments. For example, American Studies students from a university in Australia undertake internships in government offices in Washington DC, America; social work students might undertake part of their programme of study off campus in a welfare organization; and students from any discipline might undertake service learning experiences in community-based organizations such as homeless shelters or drug rehabilitation centres.

Work integrated learning itself is not new and has a long history in higher education. One prevailing view is that, historically, the role of universities has been to conduct research that will generate ideas, ideologies and theories, or discover facts about nature, society and the universe, which are then transmitted to its students through education. The contemporary image generated by such a view is one of researchers in laboratories, people in front of computers, lecture halls full of students taking notes while attending to a single expert lecturer, and intense circles of students debating in tutorials. This is largely the way that life in universities is communicated to, and construed by, those outside them. While this is partly true, a significant component of the learning experiences of more than a third of all university students in any one academic year occurs not in university classrooms but in workplaces and communities. The intentions underpinning this mode of university education are varied and will be discussed in various ways throughout this book. Common to all sets of purpose is a desire for the interpretation and integration of observations of everyday life and workplace practice with conceptualized ideas. There is a prevailing intent for students to engage in work in order to learn workplace literacy, social awareness and responsibility, career awareness, professional knowledge and vocational skills as elements of their formal studies. This learning may happen in a professional or industrial workplace, a formal community organization or geographical community.

These intentions are not new. Many early European universities had their genesis in the study of theology and medicine. Both disciplines are intimately concerned with the application of theory to professional practice and everyday living. Since its inception, technical education has also had curricula and learning practices that incorporate apprenticeships, cadetships and internships grounded in partnerships between industry, professional regulatory bodies and educational systems. But something has changed. What is new is the scale and diversity of student engagement in workplace and community-based learning. This change has occurred because learning in and through workplace practice and community service is being driven by new strategic institutional imperatives and new motivations. This shift in locus in the drivers of curriculum initiation has created a new university paradigm in work integrated learning.

The old paradigm: the cottage industry?

Before we explore the new paradigm, it is important to understand the old, largely tacit paradigm. Initially, integration of theoretical study and learning with work had its genesis in professional education where gaining a degree was also an essential pathway to professional registration. Professional registration bodies laid down requirements for university courses in terms of content coverage and the amount of time that students should spend in workplaces in order for the course to be accredited. Students who graduated from these accredited degree programmes were able to become registered professionals eligible for employment within the field. Leadership in this approach came from the professions, driven by their expert knowledge of the workplace practices and requirements. Those in the university who implemented or coordinated these programmes were often 'of the profession' themselves. The development and motivations that drove these programmes were based on the commitment of individual academics to their primary practice professions. These academics' strong external links and networks within the professions assisted in gaining work integrated learning spaces.

One tacit and poorly considered aspect of this field of leading and managing work integrated professional learning programmes is that it often occurred at the expense of an academic's personal success. Time spent in establishing and maintaining programmes constrained their engagement in research. In addition, it needs to be recognized that the task of work integrated learning programme coordination has often been an isolated responsibility within a department; a 'short straw job' that was learnt 'on the job' with little or no induction or mentoring and often a job for 'the girls' not the boys. Furthermore, there have been few opportunities for forging connections and sharing 'wisdom of experience' between coordinators in other disciplines with similar responsibilities.

The particular point to be noted here is that university leadership and management of work integrated learning was not located at the institutional level. It was located at the specific programme coordination level within disciplines and academic departments. This meant that work integrated learning programme coordination was largely invisible in university infrastructure and policies, and the quality of management varied across the institution, being best characterized as a *cottage industry* (Orrell 2005a).

The activities and processes of work integrated learning as a cottage industry, led and managed from within its academic organizational unit, remained largely invisible. This was true in curriculum approval systems, assessment moderation and duty of care protection processes as well as in academic profiles, and workload and promotion systems. Few universities could quantify adequately the scope of involvement of students, staff and workplaces in work integrated learning systems. Nor could they report on the approaches taken by various programmes or account for the associated costs and benefits. In many ways work integrated learning was an undervalued, underutilized resource despite having considerable underdeveloped potential for assisting the universities to develop comprehensive and authentic partnerships with their related industries and communities.

As a result, work integrated learning was largely under-resourced, under-researched and undertheorized. It was managed at considerable personal and professional cost to the individual academics responsible for managing it (Cooper and Orrell 1999). The highly demanding administrative problems experienced in gaining, developing and maintaining cooperative relationships and partnerships with industry, as well as managing challenging difficult and ethical dilemmas with students, were mainly perceived as problems for individual academics to solve. This work was carried out largely without the benefit of dedicated policies, infrastructure and systems.

Another worrisome feature of the invisibility of work integrated learning coordination was that its management was learnt on the job without the benefit of expert ethical and legal support and advice in what is clearly a high-risk aspect of university learning and teaching. Students were often assigned to workplaces without the benefit of agreements between institution and workplace. This meant that expectations of student participation and its limitations were unclear. Reporting and communication systems for dealing with contentious behaviour or incidents, or matters that might eventuate in institutional insurance claims, were also unclear. Ethical, legal and legislative matters and risk management generally were left to personally acquired understandings. Mechanisms for attending to such matters were developed on a case-by-case basis (Orrell *et al.* 1999).

Because this aspect of university education was so invisible and so under-researched, the full scope of risks involved did not come to the attention of institutional management and governments until this last decade. Furthermore, the mechanisms put in place were short-term and short-sighted, demonstrating very poor understanding of the precise nature and needs of work integrated learning.

The Australian Federal Government first turned its attention to work integrated learning in 2001. In so doing, it reduced funding to many university programmes because it understood that many of the teachers were not university staff but were out in workplaces and, as a result, not paid for their services. This showed a deep misunderstanding of what is required to establish and maintain effective work integrated learning programmes. A similar government initiative was not introduced for online, independent student options that might have some operational similarities. The initiative cost many universities dearly through lost funding. It failed to account for the considerable amount of work that university staff undertook in locating work integrated learning experience places, preparing and negotiating learning environments within the workplaces, briefing and debriefing students before and after their work integrated learning experiences, and in supervising, supporting and assessing learning outcomes. Most institutions failed to recognize the government's mistake; they neither resisted nor proposed an alternative.

Whilst this is just one nation's response to work integrated learning, it demonstrates that when so little is known publicly about the nature of, and resources required for, work integrated learning, many potential benefits can be lost through inappropriate management responses. It suggests that there is a need for systematic multi-institutional, multidisciplinary research to understand the needs and benefits so that there can be an evidence-based approach to institutional and national policy development and infrastructure provision in relation to work integrated learning.

The new paradigm: work integrated learning as a higher education enterprise

In recent decades there has been a growth of university courses requiring students to learn in workplaces as well as classrooms. Increasingly, more generalist vocational programmes have elected to include workplace and community work integrated learning experiences as required or elective elements. Leadership and management of these programmes has generally been located at the academic organizational unit level. Management is therefore still reliant on the commitment of individual academics who are, hopefully, well linked to their related industry partners in areas as diverse as forensic chemistry, business, environmental management, local government, community health centres, and cultural and environmental tourism.

There is also increasing emphasis on service learning as a model of work integrated learning (described in depth in Chapter 2). This North American initiative has taken hold in universities internationally. It is a teaching and learning strategy that integrates meaningful community service with instruction and reflection to enrich the learning experience, teach civic responsibility and strengthen communities (National Service-Learning Clearinghouse n.d.). Its focus is on ensuring students graduate with well-developed dispositions towards responsible citizenship, engendered through a curriculum-enhanced programme of service contributions to the community involving student engagement with communities and making active contributions towards their needs.

Whilst it is clear that work integrated learning is not a new element of university studies, the drivers for its practice are new and the locus of leadership and imperatives for management have changed. These new drivers promise a significant, positive impact on actual practice, management, curricula, external partnerships and, most importantly, student learning experiences. The most significant change is that work integrated learning has become an important element in institutional and national agendas. It is no longer an optional aspect of university education. The emerging new agenda is more frequently led by an institutional vision.

The new and emerging trend is for institutions to be the instigators of visions, targets and priorities that call for far greater involvement of students in work integrated learning, including service learning, during their course of studies. The earlier programmes were driven by the need to meet professional requirements or aimed for educational enhancement at the department level. Institutional instigations for the new work integrated learning paradigm incorporate other goals such as gaining a competitive edge in the market of student enrolment and forging authentic, comprehensive industry and community partnerships. An additional need is engagement with national government agendas to have work-literate and workforce-ready graduates.

Increased institutional involvement in work integrated learning has resulted in the work entailed in its design and management becoming more visible, and in the emergence of new and important roles and tasks for institutional leaders, namely:

- articulating a vision that sets the direction for future planning;
- promulgating the vision in and beyond the institution, motivating and gaining support and cooperation of the various faculties;
- providing direction and priorities through strategic planning;
- ensuring that appropriate support and preparation are available to those who must implement the vision;
- providing resources and infrastructure, policies and procedures for education-ally effective practice;
- ensuring practices meet legal and ethical standards for safe duty of care;
- recognizing related academic work;
- ensuring coherence between the various elements of implementation.

Challenges that were once met by individuals are now adopted as institutional concerns involving development of policies, infrastructure and resources, as well as provision of systematic professional development. Importantly, the cost of work in this field can rightfully be calculated and accounted for, and the quality of students' work integrated learning experience taken into account in institutional systems and national agendas. Recognition and reward systems, such as promotions and awards for practice, will also acknowledge the outstanding and innovative contributions of individuals and groups. For example, in Australia, universities and the Australian Awards for University Teaching specifically focus on work integrated learning and institutional engagement with their communities. Similarly, universities and the Australian Council for Learning and Teaching (ALTC) have prioritized grant funds for investigating and further developing work integrated learning.

It is clearly apparent that this cultural shift from work integrated learning as a cottage industry to a new higher education enterprise regime must become observable in authentic partnerships with related industries that exploit the poten-tial mutual benefits for all stakeholders (Moody 1997). The success of the shift to the new paradigm is dependent on engaging all stakeholders by establishing a new vision and new management processes that reflect the new values and goals.

The critical differences that have emerged in the new culture of the new para-digm are illustrated in Table 1.1.

The shift from cottage industry to institutional enterprise is not simple and, in an era of increased focus on academic leadership practice, needs careful examina-tion as to the implications for its management. As Table 1.1 indicates, the old cottage industry culture did not call for a dedicated institutional infrastructure. As issues arose or gaps in provision of services or infrastructure were noted, solutions were developed at the local level to meet the immediate requirements. Student

Table 1.1 Contrast between the old and new work integrated learning cultures (Orrell 2005a)

Old Culture	New Culture
Cottage Industry • voluntary • atomistic • learnt 'on the job'	*Higher Education Enterprise* • intentional • comprehensive • responsibility induction

Value-added Approach
• students as workers
  — *Learning to work*
• individualistic
• students as observers
	Stakeholder-partnership Approach
	• students as learners
	  — *Working to learn*
	• shared goals/mutual benefit
	• students as participants

participation in the workforce and community as part of their studies was accepted as either a legislative requirement for professional registration or an 'educationally good thing' for service or vocational education. It was conceived as a value-adding activity, quite often independent of core curricula. These programmes were not formally linked with institutional or national agendas. Developments such as widened participation in higher education and the equity agendas were attended to atomistically as constraints to localized work integrated learning. Failure to include work integrated learning in the overall institutional leadership vision and management agenda has meant that its intersection with new higher education agendas has also failed to be considered and the appropriate challenges anticipated.

The new paradigm of work integrated learning as an institutional or higher education enterprise is recognizable in Moody's (1997) and Harvey *et al.*'s (1997) concept of a stakeholder approach. Within this new paradigm all stakeholders are considered; their rights and their needs are accounted for in the vision and the management systems. Stakeholders are inducted into their various roles and responsibilities rather than learning on the job. Within this paradigm, the work-place is regarded as a learning environment within which two learning agendas are managed proactively so that students *work in order to learn* and at the same time *learn to work*. These two very different but complementary learning agendas are recognized in terms of the instructional and supervisory arrangements, and legal, ethical and duty of care considerations. These are large agendas that have always been present but, for the most part, have been tacit, hidden and managed only as they have become apparent. New leadership is calling for these agendas to be included in the institutional conceptions and management arrangements.

Harvey *et al.*'s (1997) contrasting concept is that of a 'value-added' approach in which each participant engages in an exchange that complies with the needs of the other in order to have their own needs met:

• The institution meets its own needs for work integrated learning experience venues and compliance with professional accreditation requirements in exchange for providing students who are potential recruits for the organization and are, in many cases, unpaid workers.

- The student learns indirectly 'on the job' in order to meet professional credentialing requirements in exchange for unpaid work.
- The organization provides work integrated learning experiences in exchange for the opportunity to recruit with reduced risk and cost, and to access an unpaid workforce.

Harvey *et al.* (1997) argue that the stakeholder approach, signified by collaboration rather than compliance, is preferable to the value-added approach. The stakeholder approach results in all parties being more knowledgeable about, and more engaged in, each other's purposes. Harvey *et al.* (1997) also argue that mutual benefit is a key factor to the success of the stakeholder approach; if this fails, so too does the partnership.

Drivers for work integrated learning

Various imperatives and interests drive the implementation of work integrated learning. Whilst the two agendas 'working to learn' and 'learning to work' are evident in work integrated learning programmes, they are not incompatible, but the diverse interests of each need to be managed. These two sets of expectations have the potential to become oppositional in that universities want their students to engage in work and community service as a vehicle for learning, whilst organizations and industries provide work integrated learning experiences so that students learn to work in order to be work-ready on graduation. A balance between university and workplace agendas creates an environment of 'complex inter-relationships between the development of graduate skills, student learning', employee capability and progression, and workplace structure, all of which challenge prevailing institutional and organizational ethos in relation to both learning and work (Harvey *et al.* 1997: 11).

The emphasis on any one particular driver has potential implications for curriculum design, management and resourcing. Drivers include:

Professional accreditation	A period of time, established with a professional accrediting body, is required in the curriculum for work integrated learning experiences which have associated learning outcomes to be achieved, e.g. medicine, nursing, law, allied health.
Learning enhancement	Students are provided with the opportunity to explore the world in relation to their discipline, e.g. parliamentary internships, environmental management, with the goal of developing social literacy.

Career selection, confirmation and development	Students are given early exposure in work integrated learning experiences related to their field of study to confirm their career choice or to enhance their understanding and assist them in finding relevance.
Social service	Service learning in which students are encouraged to make a contribution and in doing so, increase the capacity to function as responsible citizens.
Workforce development	Students apply and transfer their generic capabilities engendered by their studies into novel workplace contexts in order to become 'work-ready' upon graduation.
Knowledge transfer	Students are encouraged to explore and share their classroom learning in workplaces and critically reflect on it in the light of everyday practice. The goal is that both universities and organizations learn and change as well as the student.
Enhancement of university/ industry partnerships	Student work integrated learning experiences are part of a much wider agenda of collaborative research, consultancies, continuing professional development for industry-based staff, industry placements for academics, and shared curriculum development and innovation.

Leadership and management of work integrated learning: What should it look like?

Leadership and management of learning and teaching have become increasingly interesting and important as both discipline and enterprise to scholars and leaders of higher education. Marshall *et al.* (2009), building on the work of Kotter (1990), Leithwood *et al.* (1996) and Stace and Dunphy (2001), argue that envisioning the future of learning and teaching enterprises and creating circumstances by which they can be realized are defining features of effective leadership and management. What does this mean in relation to work integrated learning? How can institutions organize and develop capacity to identify, support and develop individuals capable of implementing this new vision in work integrated learning programmes within their institution at faculty, department or discipline level?

Kotter (1990) espouses that, on the one hand, leadership is focused on effecting change, establishing a vision for the future, engaging and aligning the efforts and commitments of key stakeholders with the vision, and motivating and inspiring them to contribute to the realization of the vision. Management, on the other hand, is focused on maintaining predictability and order by developing plans, budgets and staffing, and organizational arrangements to implement, monitor and, where necessary, solve any problems that might prevent realization of the vision. The leadership and management roles are rarely discrete: they are inextricably engaged and may be included as responsibilities within single roles.

In their research on leadership and management of learning and teaching, Marshall *et al.* (2009) identified four key domains of practice that distinguish the leadership and management of learning and teaching from leadership and management in other areas. The four domains are:

1 *Curriculum.*
2 *Staff* involved in, or supporting, learning and teaching.
3 *Students.*
4 *Organizational enablers*, or those aspects of the organizational environment that enable or support learning and teaching, such as policy, organizational infrastructure and IT infrastructure.

The key tasks of leaders in each of these domains are to:

• establish a vision;
• gain alignment between various elements, plans and priorities within the institution in relation to the vision;
• motivate the various divisions and sector interests to engage with the vision;
• develop strategic plans to enable the vision to be implemented;
• establish infrastructure and systems to support development and implementation of the vision;
• establish evaluation systems to monitor implementation of the vision.

The task of management in relation to the four domains of practice is to:

• establish a direction for plans and priorities;
• assist in translating the vision into the culture, language, and priorities, goals and everyday concerns of the various faculties, departments, schools and services of the institution;
• achieve an effective level of engagement with the vision at the workplace level;
• prepare budgets and provide resources to enable implementation of the vision;
• provide and induct dedicated staffing for the initiative, and coherence with all the policies and procedures that involve the management and support of staff;
• engage in formative evaluation, problem identification and troubleshooting to ensure progression in the plans and priorities that are part of the vision.

In universities, leadership and management activities will have to occur at multiple levels, namely within a degree programme, within a department or school, within a faculty or division and within the institutional central system. With this model in mind, the new *higher education enterprise* paradigm now necessitates another level of involvement and coherent engagement throughout the institution. Looking from the perspective of this model, the inefficiencies and the risks of atomization and inconsistency inherent within the old *cottage industry* paradigm become apparent.

Work integrated learning challenges the model of leadership and management that works so well for other aspects of university learning and teaching because it requires insertion of another level for which management and leadership must account, namely external partners. How might institutions appropriately engage the external government, industry and community partners? The challenge to leadership in this case is to respond to, and engage with, groups that are both external and internal to universities in order to stimulate and encourage a reconsideration of current practices.

A second challenge is the primacy of the student learning experience in policies, infrastructure and practice. This can no longer be sustained in work integrated learning because the prevailing centrality of student learning must compete with the centrality of their workplace organization's mission and the interests and well-being of its clients. It is this challenge that distinguishes work integrated learning from the learning that occurs in more traditional face-to-face and virtual classroom-based learning environments. This difference calls for careful review and adaptation of education policies, infrastructure and support for students and staff.

Leadership of work integrated learning must define a vision that ensures that distinctive issues will be taken into account in:

- curriculum design and development;
- staff capability, induction, support and engagement;
- student preparation, support and protection;
- engagement with, and utilization of, organizational enablers that facilitate and support the placement of students in host organizations;
- delineation of partnerships with host organizations and communities.

If work integrated learning initiatives are to be successful, the initial and primary concern of institutional leadership must begin with an understanding that the leaders' role is to ensure that all key stakeholders embrace or support the vision or direction for development. Thereafter, institutional leaders need to remain motivated and committed to supporting their realization through appropriate recognition and reward systems.

The issues and questions that drive the leadership agenda for work integrated learning include:

- Is the vision articulated and expressed in such a way as to capture or change the understanding of all those involved with the implementation, namely discipline leaders, curriculum committees, students, professional associations, potential host organizations and other internal enabling services?
- Do students understand the vision and its contribution to their future success?
- Is there a programme of support to induct and educate academic teachers to new approaches to programme design and delivery, and to the legal and ethical matters involved in sending students out to host organizations?
- What enabling services and providers are needed to assist academic units to

design and implement the programme? Do they have an adequate understanding of the vision and its intentions?

- How might industry and communities be meaningfully engaged not only in developing but also in conceptualizing the vision and giving it direction?

These are all big picture agendas for institutional leaders. Few instances can be found of institutions giving these agendas thorough attention. Even where this has occurred the challenges are not small and not attended to quickly. This development involves a major cultural shift. One institution attending to the above agendas is Victoria University, Australia, which is used here as a best practice case study to illustrate the whole of the cultural shift required in institutions.

In 2006, Victoria University (VU) undertook to remake itself. It is a large, dual sector university, resulting from the merger of a technical and vocational education institution with a higher education institution. In its remake, the university made five commitments. These were:

1 *Collaboration* with industry and community.
2 *Career* focused for their students.
3 *Choices* for students to customize their learning experiences.
4 *Connected* with their related industries and communities to contribute to workforce development.
5 *Community* focused on three specific initiatives (increased participation in post compulsory education; reducing incidence and impact of diabetes; creating a centre of excellence in sport and exercise) in a specific locality (Melbourne's western suburbs).

This new mission aims to respond to the changing nature of work, and national and international workplaces; have strong community values; blend vocational, professional, conceptual and creative pursuits; challenge conventional thinking. Commitment 2 (Career focused for students) espoused the goals of producing graduates who were work, career and future ready and capable, with the skills and capacities to continue to learn, contribute to, and be adaptable citizens of the changing world and their communities (Kay and Russell 2008). VU established a goal that a minimum of 25% of course assessment will be based on a range of Learning in the Workplace and Community (LiWC) activities and models. These LiWC models and approaches may include but are not limited to, practical, cooperative and clinical placements, projects in a workplace or community setting, fieldwork and internships, guided by ten principles, namely:

1 The activity is beneficial for all parties: learner, university and partner organization.

2   Learning in Workplaces & Community (LiWC) is an integral part of the curriculum.

3   Intended learning outcomes that include generic skills are clearly defined.

4   Critical reflection and debriefing on learning from experiences in the workplace and community are an integral part of the activity for students, Workplace Supervisors and VU staff.

5   Assessment tasks accurately reflect intended learning outcomes and emphasize authentic products and processes.

6   Assessment criteria, including levels and standards, are clearly defined.

7   All parties are adequately prepared for the activity.

8   Learners are supported in the workplace and community.

9   The quality of the activity is subject to continuous review and improvement.

10   The activity is resourced appropriately (Victoria University 2008: 3).

Sources:
http://tls.vu.edu.au/vucollege/LiWC/resources/LiWCguidelines20090109FinalV3.pdf
http://tls.vu.edu.au/vucollege/LiWC/managinglearning.html

What is unique about this vision is its systematic translation into establishing infrastructure and allocating resources that make visible and support each of the five commitments. Policies were reviewed and rewritten to ensure that they supported the new vision; the concept of curriculum was revisited; and opportunities for the professional development of all staff and for conversation and research were established so that internal staff and external stakeholders could appreciate and engage with the vision. This whole institution initiative is in its early stages and not without challenges and challengers. Its progress, however, is worthy of close observation because it represents one of the clearest, most comprehensive conceptions of an enterprise approach to engagement with community and industry, and deep commitment by, and day-to-day engagement of, the senior level institutional leaders.

Managing implementation of the new agenda for work integrated learning also needs to attend to the practicalities of how the vision and directions will be realized. This will involve:

• the development and implementation of strategic plans, policies and processes which will include reviewing current practice and renewing practices;

• provision of professional development and managing performance of staff who will be directly involved with establishing and coordinating work integrated learning programmes;

• designing and establishing organizational structures that will enable and monitor establishment of contracts with host organizations, defining roles and responsibilities of individual stakeholders and groups;

- establishing and maintaining quality assurance and duty of care strategies, policies and processes;
- monitoring quality of initiatives as they are implemented to assure and enhance the quality of the various programmes, and to ensure that they adhere to the vision.

Regardless of the constant changes that influence the higher education institutional culture, some things remain constant. The institution has a responsibility through its management policies and infrastructure to:

- ensure that the curriculum process accounts for, and maintains, the visibility and educational intentions of the work integrated learning programmes;
- ensure that staff are sufficiently inducted into the educational, legal and ethical aspects of work integrated learning programmes;
- understand, address and meet student needs in general, and those needs specific to readiness to participate in off-campus placements and projects;
- understand the needs of the participating workplaces and communities, and to work with them to ensure maximum institutional involvement in, and contribution to, the wider community.

Conceptions of work integrated learning within higher education institutions

The preceding discussion has reflected the ideals of the authors, who have a long history of participation in work integrated learning, and has been explored largely from an 'outsider' view of universities and their place in society. It must be noted, however, that strong resistance towards institutional work integrated learning initiatives is being expressed by some sectors within universities who regard classroom and practice teaching and learning as competing rather than complementary modes in the education agenda. Work integrated learning is sometimes regarded as a challenge to the academic status quo and disciplinary expertise, and an additional burden for students. For some students the opportunity to have real-life exposure to the actual work of their chosen career is profound, confirming or challenging their previous conceptions of the path they have chosen (Cullen and Mills 2006). For others, however, the experience can be vacuous and so poorly linked to their classroom learning and the curriculum generally that they regard it as a needless interruption to the primary focus of their studies. Many academics share this latter perception, regarding learning in the workplace and community as a challenge to limited curriculum resources and time.

Universities need to look to their current polices to ensure that they address the needs of students and staff involved in work integrated learning. In particular they need to consider the impact on staff workload of establishing and maintaining external partnerships, and that institutional criteria used for awarding promotions account for the achievements that are germane to work integrated learning programmes. Universities also need to ensure that appropriate continuing professional development is available to prepare and enhance academic management practice and the entrepreneurial activity required in coordinating such programmes. One example is Flinders University in South Australia where it is mandatory for new appointees to work integrated learning programme coordination roles to participate in an induction programme to ensure they are sufficiently aware and knowledgeable regarding educational, legal, ethical and duty of care matters, and have, and know how to access, support resources and experienced coordinators who can play a mentoring role.

Beyond the theory/practice divide: making the whole course count

At its best, learning in the workplace and community can be valuable for all stakeholders in the enterprise (Billett 2006; Keating 2006). Theoretical learning and practice learning can be complementary parts of a whole, each elaborating, extending and challenging the other. This very positive impact is rarely accidental. It requires intentional curriculum planning, well-prepared students, authentic workplace relations, capable and work integrated learning literate teachers and supervisors, as well as constructive, mutually beneficial alliances between university disciplines and their related industries and community groups. Preparation of students for learning in workplaces and preparation of workplaces to provide quality work integrated learning environments are key requirements.

It is important for the success of this initiative that neither theoretical nor practice learning is construed as either overtaking or suppressing the other. In the United Kingdom in the 1990s, a major government-funded project established to transfer nursing education to universities coined the phrase of 'making the whole course count' (Cast 1995). This project changed the balance by shifting learning from the workplace into the university. In doing so, it faced the same challenges as shifting learning from the university to the workplace. It is mentioned here because it signals how important it is to recognize and anticipate the potential dilemma of allowing theory and practice to be construed as competing domains. Partnerships between theory and practice need to be promoted in the university as important synergistic parts of a whole, where each is an agent for progress and change in the other. This focus cuts to the heart of contemporary concerns regarding the new emphasis on work integrated learning in universities.

Establishing and maintaining partnerships

Effective partnerships between higher education institutions and their related industries and communities require a number of elements. Developers of service learning have generated a detailed examination of the characteristic elements of effective partnerships and the fundamental values and actions required to maintain them. Trust and the opportunity to work on problems and issues of mutual concern to produce substantive results are two important elements in developing high-quality relationships. Harkavy (2003, xiii) explains how these elements are interdependent, each reinforcing the other. Jacoby (2003: 5) adds that effective partnerships to support service learning are best grounded in the concept of reciprocity and are multidirectional in terms of acknowledged needs and benefits. She contrasts this with earlier unidirectional approaches to service learning such as volunteerism. Elevating new partnerships to a position of reciprocity calls for shared values and reciprocal learning in a process of social and educational exchange.

For too long educational institutions and practice communities have been merely interested, disconnected observers of each other. For reciprocal partnerships to be established there needs to be synergy between partners, so that if there is a major shift or change of direction or values in one, it will impact on the other; like two acrobats in a balancing act there must be synergy and connectivity. Additional elements are the generation and negotiation of shared goals, and collaboration in achieving those goals.

Jacoby (2003) describes an agreed suite of Campus Compact Benchmarks developed to support campus/community collaborations (Torres 2000: 1). A significant shift in orientation suggested by the Compact is that rather than beginning with a focus on service learning, the advocate should begin with the deeper issues of establishing reciprocal democratic partnerships. The aim of the Compact is to integrate the intentions of these partnerships in the academic mission of the universities and to sustain the partnerships by using the strengths of each partner to transform both the university and the external communities of practice (Jacoby 2003: 9–14). The following is a synthesis of principles proposed by service learning theorists upon which the design, establishment and maintenance of partnerships can be grounded:

- A shared vision and clearly articulated values.
- Shared goals that are mutually beneficial to partnering institutions.
- Multi-level relationships based on trust and mutual respect.
- Balance of power amongst the partners.
- Multidimensional participation of multiple sectors that act in the service of a complex problem.
- Sharing of strengths and resources.
- Integrating institutional mission and support systems of the partnering institutions.
- Clear communications, decision-making processes and feedback mechanisms for all stakeholders.
- Shared credit for the partnerships' accomplishments.
- Regular evaluation with a focus on both methods and outcomes.

(Adapted from Community-Campus Partnerships
for Health 2006; Torres 2000: 5–7)

These principles have relevance for the new higher education enterprise formation of work integrated learning partnerships. It is now time for universities to recognize that their work integrated learning programmes provide mechanisms for establishing authentic, multidimensional relationships with their local communities and related industries, and to value them because of this potential, not merely as a means of producing work-ready graduates. Starting with a partnership expands the agenda beyond learning to wider institutional agendas, including research. Adopting an intentional approach to the formation of partnerships, grounded in these values and processes, can derive as yet unimagined benefits. Unfortunately, many established links with communities remain utilitarian, value-added exchanges that fail to sustain or transform either partner.

Evaluation

Evaluation is often overlooked in work integrated learning. Where it does occur, it is overly reliant on student feedback on their experience to the neglect of other information sources. Furthermore, student evaluations are gathered routinely but the information is underutilized (Pallett 2006). Jones (2003: 161) argues that once established, successful partnerships must be evaluated continually and involve all participants. There are sensitivities in conducting all-encompassing evaluations of university/community. One fear is that the relationship will break down if external partners perceive that they are exposed to being criticized. Genuine inclusive evaluation begins with asking questions about what is most important and seeks sources of information that go beyond those which are student-based. Genuine democratic partnerships to support transformative learning experiences are what are important in work integrated learning. Effective evaluation involves developing valid methods and indicators and multiple sources of data in order to determine what has been achieved and to identify what must be done to improve the outcomes. Adopting a cyclical approach to evaluation and closing the loop through critical reflection, constructive innovation and change, together with sensitive communication, promotes the continuance of the shared transformative learning agenda that the partnerships set out to achieve.

Summary

The higher education sector, in response to changing government agendas, is developing a new vision of their relationship with their communities and workplaces. Institutions seek to form effective partnerships with these workplaces and communities to sustain expanding agendas in the education of their students. Increasingly, institutions espouse the intent to produce work-literate and work-ready graduates who have been educated to be responsible, socially aware, actively contributing local and global citizens. It is important that institutions are aware that this intent has established a new enterprise for higher education which needs to be visible in their infrastructure, policies, internal processes and the ways they relate to their new partners. Done well, this new enterprise can be a catalyst for more authentic relationships between institutions, their communities and workplaces. It can contribute to integration of theory and practice, teaching and research in the process of creating a knowledge-based workforce better adapted to changing technologies and consumer demands, thereby maintaining a competitive edge in the global marketplace (Pont and Werquin 2001). Various models of work integrated learning are in use with the aim of achieving this outcome. Three of these models are the focus of Chapter 2, which also identifies and describes seven underlying domains common to all models of work integrated learning.

Chapter 2

A Conceptual Framework for Work Integrated Learning

Introduction

This chapter provides a conceptual framework to define what is referred to throughout this book as 'work integrated learning'. The term work integrated learning is an umbrella concept encompassing a variety of terms used in professional, vocational, liberal arts and sciences education. Whilst many similar terms are in common use, not all of these refer to work integrated learning as defined in this chapter. There is much overlap, ambiguity and difference between these terms depending on national, institutional and local practices.

The major focus of this chapter is to describe three discrete work integrated learning models – professional learning, service learning and cooperative learning. To clarify the concept of work integrated learning used in this book, some of the different terms used to describe work integrated learning will be outlined. Following this clarification, seven key interrelated dimensions characteristic of all work integrated learning models are outlined as an introduction to describing the three models. The chapter provides a conceptual basis for understanding the forces shaping and promoting work integrated learning, and its outcomes for students, the university, academic staff, the workplace, the workplace learning guides and the general community.

Work integrated learning terminologies

Terms classified as work integrated learning include practicum, internships, fieldwork, cooperative education, field education, sandwich course, service learning and international service learning. Table 2.1 shows a list of terms that fit the classification of work integrated learning.

Regardless of the terms used, all work integrated learning is characterized by seven key dimensions: *purpose*; *context*; nature of the *integration*; *curriculum issues*; the *learning*; *partnerships* between the university and the workplace or community; and the *support* provided to the student and the workplace. The value of work integrated learning is that it takes the strengths of the theoretical orientations of academic education and blends these with the rich, tacit practice knowledge

Table 2.1 Description of terms used for work integrated learning

Work integrated learning terms	Description
Practicum	Involves extended periods of time in an organization to develop skills and competencies associated with professional training. Students have theoretical training before commencing their practical experiences in upper level years. Classroom teaching is often concurrent with practice. Students are expected to achieve skills and competencies, and are supervised by more experienced professionals to develop these outcomes. Students complete the practicum as part of their course. It is not paid work. Practicums may be completed in a block of time in overseas locations.
Internships	The term 'internship' is used interchangeably with 'practicum' and has similar characteristics. It extends over a long period of time, with practice supervised by more experienced practitioners. It is part of a course of study and taken as credit. Sometimes an internship refers to study after a course is completed. In this latter situation, it may not be work integrated learning. Internships can be paid or unpaid.
Fieldwork	Fieldwork refers to short periods of time in a workplace where the student is able to observe and participate in work. In some professions and disciplines, 'fieldwork' is used interchangeably with 'practicum' or 'placement'. Students are not paid for fieldwork experiences. Fieldwork is linked to students' academic programmes and is supported by the academy.
Cooperative education	Cooperative education refers to periods of work experience which are integrated into classroom studies. The work experience is aligned to the student's future career goals. There is a strong emphasis on the integration of theory and practice in the curriculum, and on partnerships with employers and industry. There is recognition of the work-based experiences in the student's academic transcripts. Some students are paid to undertake cooperative education experiences.
Field education	Field education is an integral part of professional education. Through this component of professional courses, students are prepared for professional practice. Students are expected to achieve professional competencies and are supervised, assessed and supported in the development of these outcomes.
Sandwich course	In these courses students are placed in business or government organizations to gain work experience and to apply the knowledge from the classroom into the real world. Generally sandwich courses are held over the vacation period between the years of the degree, with paid employment as part of the arrangement. Sandwich courses are assessed by an academic supervisor.

Work integrated learning terms	Description
Service learning	Service learning is a course-based programme, taken for credit, where students engage in a range of community activities that meet the needs of the community. Students use community activities to gain an understanding of their course material and to develop an appreciation of civic responsibility. Learning depends on reciprocal relationships between the institution and the community.
International service learning	This is similar to service learning except that students are linked to service in international non-government organizations. This learning is supported by the academic institution.

of workplaces and communities. This integration is achieved through focusing on the seven key dimensions when planning and implementing work integrated learning programmes.

Seven key dimensions of work integrated learning

Purpose

Defining the purpose of work integrated learning experiences for students guides decisions about which work integrated learning model to use. Having a clear purpose beyond simply integrating theory with practice means clarifying goals, expectations and intended outcomes for students, the workplace, the university and community to ensure strong partnerships in suitable contexts that facilitate integrated, supported student learning.

Context: The workplace

Workplaces, including government organizations, large and small businesses, industries and not-for-profit organizations, are increasingly becoming important contexts for practice learning for the professions, and for cooperative and service learning in other disciplines, with learning being achieved through work. Many workplaces have structured curricula and afford new recruits opportunities to learn outside the classroom (Billett 2001). Learning in these workplaces is facilitated through a variety of strategies, including guided learning, mentoring and coaching. The learners are immersed in a community of practice where they move from the periphery to full participation (Lave and Wenger 1991). The value of workplaces is that they can provide sites for learning vocational, professional, disciplinary and service expertise.

Integration

Integration is the act or process of making whole or entire. It aims to construct one system that uses all available knowledge from several separate sources. Integration is achieved through a synthesis of experiences, theory and practice (Kelton 2009). In relation to work integrated learning, integration is the process of bringing together formal learning and productive work, or theory and practice, to give students a complete, integrated learning experience. Integration involves the application of formal theory with real-world problem solving, abstract thinking and practical action, and discipline-specific and vocational skills. Integration is not an event but a learning process encouraged in the workplace and academy through dialogue, reflection, tutorials and assessable work, resulting in students putting knowledge into action and developing the ability to 'act knowledgeably and responsibly in the world' (Association of American Colleges and Universities 2009).

Integration occurs at the individual level, the organizational level and the system level (Stenström and Tynjälä 2008) through connectivity and transformation. Connectivity refers to processes that enable the development and maintenance of close relationships. Transformation means changes in developmental and policy processes as a result of connectivity. At the individual level, the classroom teacher and student work closely with the workplace that provides the work integrated learning experience. Theory and practice, thinking and action are connected. Transformation of thinking and action is felt at the organizational levels of workplaces and universities. Their connectedness allows transformation of issues into policy and practice that can then be considered at the systems level. At the organizational level, the specific university administrators and coordinators connect with a variety of work organizations, supervisors, mentors and trainers. At the systems level, universities concerned with policy and systemic issues connect with employers and governments representing labour markets.

Curriculum

Biggs (1999) noted that the difference between declarative knowledge and functional knowledge is fundamental to the work integrated learning curriculum, in which learning at work must be part of, and integrated with, the overall learning. In other words, learning in the workplace is included in the curriculum. Declarative knowledge is the information passed on in books and lectures about theory, whereas functional knowledge is the application of declarative knowledge in real-world situations where students are required to problem solve, prioritize, act like a professional or demonstrate civic commitment. This functional knowledge may be found in, and learnt through, the (tacit) workplace curriculum. Thus, in work integrated learning, teaching and learning are part of the whole system of the university and the workplace.

The process of thinking about and developing the curriculum is complex and contested. The curriculum model included here was developed by John Biggs (1999) and is based on the concept of constructive alignment, 'an approach to curriculum design that optimizes the conditions for quality learning' (Biggs n.d.). Constructive alignment is best understood by starting with the learning outcomes students are expected to achieve. The teacher's responsibility is to align learning activities, methods and assessment with the intended learning outcomes. There are four important steps in thinking about the curriculum:

- defining the intended learning outcomes;
- choosing teaching/learning activities to lead to the intended learning outcomes;
- assessing students' actual learning outcomes to see how well they match what was intended;
- arriving at a final grade.

Whilst constructive alignment was designed for learning in formal contexts, it provides a structure for designing work integrated learning, as students are expected to achieve competencies and behaviour in the workplace that meet professional, vocational, industry or civic requirements. The assessment process should align with these real-life actions or performances so that a grade can be determined.

Learning

Work integrated learning involves student engagement in experiential and situated learning, guided by clearly explained learning intentions and expected learning outcomes. Students participate in a spiral learning process where theory and practice are conceptualized and reconceptualized, with each spiral deepening the students' understanding. This transformative process results in changes in understanding and interpretation of theory, personal perspective, beliefs, values and practice. Kolb (1984) has described experiential learning as beginning with concrete experience, followed by reflective observation, abstract conceptualization and active experimentation. Learning begins with experiences that allow participants to observe, review and reflect on what they have practised. In the next stage learners are able consciously to link their experiences to theory or previous experiences. They then experiment with new ways of working. Whilst Kolb's model is presented as a sequential, staged process, this process is not so apparent to learners, their colleagues or experts in the workplace.

Situated learning (Lave and Wenger 1991) involves students participating in a work environment in a series of collaborative social interactions with other workers and students who have equal or more advanced skills. The learning depends on the context, the activities undertaken by the student, and the social and cultural norms, attitudes and values within the workplace. Participation means negotiating with others and interpreting, evaluating and translating meaning. Students learn from, with and through other people in a community of practice (Wenger 2000):

a group of people with diverse practice experience. In this community the student is able to analyse and reflect on their previous and existing experiences in order to construct meaning and to share the tacit knowledge about the workplace – the cultural knowledge and the practice or 'doing' knowledge.

Partnerships

It is not possible to have work integrated learning without strong partnerships between industry and educational institutions. Bringing partners together means that diverse interests are represented, strengths and issues identified, and new ways of improving and developing common goals addressed. Through partnerships, industry and the university can understand each other's interests and improve the quality of education in both the university and the workplace. Partnerships exist at the individual practitioner and institutional level. They may be transitory or ongoing, formal or informal, and involve single or multiple workplaces. Mechanisms such as advisory committees provide support for partnerships.

Support

Students and workplaces require support before, during and after any work integrated learning programmes. Students come to higher education with diverse and unique experiences. Some students may be first generation tertiary entrants, indigenous, migrants or from an impoverished background. Students are diverse in terms of ethnic or cultural origins, spiritual and religious views, sexual preferences, or abilities and disabilities, and with much or no experience of the world of work. All students have special needs and accommodations which should be accounted for in any support. For young students who have had little employment, voluntary or professional experience, work integrated learning can be challenging, creating anxiety and uncertainty. Students need support in knowing how to approach organizations and present themselves to employers, as well as in knowing what to expect and how learning takes place.

Support can take a variety of forms, from practical and administrative assistance to educational and emotional support. Administrative support refers to assistance with policies and procedures at all stages of the work integrated learning process. Both workplaces and students, especially those that have never participated in work integrated learning programmes, need help in this area. Educational support is also necessary as students learn about workplace and institutional expectations, the challenges of learning in the workplace, making sense of their experiences in working with others and developing an understanding of reflection.

The seven key dimensions of work integrated learning described in this section have been used to provide a framework for classifying programmes as work integrated learning or non-work integrated learning. All seven dimensions are required for a programme to be classified as work integrated learning.

We now describe those student learning experiences in the workplace that do not meet these criteria for categorization as work integrated learning experiences. This description makes a clear distinction between the work integrated learning experiences outlined earlier in Table 2.1 and the non-work integrated learning experiences (work experience) outlined in Table 2.2.

Non-work integrated learning experiences

Work experiences that are not integrated with the academic curriculum, do not promote learning through a process of reflection and analysis, do not provide student support, and in which the learning is not situated, constructed and experiential, are not work integrated learning. Harvey *et al.* (1998) outline a variety of such work experiences, which they term 'organized' and 'ad hoc'. These are external to the programme of study and, whilst not fitting the parameters of work integrated learning, can provide important learning experiences for participants. These work experiences are summarized in Table 2.2, with comments outlining why these are not work integrated learning.

With the conceptual groundwork laid about what is and what is not work integrated learning, we move on to describe three models of work integrated learning.

Models of work integrated learning

The three models described here are work integrated learning in *professional programmes, service learning* and *cooperative learning*. The unique characteristics of each programme are described, followed by a summary statement about the model's fit to work integrated learning.

Professional work integrated learning model

Professional work integrated learning programmes have many names. These names reflect different historical and cultural factors as well as factors related to the professional body, the nation or the university. Despite differing terminologies, professional work integrated learning programmes are an increasingly critical part of professional education for many professions, including nursing, medicine, dentistry, social work, teacher education, law, surveying, forestry, speech pathology, physiotherapy, occupational therapy, engineering, veterinary practice, pharmacy and optometry. Workplaces in which these professions practise include schools, the court and broader legal system, hospitals, specialist clinics, health, education and research institutions, government agencies, the not-for-profit sector, private industrial and business enterprises as well as in the community and broader field settings (veterinarians, for example, may practise their profession in a zoo, a wildlife park or out in the ocean).

A defining feature of professional work integrated learning programmes is the existence of regulatory requirements regarding student learning outcomes, expectations regarding learning, length and timing of placements, supervisory

Table 2.2 Non-work integrated learning experiences

Organized work experiences	Description
Structured vacation work programme aims to provide students with relevant work experience	• An organized programme of work during vacation • Application and selection to programme • Project-based • Work experience relevant to subject areas • Skills related to work experience • Paid but not full market rate
Work experience vacation placement provides students insights into work and businesses with an opportunity to scrutinize graduates	• Application and selection process • Highly competitive because of stringent selection criteria • Paid but not full market rate
Organized world-placements aim to deepen understanding of cultures and languages	• Placements arranged by international organizations • Placements limited • Students expected to pay travel costs but may have minimal financial support on placement
Short vacation courses and periods of induction assist with awareness of workplace and development of skills	• Specific courses with companies • Limited to several days in the workplace

Ad hoc work experience external to the programme of study	Description
Traditional vacation work allows students to earn money and simultaneously gain experience	• A wide variety of experiences that may not be relevant to degree or future employment • Seasonal work • Paid
Term work, part-time work allows students to earn money and support themselves	• Not always formal jobs • Paid and could be cash in hand • Not linked to career direction
Working in a family business provides work experience	• May not be regarded as a serious learning experience • Paid in cash or in kind • Not linked to career directions
Volunteer work, term time enables students to gain experience that links to a career or to broaden experience	• Not linked to subject areas or after graduation employment • Unpaid • Useful to include on curriculum vitae

Ad hoc work experience external to the programme of study	Description
Volunteer work, vacations and after graduation enables students to gain experience that links to a career or to broaden experience	• Generally organized by not-for-profit organizations • Matching of student's skills with the organizational needs • Unpaid • Allows the development of particular skills
Time off during the programme will assist students to broaden their experiences	• Negotiated between student and academic unit • May be linked to discipline, professional programme or subject specialization
Gap year assists students to gain work experience and develop social skills	• One year before completing secondary school and undergraduate programmes • Generally taken internationally

Adapted from Harvey et al. (1998)

requirements, and the type and nature of the learning experiences. Regulatory requirements are strict, codified and governed by the different professions' registration prerequisites.

The aim of professional work integrated learning programmes is to provide students with those professional skills and responsibilities that develop through engagement in professional workplace activities. In professional workplace settings, students are exposed to real-world problems that typically represent the variety of work a professional might experience in their particular field of practice. According to Schön (1983), practice problems are the ill-defined problems of the swampy lowland. These practice problems are not neat technical problems that are easy to resolve; they are complex and their resolution requires both theoretical understanding and practice knowledge.

Many professional bodies place particular importance on specifying their expectations of a developing professional as well as the roles of professional mentors and supervisors in teaching students, and the nature and structure of student learning. Supervisors or mentors are important for a variety of reasons. They bring together expectations of the profession, the workplace and the university. Specific supervisory requirements are commonly imposed by all parties, but most frequently by the educational institution. In a study on the clinical practicum experience in Canada, Ralph et al. (2008:163) noted the importance of the mentoring process, which consists of the supervisor working closely with the student to:

• establish professional and practice goals;
• observe the learner as they work in their professional roles;

- supervise, mentor or coach the students through the process of developing professional competence;
- provide feedback to the student about their performance as a formative or learning process and as evaluative statements at the completion of the practicum.

Professional organizations have clear mission and goal statements on both professional education and practice. These goals are reflected in the educational aims of the professional work integrated learning programme and in student learning *in situ*. Understanding the profession's mandate, values, ethics and professional identity are particularly valued. Some professions regard professional socialization as a critical part of learning. This socialization takes place through supervision or mentoring by a more experienced professional in a community of practice of like-minded professionals with differing levels of experience. It is reinforced by the theoretical and practical components of the university course.

Professional work integrated learning programmes fit the concept of work integrated learning used in this book because the learning takes place in specialized professional work settings, the focus is on experiential learning with guided learning, the students are expected to achieve specified professional competencies, and they are supervised, supported and assessed as part of the integration between the university and the professional practice setting.

The next model we describe is service learning, which is differentiated from the professional model by its greater focus on civic participation and civic engagement.

Service learning model

The practical foundations for service learning were laid by the intellectual considerations of John Dewey and the cooperative education initiatives of Professor Schneider in the United States (Sovilla and Varty 2004). Civic participation was promoted in the years following the Great Depression, presenting a variety of opportunities for young people to participate in and enrich communities. Although American educational institutions began introducing college-level programmes, it was not until the 1980s that service learning was actively adopted in higher education. In current times, service learning involves educational institutions being fully involved with their communities to jointly achieve common goals (Madden 2000; National Service-Learning Clearinghouse n.d.).

Jacoby (1996: 5) defines 'service-learning' as a 'form of experiential education in which students engage in activities that address human and community needs together with structured opportunities intentionally designed to promote student learning and development. Reflection and reciprocity are key concepts of service-learning'. Jacoby hyphenates service and learning deliberately to emphasize their connectedness, with neither component dominating the other; she has integrated service and learning.

Jacoby's definition of service learning precludes some of the features found in professional or cooperative education. For example, to meet her criteria, civic engagement is critical in service learning, meaning that the university connects only with the not-for-profit sector and students are not paid for their work in community organizations, nor are they regarded as volunteers, interns or co-op students. They come to the sector as learners. Service learning is not, in these terms, part of a professional work integrated learning programme and does not include shadowing more experienced workers or observing people in a workplace. As specified by Jacoby (1996), 'service-learning' is experiential, meaning that students go through a cycle of experience, reflective observation, conceptualization and active experimenting on the basis of the experience.

Students' active involvement in community activities and problems means they learn more about the nature, causes, distribution and consequences of issues. They are then better able to use their knowledge of issues from the classroom and their experiences to reflect on, rethink and reconceptualize their understanding, and then work to improve how they might re-engage with community issues. Through this learning process, students come to understand particular communities and populations, and the complexity of the human condition. They also develop personal and work-related skills.

One criticism of service learning is its normative focus (Butin 2005). Critics argue that service learning could or should be transformative. Whilst Butin does not specify 'normative', it is assumed to mean that students acquire new information and understandings without processing the emotional and intellectual challenges to their perceptions, values and attitudes. Whilst there are many examples of apparently normative models, even such simple community tasks as tutoring algebra can provide students with an intellectual and emotional challenge; it may enable them to see the impact of the intersection of race, gender and poverty on high school students. There is some debate, however, about whether this changes how students see social problems per se, or whether it transforms their perspectives and assumptions about society. Eyler and Giles (1999: 148–9), for example, in their study on learning outcomes in service learning, say that transformation of perspective is rare amongst students. Even so, high-quality placements where students have responsibilities and face challenges are more likely to result in students seeing social problems in different ways. Furthermore, the classroom teacher who integrates services with theoretical understandings is likely to challenge conventional understandings. Transformational opportunities come with the challenges provided by the classroom teachers and community groups.

There are many opportunities to work with people who are oppressed or experience multiple forms of oppression when working with community organizations. The transformative learning model challenges the bifurcation of the university and community, and has the potential to transform students and academics because students in community settings can experience issues such as race, ethnicity, religion, gender, sexual orientation, age and poverty. Service learning, Butin (2005) argues, should be located in the social justice and social change traditions. This may include working in areas such as human rights, with refugees and migrants, advocacy organizations, food banks or in violent communities, as illustrated in the following case example. This transformative view fits with Mezirow's (1994) theory of adult development.

> The University of Alberta has a CSL course entitled Oil and Community: Gendering the Boom. This Faculty of Arts programme explores the intersectionalities of gendered relations in the boom/bust economy and beyond the oilfields. Issues include 'boom' masculinities, migrant labour, homelessness and the sex trade. In this service learning course, students work in 'interdisciplinary groups to learn community-based project development and research skills'.
>
> http://www.uofaweb.ualberta.ca/arts/spring_immersion.cfm

Although this example does not specify how students will work with community service organizations, it is assumed the students would partner with women's organizations interested in advocacy, domestic violence or homelessness.

Service learning is structured to enable students to undertake service experiences concurrently with their academic work. These service experiences may be two hours per week in a workplace over the course of the semester, a project activity with less structured time constraints or a research task. Eyler and Giles (1999) have described learning outcomes for students undertaking service learning as including: personal and interpersonal development; the understanding and application of knowledge to community problems; engagement, curiosity and reflective practice; critical thinking; perspective transformation; and citizenship. Workplaces offering community service learning experiences include: indigenous organizations; volunteer centres; women's organizations; schools; elderly care facilities; mental health and community organizations; shelters for the homeless; food banks; health organizations such as AIDS services; organizations providing services for developmental or learning disabilities; advocacy groups; environmental groups; culture and recreation bodies; hospices; social service bodies; and social planning councils. In the university, these service learning courses may be connected to programmes such as sociology, business and economics, science, psychology, speech pathology, physiotherapy, geography, political science and global studies, women's studies, human rights, education, child and family welfare, social work, human nutrition, sports sciences, engineering and architecture. Table 2.3 provides some examples.

There are three major foci in service learning: the scholarly agenda for faculty and students (curriculum and learning); civic engagement (purpose, context and integration); and the partnership between the academy and the community. Support is implied across every facet of the service learning programme.

The *scholarly agenda* refers to the learning component of service learning. Undertaking service learning does not mean a student's experience is remote from the classroom teaching. From our understanding of constructivism, we know that

Table 2.3 Examples of service learning

Focus of course in educational institution	Example of activity in service organization
Business communication	Business research in service organizations
Algebra	Tutoring students in maths classes
Architecture	Design of a rehabilitation centre in a residential facility for older people
Kinesthetics and physical development	Teaching dancing to migrants in care facilities or providing physical activities for children
Music	Providing community education programmes to community groups
Computer art and design	Providing graphic design services to community organizations
Psychology (development)	Reading to children with learning difficulties
Ecology	Assisting with a biophysical inventory of a habitat; planting of native vegetation
Marketing	Assist social service organizations with development of a marketing plan
Engineering	Design ramps for wheelchair access
Global studies	Assist with a campaign for disenfranchised groups

students learn when they build on their previous experiences, have authentic learning tasks and engage in meaningful activity, and have social interaction and critical dialogue around social issues confronted during their workplace experiences. It is assumed that in addition to completing their learning tasks, students will have the opportunity to discover new learning; to integrate learning from their workplace experiences with learning in their classroom; interpret, analyse and explain their new understandings; and be able to apply this knowledge to develop theoretical insights or enhanced practice understandings (Zlotkowski 1998).

Civic engagement is a concept strongly influenced by two educational theorists: Dewey (1927, 1933, 1938), who wrote about the responsibilities of education in a democratic society, and Boyer (1990, 1996), who addressed the scholarship of engagement. The university is an important part of the community in which it is located. Civic engagement refers to the activities of the university, the faculty and students who work with their local community to make a difference and improve its members' quality of life. The university, faculty and students not only learn to understand social problems, but also to understand better how to address these problems through social change processes.

Service learning participants recognize that community issues are public issues, that private troubles are a manifestation of public policy, and that they, as citizens, have a responsibility to respond to social problems (Mills 1959). Civic engagement means that students engage in community activities and use their knowledge and expertise to resolve social problems. This engagement is supported by an academic curriculum, which encourages students to understand their responsibilities as citizens. There are five important elements in engaging with the community: values; knowledge; skills; efficacy; and commitment (Eyler and Giles 1999: 157).

Partnership between the academy and the community follows on from civic engagement. Here the academy works on behalf of its students and faculty to partner with community groups in developing learning experiences that build on civic engagement. The partnership builds on an understanding of both partners' strengths and partnership opportunities for service learning. From the student's perspective, this means understanding that they must reach out for, listen to and understand the community voice. This partnership leads to more purposeful and deliberate actions that arise from effective civic engagement.

The focus of service learning programmes on civic engagement is very different from the focus of cooperative learning programmes, the third model to be described in this book. Cooperative learning programmes have strong employer–academy links and facilitate employer recruitment of students to the workforce.

Cooperative learning model

Cooperative education is a structured work integrated learning programme where academic work and actual work experience are structured across programmes of study. The cooperative programme is counted as part of the degree and is recognized in academic transcripts. In many degree programmes, cooperative education is not compulsory – students elect to do it. In other programmes it is a required part of the students' education. Workplace selection may be done by employers and confirmed by the programme, or arranged and organized by students themselves. Generally, this work integrated learning experience is undertaken in blocks of time over the summer breaks, enabling students to understand better the complexities of workplaces, discipline and academic interests.

Although there is evidence of cooperative education in other nations, it was launched in Cincinnati in the USA by Herman Schneider in 1906. Schneider, an engineering professor, was concerned that he could not teach the skills necessary for engineering practice solely in the classroom and therefore launched the alternating of on- and off-campus study (Sovilla and Varty 2004). Cooperative education was originally an attempt to link theory with practice in an occupational field. The work was planned and linked to the educational curriculum. At a later stage, development and maintenance of strong connections to employers in this learning process was recognized. These relationships were reciprocal because cooperative education provided students with an opportunity to explore career goals, and gave employers an opportunity to review student competencies and abilities.

Whilst the original meaning of the term 'cooperative education' is clear, the term is sometimes used to encompass a variety of other terms with similar but different meanings. For example, Groenewald (2004:19) asserts that these alternative terms include 'apprenticeships', 'exchange programmes', 'field-based learning', 'field placements', 'professional practice', 'work-based education', 'service learning' and 'experiential learning'. For the purposes of this chapter, we use the National Commission for Cooperative Education's definition, in which cooperative education is:

> a structured educational strategy integrating classroom studies with learning through productive work experiences in a field related to a student's academic or career goals. It provides progressive experiences in integrating theory and practice. Co-op is a partnership among students, educational institutions and employers, with specified responsibilities for each party.
>
> National Commission for Cooperative Education (2002)

Strong and effective relationships with employers are characteristic of cooperative learning. Employers are key participants in the delivery of cooperative education placements. Employers participate if the cooperative programmes provide access to students who meet their needs as employers, that is, students who have a strong understanding of their discipline or vocational area, are work-ready and able to respond to competitive workplace challenges. These partnerships are reciprocal: in turn, employers provide student access to employment and opportunities to apply current theories to the workplace, and can provide feedback to the academy about the relevance and strengths of various programmes for business and industry. Academy–employer relationships go beyond access to cooperative opportunities and include participation in on-campus educational activities and various industry events, such as Career Fairs (Canadian Association for Co-operative Education 2005).

The aim of cooperative education is to alternate work experience with classroom study so that students are able to integrate theory with practice and practice with theory to enable a deeper understanding of both the theoretical and the practical. The focus of cooperative learning is on the skills learnt in particular workplaces, especially on the generic skills and work literacy that enable students to explore academic and career interests in a practical setting. It differs from professional learning in that the learning outcomes will vary depending on the workplace, rather than on professional regulatory requirements. Linking learning in the academy with learning in the workplace strengthens broader links between institutions and employing bodies. Cooperative education is available to students in a variety of programmes including the arts and sciences, business and economics, engineering and computer science, and in other vocationally-based programmes.

Some structures and criteria for cooperative placements have been defined by the Canadian Association for Co-operative Education (2005) and the National Commission for Cooperative Education (2002). These criteria include:

- The work is designated as a learning experience by the academy.
- There is a clear job description and opportunity for learning in the workplace.

Students are expected to do work rather than observe or shadow the other employees' work.

- There are minimum and maximum periods of work depending on whether the programme is alternating or concurrent. In concurrent programmes, the hours per week will be shorter than for full-time programmes.
- The student and their work are monitored by the academy and by employers, with feedback provided about performance.
- The student has a guide in the workplace to assist with learning.
- The workplace learning is evaluated by the academy and the employer.
- Students reflect on their experiences in the workplace as an important form of learning.
- Students are remunerated by employers for their contribution to the workplace.

It is worth noting the importance of remuneration by employers. Remuneration and competition for places are features of many cooperative education programmes in North America. In other nations, such as Australia and New Zealand, there is a diversity of models, with some remunerated and competitive and others being a requirement for all students with little expectation of payment.

The legitimization of work experience as learning has long been debated in cooperative education. These debates have focused on whether cooperative education has an educational orientation resulting in generalist competencies, or is simply a training strategy enabling students to learn work skills. According to Eames and Cates (2004), for some years cooperative work placements were not seen as educative. In the late 1970s, the US government commissioned a study into the educational outcomes and assessment of cooperative education. The study concluded that there were many learning objectives suitable for incorporation in cooperative learning activities. The end result of these debates was intensification of a pedagogically sound placement process. One area for intensification lies in the specification of outcomes for the students, the employers, the academy and society.

Student learning is important in cooperative education. It takes place through specification of outcomes, formative and summative assessment, and student reflection on their experiences in individual or group sessions in written or oral format (Canadian Association for Co-operative Education 2005; Hodges *et al.* 2005). Student outcomes include academic, personal and professional (National Commission for Cooperative Education 2002). Whilst outcomes depend on employer, student and academy arrangements, many are frequently expressed as generic skills including such things as willingness to learn, teamwork, analytical thinking, computer literacy, written communication, and concern for order, quality and accuracy. An example of student learning outcomes is provided in Table 2.4.

A critical part of the cooperative learning process is student assessment as a process and outcome. It can be achieved through using feedback from workplace mentors and by submission of work to the university. Portfolio assessment is often used as a way of securing reflection on learning and specifying outcomes achieved.

Table 2.4 Student learning outcomes

Academic	Professional	Personal
Ability to integrate classroom theory with workplace practice	Clarity about career goals	Maturity
Clarity about academic goals	Understanding of workplace culture	Determination of strengths and weaknesses
Academic motivation	Workplace competencies	Development/enhancement of interpersonal skills
Technical knowledge through use of state-of-the-art equipment	New or advanced skills	Earnings to assist college expenses or to support personal financial responsibilities
	Career management	Productive and responsible citizenship skills
	Professional network	Lifelong learning skills
	After graduation employment opportunities	

Source: National Commission for Cooperative Education (2002)

During a student's experience in the workplace, learning is enhanced through support and guidance of workplace learning guides. Groenewald (2004: 22), a South African academic, specified the criteria for successful cooperative learning, which we have summarized in Table 2.5.

Academy and employer partnerships enable employers to identify those academies that have particular educational approaches which provide an integrated curriculum that enables student recruitment and facilitates excellent employment outcomes. These universities will have an enhanced reputation amongst employers.

Table 2.5 Criteria for success of cooperative education

- Learning in the workplace is experiential and recognized in the curriculum.
- Students are registered into cooperative programmes and assisted with finding placements.
- Orientation to experiential learning and workplaces is provided.
- There is planning of the student's learning experience with contracts between parties.
- A workplace mentor or learning guide is provided in the workplace.
- Monitoring is provided by the academy.
- Formative and summative assessment is a critical part of the learning.
- Reflection on learning is an important part of learning.
- The learning is recognized by attainment of academic credit.

In those situations where alumni connections are important for donations and fundraising, cooperative learning opportunities provide students with strong connections to their academies and increase the likelihood of their giving to the institution after graduation. Similarly, employers strongly connected to the academy may be approached more comfortably for financial contributions.

The societal outcomes are a better prepared workforce that can better contribute to the knowledge economy, and stronger reciprocal relationships between employers and higher education, enabling greater connectivity between the practical challenges in workplaces and the theoretical initiatives of the academy (National Commission for Community Education 2002).

The value of using models

The three models outlined illustrate how work integrated learning takes place in workplaces that operate in professional, industrial and community contexts. This situated learning facilitates better integration of the theory taught in the classroom with real-life practice outside the university. It begins experientially *in situ*, and is then deepened and enhanced when students reflect on and process their experiences. Integration occurs when theory is used to understand practice and practice is used to rethink and critique theory.

Learning is most effective when the university and the workplace or community combine in a reciprocal relationship to further the development of student learning. Work integrated learning is structured and sequenced, with clear expectations, goals, outcomes and assessment, and is embedded in the whole academic programme. It provides the student with support in the classroom, the workplace and the community to facilitate their development into a graduate ready to face the challenges of the world.

Summary

The term 'work integrated learning' covers a vast array of terminologies and programmes internationally. We have defined work integrated learning programmes as those incorporating and working from seven key domains: purpose; context; nature of the integration; curriculum issues; learning; partnership between the university and the workplace/community; and support provided to the student and the workplace/community.

The three models of work integrated learning discussed in this chapter – professional learning, service learning and cooperative learning – serve as the basis for demonstrating how the seven concepts are integrated into the practical implementation of work integrated learning programmes. The models provide an introduction to Chapter 3, 'Working to Learn, Learning to Work', which focuses primarily on the curriculum, context and learning dimensions of work integrated learning.

Section 2

Learning, teaching, assessment and supervision

Working to Learn, Learning to Work

Introduction

This chapter is the first of four focusing on the curriculum and pedagogical elements of work integrated learning. The term work integrated learning is used here as a metaconcept to include three different models of work integrated learning, namely the professional, service and cooperative learning models described in Chapter 2. The concept of curriculum is used in its broadest sense to include all aspects of the learning agenda. Curriculum includes pedagogy, intended outcomes and unintended consequences, the environmental context, learner characteristics, and learners' interactions with the learning agenda and environment. Teachers and teaching, assessment and the distinctive role of supervision as they all relate to work integrated learning are also elements of the curriculum, but are not included in this chapter. They are addressed in Chapters 4, 5 and 6 respectively.

The learning agenda for work integrated learning programmes is unique. It will be explored in some depth, as will the unique characteristics of, and unique challenges presented by, learning in work integrated learning experiences. The discussion in this chapter will contrast the distinctive characteristics of workplaces and classrooms as learning environments, and will note the implications of these for supporting student learning. Diversity amongst learners is also of special importance, having implications for the ways learners engage with, and perform in, work integrated learning contexts. Whilst acknowledging that all stakeholders in the work integrated learning process become learners within a community of practice, we will restrict the discussion of 'learners' to students participating in work integrated learning experiences as part of their programme of study.

The work integrated learning agenda

The challenge for designers of work integrated learning curricula is to capture conceptual diversity and the complexity of multiple agendas in a single curriculum. Similarly, the challenge of capturing the many ways of thinking about work integrated learning in a single chapter in a book has required a degree of selectivity. We have been discerning in presenting what we believe are core conceptual frameworks about learning and learners that need consideration when designing and managing work integrated learning programmes.

The decision to include work integrated learning experiences as a significant element in a programme of study signals a specific and distinctive learning agenda in the higher education curriculum, namely, drawing on the potential learning opportunities inherent in work and practical action. The primary curriculum agenda is learning 'through' work, whether that work occurs in an industry, profession or community organization. This curriculum agenda is referred to here as *working to learn*. Within this process of working to learn students might also *learn to work*, benefitting from all that this implies in terms of knowledge, skills, capacities and dispositions. Learning to work is only one goal of the broad work integrated learning (working to learn) agenda.

The broad agenda

Work integrated learning agendas aim to provide students with unique opportunities to:

- identify, develop and use theory to interpret, explain and intervene in the real world;
- affirm personal career choices and develop intrapersonal awareness;
- assume roles in which they must function as responsible members of society, contributing to their community;
- develop their interpersonal communication capabilities;
- learn the particular competencies and cultures of specific professions, industries and community contexts.

Because these learning intentions are elements of a formal curriculum, they need to be identified explicitly and communicated to students and other stakeholders involved in work integrated learning. Clear communication contributes to common understandings and expectations regarding achievement of generic and specific learning outcomes designated in work integrated learning curricula.

The broad aim of the work integrated learning agenda is that students should achieve professional competence, not merely as a professional in a specific field, but in terms of mastering the skills and attributes required to function effectively in diverse situations in diverse real-world contexts. Worth-Butler *et al.* (1994: 226–7) propose that such competence requires a combination of 'capability' and 'performance'; that is, a combination of 'unobservable attributes including attitudes, values, judgemental ability and personal dispositions' and measurable, 'observable behaviour'.

Generic learning outcomes

Specific learning outcomes for work integrated learning will differ across disciplines, various models of work integrated learning, workplace contexts, and also according to the primary purposes of the work integrated learning programme. Despite these differences, all work integrated learning programmes aim to develop in students a set of generic learning outcomes or capabilities, which include students becoming:

- self-aware as proactive and intentional learners;
- effective in forming productive relationships with a diverse set of people and functioning in different roles;
- competent and astute in applying conceptual learning to transform and explain practical/functional knowledge and action;
- collaborative workplace learners;
- confident in themselves as learners;
- confident in themselves as members of a community;
- able to balance practical and theoretical expertise;
- culturally aware and respectful of differences in individuals, amongst cultures and within communities;
- competent, responsible, civic-minded citizens;
- responsible and contributing workers and citizens.

In short, work integrated learning aims to develop students' capacity to be proactive, adaptable, motivated and responsible. These are qualities sought by potential employers (DEST 2005; Orrell and Bowden 2004; Smith 2005).

A particular challenge in establishing the work integrated learning agenda is to communicate effectively to students what is expected of them and what these expectations look like in everyday practice. Students are often unaware that workplace supervisors are looking for evidence that they possess the qualities just outlined, and, therefore, are unaware of the need to demonstrate them explicitly. The challenge for students and their workplace learning supervisors/guides is to identify what activities will assist students to develop these capabilities, and what constitutes evidence of students having achieved them. These issues will be discussed in Chapter 4 (Teaching) and Chapter 5 (Assessment) respectively. The issue of importance here is to ensure that students are informed of the expectation that these capabilities will be developed. An explicit communication agenda will ensure that students, workplace personnel and the academy are made aware of the indicators that will be used as evidence that students have attained these capabilities.

Workplace literacies

Students will need to develop specific workplace literacies as part of the process of attaining the more generic capabilities. Workplace literacy, therefore, is an espoused goal of the work integrated learning curriculum. The aim is for students to develop, understand, continuously evaluate and update the knowledge, skills and attributes that constitute workplace literacy. The broad concept of workplace literacy encompasses six categories of literacy. Each category focuses on one distinctive element, namely organizational matters, legal and ethical issues, profession-specific concerns, career learning, social learning and cultural learning (Cooper *et al.* 2003). Each category has a set of knowledge, skills and attributes that develop through student engagement in the unique working to learn agenda. These are outlined here in brief. A more detailed list is provided in Appendix 1.

Organizational literacy refers to students' understanding of workplace organizational values, priorities, structures and culture. Within work integrated learning programmes there are opportunities for students to learn to adapt to different situations; adjust to and cope with uncertainty; recognize and understand different learning pathways and affordances; appreciate the value of good and bad work integrated learning experiences; demonstrate initiative; and respect and work within the workplace culture.

Legal and ethical literacy refers to knowledge of, and behaviours appropriate to, universal, national, local and workplace-specific legislations, and policies and procedures related to these in the workplace. Examples include the Universal Declaration of Human Rights; occupational health and safety legislation; and equal opportunity, anti-discrimination and sexual harassment legislation. As a consequence of participating in workplaces students will gain awareness of, and behave in accordance with, requirements for client confidentiality and privacy, copyright, trade secrets and intellectual property, duty of care to those with whom they work, the workplace, the university and the wider community, and risk mitigation and management.

Profession-specific literacy refers to student understanding of profession-specific expectations, standards and competency requirements. Through participation in workplace experiences students will be expected to demonstrate a willingness to learn and practise profession-specific skills and ways of being. They will also be expected to exhibit particular professional attitudes, develop procedural knowledge (rules and procedures) and conditional knowledge (situation-specific), transfer conceptual knowledge between situations and exhibit practical knowledge in their day-to-day functioning.

Career literacy refers to students identifying and confirming their personal areas of interest and strength in terms of their career choices. Through participation in workplace experiences students gain first-hand opportunities to research their interests by observing mentors and role models in the workplace and seeking their career guidance. Students will be able to reflect on their current knowledge, skills, attributes and values, evaluate the realities of their currently identified career path and make modifications.

Social literacy encompasses the capacity to work with others, including collaboration, conflict resolution and mediation. Whilst working, students might have the opportunity to undertake diverse team roles, including leadership. This role diversification provides challenges for students' communicative competence and capacity for diplomacy. Workplaces provide opportunities where students can experience judicious use of personal and official power, and exercise workplace etiquette. One challenging opportunity is for students to gain an understanding of their status in the workplace context, including insight into how this status interacts with their personal values, strengths and limitations in that context. The social learning opportunities are powerful when students are required to ensure responsible, rational decision-making and balance it with their affective responses to experiences.

Cultural literacy refers to students developing the ability to value difference through understanding and respecting others' perceptions, values and needs. The challenge in work integrated learning experiences is for students to interact with others in a non-judgemental way, to see the benefits of diverse cultural input and to confront controversial issues such as racism, elitism and sexism in everyday practice.

Explicit development of students' workplace literacy within the work integrated learning agenda requires the deliberate exploitation of affordances that tap into tacit workplace knowledge and culture. That is, achieving this agenda demands an awareness of its importance and the need for explicit engagement between local experts who have the tacit knowledge or 'wisdom of experience' (Orrell 1997) and student participants.

Learning tacit workplace knowledge

Tacit knowledge is a rich body of knowledge that is not yet explicit and is the basis of much workplace activity. Research into expert health care practitioners and education of novice practitioners (Benner 1984; Bordage 1994, 1999) identifies that expert knowledge in workplaces is largely 'compiled', case-based knowledge enabling experienced workers to make rapid decisions and take appropriate action. Experts perceive cues in the environment that trigger recall of similar previous instances or 'cases'. They then select and implement solutions based on their holistic experience of previous cases and modify them to account for distinctive immediate conditions. Experts are often unable to explain their reasoning processes in problem solving and novices often fail to perceive that any problem-solving process has occurred. Experts commonly explain their choices as intuition: *I just know*. Students often do not recognize or get access to this knowledge in operation and thus fail to understand the rationale behind the short cuts experts take in everyday practice that seemingly contradict formal protocols taught in on-campus classes. Enabling students to recognize, access and understand this tacit knowledge in operation is a key driver of the work integrated learning agenda that must be embraced by learning supervisors/guides.

Developing specific workplace literacies and generic capabilities in students, and enabling students to access tacit workplace knowledge through work integrated learning, does not happen by chance. Structuring of learning in the ill-defined environments of diverse workplaces is needed to address individual student needs and reduce potential difficulties in the work integrated learning partnership.

The learning process: learning through work

Learning is the product of students' efforts to interpret, evaluate and translate what they experience in order to make meaning of it. Learning is only learning when it results in changes in behaviour, which include new ways of both thinking and doing. Learning occurs when attempts are made to make sense of a new environment or to master a new skill. Heraclitus said, 'You can never step twice into the same river, for fresh waters are ever flowing in on you' (Harré 1983). When past experiences are reviewed in light of new events and experiences, the way the world is interpreted is changed forever; when students interact differently with their world, trying out new behaviours in new social roles, they forge new identities. Learning processes such as these are the product of students' attempts to cope with new situations, resulting in the expansion of their cognitive, social and emotional capabilities.

Work integrated learning is a formal activity deliberately selected by curriculum leaders for the unique learning opportunities it provides. It is also an informal, social, lifelong, everyday activity. Both the formal and informal manifestations are vehicles through which students can change by learning ways to adapt to new environments and challenges.

In this section the discussion will focus on issues related to the learning processes that need consideration when designing the learning for work integrated learning programmes. The section begins by emphasizing the importance of structuring learning in workplaces, and then highlights learning and development factors that impact on the quality and quantity of work integrated learning that students achieve. These factors include student approaches to learning, the developmental nature of learning and different individual ways of knowing.

Structuring the learning in workplaces as learning environments

The unpredictable nature of work integrated learning environments necessitates structuring the learning through explicit use of intended learning outcomes. This learning design strategy ensures shared appreciation of the specific learning expectations inherent in learning outcomes. Structuring learning through stated learning outcomes defines for students what must be learnt and the culture of the workplace.

One strategy for defining intended learning outcomes and communicating these to stakeholders in the work integrated learning enterprise is the development and negotiation of a three-way learning contract between student, workplace and university. The contract clarifies expectations; contains criteria or indicators for observing practice behaviour; sets out agreed learning outcomes; and can be developed into a record of negotiated learning assessments. To be effective the contract must be explicit about credit for the learning achieved (Marshall and Mill 1993: 144).

Structuring the learning with a three-way learning contract can help students become proactive learners in the workplace. It is up to students to seek out and take every learning opportunity available, within safe limits, all the while maintaining a focus on the particular intended learning outcomes of their work integrated learning programme. Being proactive requires students to have high self-awareness and knowledge of their personal limitations. The process of developing the three-way learning contract will not only help students clarify learning outcomes that structure the types of learning opportunities they will seek, but also help them to consider their level of knowledge and preparedness for entering the workplace.

Structuring learning through contracts can provide a map for skills development. In some cases it may contain timelines for achievement of specific competencies. This superstructure guides students and their workplace supervisors/guides as they work together towards achieving the intended learning outcomes related to student learning capabilities. Not all students will attain these intended qualities, but when intended learning outcomes are explicit, students have the opportunity to assess their current capability, determine the gaps and establish their own personal learning agenda. Where these intended learning outcomes remain implicit in the supervisory conversation, or where student motivations for, and attitudes and approaches to, learning are not within their personal control, students may find it difficult to achieve the expected intended learning outcomes. Where intended learning outcomes are not explicit, students will often discover where in the workplace they feel successful or what they do well and contrive to focus on those areas and tasks rather than challenge themselves in those aspects of work where they have the most learning to do.

The developmental nature of learning

Learning is always a work in progress and has a developmental component. The concept of development is not restricted to an increase in what is known and accomplished. The concept incorporates the learning process itself – the ways in which learning occurs and its qualities. Pertinent to work integrated learning, Piaget (1972) and Vygotsky (1978) describe the construction of knowledge and meaning through participation in activities, and Vygotsky focuses on the importance of expert guidance as a developmental tool.

Piaget's (1972) cognitive development theory describes distinctive and different learning processes that change across the early lifespan. The stages progress from learning by sensory exploration and mobility in infancy, through learning by symbolic play in early childhood, through learning by concrete experimentation in middle and later childhood to the fourth developmental stage (formal operational) in which adults develop their ability to think abstractly, analyse information and draw conclusions, as well as to consider the perspectives and experiences of other people and understand their values (Merriam and Caffarella 1999: 139; Huitt and Hummel 2003). This latter stage is particularly relevant to learning in workplace and community contexts. The capabilities developed in Piaget's (1972) fourth developmental stage are important achievements for students that enable them to function socially and learn to become global citizens through work integrated learning. Many higher education students may still be functioning in this developmental stage and in the process of acquiring these capabilities. The workplace environment has the potential to provide the kinds of challenges that provoke and enhance attainment of formal operational capabilities at this important stage of development.

Development of ethical moral reasoning

An aspect of student development selected for particular consideration here is the capacity for ethical moral reasoning, which has particular salience in work integrated learning experiences. William Perry (1999) examined the reasoning of a large sample of university students and found that individuals' ethical and moral reasoning progresses incrementally, from one level to the next, through increasingly sophisticated stages of reasoning. As individuals confront moral dilemmas, over time these confrontations can provoke 'a higher level of reasoning'. William Perry's 'Scheme of Intellectual and Ethical Development' incorporates nine developmental stages grouped into four levels that illustrate how learners form ethical and moral judgements, and perceive others' actions. These categories and their corresponding student positions are summarized in Table 3.1.

At the lowest level, Dualism, learners are absolutist, black and white thinkers, perceiving the world in absolute terms. Students who function at this level see all questions as having right or wrong answers and are reliant on the opinion of those in authority to validate their thinking. With life experience and personal growth, students' powers of reasoning progress to recognition of the possibility of multiple viewpoints (Multiplicity) about a set of circumstances. Students who operate at this level of thinking are still in search of the 'right' answer and are still dependent on authority to help them form an opinion. Students' thinking then progresses to Relativism, in which they accept that the 'truth' is different for different people, and that these truths are located in diverse world views and are explained through recognition of diverse life experiences. The difficulty for learners who operate at this level is to arrive at a personal opinion, as at this stage everything is regarded as 'relative'. The challenge for relativistic thinkers is to progress to higher levels of ethico-moral reasoning, namely that of Commitment, which involves self-knowledge, rational appraisal of evidence, and use of principles in reflecting on their own and others' knowledge and values. The highest position is 'Limited Commitment' in which the student has formed opinions based on rational appraisal of evidence, engages in active reflection and inquiry, and reserves the right to change their opinion in the light of new evidence. In other words, the highest level is observable in the habits of a lifelong learner.

Table 3.1 Summary of Perry's (1999) Scheme of Intellectual and Ethical Development

Stage		Student position
Level 1: Duality – received knowledge • A right or wrong answer to everything • Authorities know the answers	1 2	Learning the right answers and working hard will be rewarded; see authorities as knowing everything – follow authorities without questioning Aware of disagreement among authorities; choose which authorities to believe; memorize the correct answers
Level 2: Multiplicity – subjective knowledge • Conflicting answers • Trust own 'inner voices' • Still seek confirmation from authority	3 4	Uncertainty – some problems have no known solution Knowledge is just an opinion; everyone is entitled to believe in the truth of their own opinion; begin seeking own solutions to problems, but still seek guidance from authorities
Level 3: Relativism – procedural knowledge • Disciplinary reasoning methods: subjective knowledge (connected) vs. objective analysis (separated)	5 6	View proposed solutions in context, relative to supporting reasoning; recognize opinions based on values, experiences and knowledge while evaluating solutions; see everything as relative, even themselves Realize must make own decisions and must commit to a solution; begin to develop a sense of community; view themselves and authorities as collaborative thinkers; develop faith in their own decisions
Level 4: Commitment – constructed knowledge • Construction of own values and identity through rational reflection on knowledge learned from others and personal experience	7 8 9	Decide who they are; commit to their personal values Experience tensions arising from this commitment – ask what are the implications for the future? Explore issues of responsibility Come to terms with how their life is and the commitment they have made; aware of own values and those of others; settled in their own values while respecting others (even though they may not believe them to be right); realize they will undergo constant change from now on.

In the current internationalized higher education, workplace and community contexts, students who attain the fourth level are open to learning new ways of thinking and acting with and from diverse groups of people in diverse settings. They are able to reflect on the new knowledge they learn from interacting with diverse others and integrate it with their own experiences (Perry 1981: 79). University teachers and workplace supervisors/guides are wise to listen to the thinking or reasoning of the students with whom they work. This will enable them to identify student levels of reasoning development and strategically provoke challenges that will assist students to advance their level of reasoning capacity. Student reasoning will not only give indicators of their development level, it can also provide clues to students' different ways of knowing.

Students as learners in the workplace

The current internationalized and transnationalized contexts of higher education and work, and increasing use of information and communication technology (ICT), continue to expand the cultural mix of students in universities and workplaces. Greater participation of indigenous students, students from other disadvantaged socio-economic and socio-cultural groups and mature students adds to this diversity. Many students are in the workforce whilst attending university, or have been previously in the workforce. Learners in work integrated learning experiences represent a rich and complex mix of interwoven cultures, value systems, communities, professions, supervisors, coordinators, universities and other education systems, previous experiences, life circumstances and responsibilities: influences Brundage (1980: 9) summarizes as 'histories of socialization ... as part of many communities of practice'. Similarly, Boud and Miller (1996: 9) espouse that 'each experience is influenced by the unique past of the learner as well as the current context', including the influence of 'socio-cultural and historical factors' on knowledge created through experience. Therefore, it is important to have some idea of who the students are: their backgrounds and characteristics, and how these impact on work integrated learning.

Diversity requires understanding the factors that contribute to students' histories of socialization. These factors impact on students' attitudes and access to, and opportunities for, styles of learning that occur in universities, workplaces and life contexts. Consideration of these factors causes a rethink of prevailing assumptions about students. The integration of diverse cultural, social, educational and work factors produces in students a unique development of identities as human beings and as learners, workers and members of communities of practice. Table 3.2 provides a framework to assist in identifying a complex range of issues that can potentially impact on students' capacity to learn in any context. The framework emphasizes diversity in terms of privilege and power, systemic marginalization and oppression, minority groups and majority groups – the power of 'isms' (e.g. racism), 'phobias' (e.g. homophobia), 'ivities' (e.g. inclusivity, exclusivity) and 'ilities'(capability, ability, disability) that impact on relationships, communication, understanding, learning and knowledge. The framework has been developed primarily from interviews with work integrated learning coordinators, workplace supervisors and students participating in work integrated learning experiences (Cooper and Bowden 2008), as well as research into the developmental nature of learning (Perry 1999; Piaget 1972; Vygotsky 1978), factors impacting on students' learning in the workplace environment (Edgecombe 2005; Edgecombe and Bowden 2009; Rogan *et al.* 2006; Wenger 1998), and teaching and learning philosophies (Wang 2007; Wang and Farmer 2008).

Table 3.2 Factors influencing student histories of socialization

CULTURAL FACTORS AND ISSUES

Race	Ethnicity	Language	Religion	Gender	Sexuality	Age	Communication styles	Knowledge pathways	Technology
Racism; visible or invisible difference; social structures – patriarchal, matriarchal, etc.	Ethno-centrism; visible or invisible difference; sub-structures – cultures; social structures	English as international language; dialects; hidden meanings; structure; literacy level	Beliefs; visible or invisible; persecution or favour	Sexism; sexual harassment; roles; taboos; male; female; transgender; changing gender identity; bias	Homophobia; sexual harassment	Ageism; age range 17–60 years; cognitive psycho-social and moral development	Greeting styles; naming; touch; manners; eye contact; body language; facial expression; agreeing; silence; gift giving	Knowledge generation; handing down of knowledge; ownership; sharing or keeping; taboos; form	Access to, knowledge and use of ICT

SOCIAL FACTORS AND ISSUES

Family	Socio-economic status	Disability	Community	Physical environment	Everyday life
Position; responsibility; expectations; safety; trust; abuse; discipline – reward or punishment; hierarchies of respect	Access to food, shelter, education, health care, employment and ICT; poverty; wealth; support systems	Visible; invisible; capabilities; abuse; valued or devalued; mental health; discrimination	Welcomed; belonging; outsider; acceptance; rejection; valued; devalued; residency status	Geographical location – urban, regional/countryside; peaceful; violent; restrictive; expansive; weather conditions – extreme or mild; natural disasters (earthquakes)	Mainstream; minority; interaction; isolation; good experiences; bad experiences; media; use of ICT; local knowledge; interpretation of treatment and place in the world

(continued)

Table 3.2 (cont.)

EDUCATION FACTORS AND ISSUES

Formal education/classroom	Family attitude to formal education	Technology
Curriculum; success; failure; learning styles; belonging; outsider; reward; punishment; support; physical environment and institution culture; institutional teaching and learning philosophy; teachers; sponsor expectations (e.g. scholarship providers); education level; delivery mode	Valued or devalued; support; generational education history; trust or mistrust of system; work more important than formal education – 'earn not learn'	Access to and education in use of ICT

WORK FACTORS AND ISSUES

Never worked	Casual work	Volunteer work	Many jobs	Same profession for many years	Technology	Common issues
Culture shock; extra preparation; no work literacy	Culture shock of full time work – personal time and organization issues	Own boss; no evaluation of work; appreciation	Ideas of ways of working may or may not be welcome; initiative; different workplace cultures	Power and age issues; wisdom or out of date? Flexibility? Change of direction; attitude – know everything or go back to open learner mindset of starting again	Many different technologies – student experience of these?	Employer and student expectations; physical environment; organization culture; support; opportunity to practice; time; resources; previous success or failure; personality; autonomy; bullying; discrimination; trust; communication

All of the issues identified in Table 3.2 are expressed in the broad concept of life experience. How this assortment of issues affects students in the workplace as a learning environment will be as diverse as the workplaces, the students and workplace personnel. Student performance in that environment will largely depend on how students see their role within it and how they regard themselves – their self-identity.

The impact of life experiences on students' learning

It is not possible fully to account for individual human factors despite it being possible to factor disparate institutional, workplace, local, national and global cultural and economic philosophies, policies and laws into work integrated learning strategies. Student histories of socialization will shape individual physical, cognitive, psychosocial and moral development, which will become evident in attitudes and approaches towards learning in the workplace environment.

Factors impacting on life experiences (for example age, race, gender, sexuality, culture, socio-economic background and family background) will influence student attitudes to formal and informal learning, ability to develop positive, trusting, respectful relationships, and ability to continue to learn and to share knowledge with others. Understanding these factors through building learner profiles can help identify students' diverse needs.

A challenging issue for students, especially when they are removed from their comfort zone and placed in an unfamiliar workplace environment, is to understand how their cultural identity can impact on their work integrated learning experience. Culture shock can set in and the student begins to question who they really are and why they are choosing to engage in the challenges confronting them.

Cultural ambiguity – who am I?

Systemic marginalization exacerbates visible and invisible differences between cultures that combine to create a student's cultural mindset. At the heart of a cultural mindset are core beliefs and taken-for-granted assumptions regarding social structures, teaching and learning traditions, ways of knowing, life expectations and forms of communication such as silence and allowing others a respectful personal space. In particular, the different cultural nuances ingrained in specific languages are often non-translatable into other cultural contexts. For example, one student from a non-English-speaking background undertaking work integrated learning as part of her study programme in an English-speaking country said of report writing requirements: 'We cannot just understand how to write in this style; it does not make any sense to us. But our supervisor just does not understand that we cannot understand. We feel very stupid because we cannot understand' (Cooper and Bowden 2008).

Individual learner identification with a particular group and its corresponding culture and belief systems influences how they learn, what they learn, and their perceptions of themselves and others. Students may face identity crises when they cross cultural boundaries to function in unfamiliar workplace and community contexts. Issues such as adopting the language of a particular profession, steeped in cultural nuances that may be foreign to the student's culture, can place the student in 'no man's land', where they feel they belong to neither their culture nor that of their profession. Students may begin to question how they can maintain their identity, culture and connection to their cultural roots and cultural communities of practice while practising their profession (Ranzijn *et al.* 2006: 22).

Even when students ostensibly 'belong' to the predominant cultural and social education and work systems, when entering the unknown territory of workplaces they may suffer extreme anxiety and succumb to a lack of confidence (Thompson 2003). Structuring the learning process in workplace contexts provides a basis for overcoming this and other issues arising from student and workplace diversity, and the differences between the university and workplace as learning environments.

Students' ways of knowing

One of the risks in all educational discussion is to conclude that consensus exists where it does not. Assuming consensus and taking it for granted can silence and marginalize those who have the least power and influence. Students who are in this position can be labelled as unmotivated or unengaged in their learning when in reality they feel unable to contribute to an environment in which they feel excluded because they cannot conform to the prevailing values and ways of work-ing. Exclusion of some groups from particular studies, professions and workplaces results from tacit and insidious marginalization. Unintended marginalization occurs when the assumption is made that conforming world views exist within a functioning community when they do not.

Taken-for-granted assumptions of consensus effectively silence the least power-ful whose ways of knowing and knowledge often differ most from those of the dominant and privileged. Women's ways of knowing and indigenous ways of knowing illustrate the value these marginalized groups place on their own dis-tinctive ways of knowing. Work integrated learning programme designers must be sensitive to diverse ways of knowing and factor these into their programmes.

Women's Ways of Knowing

Gender has the capacity to influence ways of knowing and ways of being. Gender balance is often an issue in workplaces. Workplace leaders and managers recognize potential gender-related strengths and want their organizations to have access to the influence of both men's and women's ways of knowing and relating. Much of this thinking has been influenced by the theory of 'Five Ways of Women's Knowing' (Belenky *et al.* 1986), which articulates the concept of *connected teach-ing* as a process of collaborative knowing among learners and teachers; a process that acknowledges and builds on the importance for women of connectedness to relationships and the influence this has on their learning as adults (Merriam and Caffarella 1999: 111).

In responding to the prevailing values in workplaces or educational institutions, women see themselves as ranging from having no voice (silence – disempowered) through to having 'an authentic' voice (constructed knowledge – empowered). In this latter category, women (learners) understand knowledge as contextual; value and utilize subjective and objective ways of knowing; value their own opinions, knowledge, sense of self and ability to create knowledge; and integrate their views and identity 'with reason and the wider world' (Merriam and Caffarella 1999: 146). Developing an authentic voice for some women learners in work integrated learning programmes can be an appropriate additional learning outcome gained through immersion in workplace contexts.

Indigenous ways of knowing

Indigenous academics and leaders from diverse, marginalized, indigenous nation states remind us that their traditional ways of knowing differ from, but are equally as valid as Euro-Western ways of knowing with their scientific, socialized and racialized knowledge. Indigenous knowledge is diverse and has many teachings from various indigenous nations. What is important to recognize here is that indigenous knowledge is transported within indigenous students 'through experiences, histories, cultures, traditions, languages, and teachings' (Battiste and Henderson 2000). One indigenous community in a Canadian university reasons that 'Survival for Indigenous peoples is more than a question of physical existence; it is an issue of preserving Indigenous knowledge systems in the face of cognitive imperialism' (Battiste and Henderson 2000: 12). This particular group argues that:

- The ecology of Indigenous knowledge is based in honouring our relationship to the land and Creation.
- Indigenous knowledge is wholistic knowledge and includes our spiritual, emotional, mental, and physical ways of being. It encompasses our relationship to all of Creation and its inhabitants.
- Indigenous knowledge is ancestral and sacred. It looks at our past, present and future (Battiste and Henderson 2000: 12).

Their call was for Aboriginal students to recognize that they were 'on a learning and knowledge-gathering journey' that would benefit from the teachings they carried with them from their geographic territories. The erosion, protection and reclamation of indigenous knowledges are major concerns.

The challenge with work integrated learning is to find ways of encouraging indigenous students to value their ways of knowing in unfamiliar and often threatening environments to the extent that they feel confident enough to draw on these and talk to their teachers and workplace supervisors/guides about them. Making connections between indigenous ways of knowing and other ways of knowing can enrich the work integrated learning experiences for all stakeholders.

Student approaches to learning

Whilst student attitudes to learning and motivations for undertaking a particular course of study will be influenced by their histories of socialization, their approach to learning is more fundamental to the persons themselves, although it can be influenced by the immediate context. Students will have dispositions towards adopting a deep, a surface or a more strategic approach to learning (Marton and Säljö 1976).

Deep approach

In a deep approach, students attempt to find meaning by linking past knowledge with current information; linking information from one course with that from another course; making distinctions between evidence, rationale, argument and conclusions; and linking the information to everyday experiences. The full depth of this learning is rarely fully apparent and sometimes may not be rewarded in more traditional university courses. Such students often do well in workplace contexts where they might find theoretical relevance in what they observe and in their efforts to make meaning as they adapt and apply their theoretical learning to novel contexts.

Surface approach

Students who adopt a surface approach to learning focus on completing the task requirements without seeking meaning; they may just memorize facts. Principles and examples may be disconnected and students treat the task as an imposition, but their learning has often been rewarded in classroom contexts. Surface learners are likely to be driven by assessment tasks and often require more direction in complex situations. Work integrated learning curricula that are driven by competency schedules risk encouraging a surface approach where students tick off the incremental acquisition of specific skills and competencies. Important here is the quality of articulation of the competencies and the ways in which their achievement is managed in the workplace.

Strategic approach

Students who are strategic learners use both deep and surface approaches – whichever strategy is necessary to improve their performance. Students note the assessment requirements of every course and are motivated to pass. Their desire for achievement may prevent them from forming the authentic collaborative relationships needed in work integrated learning.

Developing deep approaches to learning in students is an ideal outcome of work integrated learning. It must be recognized that memorization has an important place in all learning, particularly in learning skills and remembering formulae. It is also an important part of the recall needed to perform effectively in workplaces. Memorization without understanding, however, can create risks, as students will be unable to adapt their actions when unexpected events or conditions occur. Students' ability to adapt to changing circumstances is influenced by their level of intellectual and ethical development, and their individual 'ways of knowing'. A student's approach to learning may reflect a personal disposition that can be overridden by the approach and expectations of a learning guide or teacher (Biggs 2003). The influence of life experiences on learners' overall development – how individuals see their place in the world – is critical to their participation in ongoing learning in diverse learning contexts.

Workplaces as learning contexts

Social learning is a strong motivator for providing work integrated learning experiences. When students enter a workplace they become part of a learning environment in which learning occurs through social engagement. Learning in the workplace involves engaging and functioning with people effectively to achieve workplace purposes as well as students' specific learning objectives (Billett 2009).

In defining learning in workplace environments, we draw on the concepts of experiential learning (Dewey 1938; Kolb 1984) and situated learning (Lave and Wenger 1991). Key principles of situated learning (Lave and Wenger 1991) include:

- Learning involving the *whole person* in a complex system of social interactions with others.
- Learning *from* others in a process of guidance and immersion in activities.
- Learning *through* our interactions with others in a culture whether an office, team, project group, professional collective or community group.
- Learning *with* other people so that practice becomes part of the collective knowledge.

Students engage in experiential learning in workplaces to develop and refine cognitive structures, and experience workplace, cultural and professional practice. Students engage in situated learning as they learn from, with and through other people while they participate in workplace activities that occur within communities of practice (Wenger 2000).

Workplaces as communities of practice

Wenger (2000: 229) defines communities of practice as 'the basic building blocks of a social learning system because they are the social "containers" of the compe-tences that make up such a system'. He has identified competence in relation to three key elements of communities of practice: 'joint enterprise'; 'mutuality'; and 'a shared repertoire of communal resources':

First, members are bound together by their collectively developed understanding of what their community is about and they hold each other accountable to this sense of *joint enterprise*. To be competent is to understand the enterprise well enough to be able to contribute to it. Second, members build their community through mutual engagement. They interact with one another, establishing norms and relationships of *mutuality* that reflect these interactions. Third, communities of practice have produced a *shared repertoire* of communal resources – language, routines, sensibilities, artifacts, tools, stories, styles, etc. To be competent is to have access to this repertoire and be able to use it appropriately.

(Wenger 2000: 229 original emphasis)

Knowledge, values and understandings shared by members of workplace communities of practice are often tacit, meaning that interaction and dialogue are required to bring this knowledge to the surface. The exchange of ideas about work practice, experimentation with unfamiliar methods and ideas, and innovations in problem solving provide rich and authentic learning opportunities for students.

Students involved in 'working to learn' programmes are required to undergo initiation processes to enter workplace communities of practice in order to become legitimate members and to gain an insight into the communities' complexity. Accomplishing this initiation is not automatic; it requires students to be open to the exposure, willing to take risks in gaining the exposure, willing to be active agents of their own learning, and realizing they will learn with, and from, many teachers. Little of this initiation process to join the workplace community of practice is explicit. The members themselves may not realize the processes students must undergo to become functioning community members. Students may not be invited or even allowed in, especially if there is a gatekeeping system in place. The possibility of students being precluded from workplace communities of practice highlights the importance of expert practitioners becoming active partners in both the design and enactment of the work integrated learning enterprise.

Characteristics of workplaces as learning environments

Workplaces as learning environments are best understood by contrasting them with the commonly understood features of most classroom-based academic learning environments. The classroom, as a site of learning, focuses on conceptual understanding. Traditional roles apply for participants in classroom learning contexts. There are tacit understandings and assumptions of the roles and responsibilities of both teachers and students. There are few taken-for-granted assumptions in workplace contexts regarding these roles, which must, therefore, be negotiated from the outset.

The classroom context is either a face-to-face interactive space or virtual domain that has become familiar over time and therefore predictable to the student during their formal course of study. In classrooms student learning is the primary purpose, yet the number of students simultaneously engaged in the teaching and learning process, and the increasing numbers studying in flexible learning mode off campus, make it possible for an individual student to remain largely invisible, individualistic, idealistic, minimally participative, silent and in control. New knowledge is frequently transmitted didactically and explicitly. Connections with the 'real world' may be introduced, but they are usually reports or simulations of real-world issues and contexts that can easily be replicated and repeated. Classroom knowledge is theoretically driven knowledge *about* a particular context.

Workplaces, by contrast, are largely unfamiliar spaces where the primary focus is on practice, and client and organizational outcomes. Students learn through experiential learning in a workplace – by doing and interacting with more experienced professionals and, importantly, clients, consumers or patients. Working with clients provides dynamic, people-laden situations that challenge the more certain, context-free and disciplinary-focused knowledge of the classroom. The contrast between the two learning environments is demonstrated emphatically in a study by Grealish and Trevitt (2005), in which student nurses talked about the contradictions between classroom learning and learning with real people. In the classroom students learn about techniques for the intimate care *of* people. It is not until they are confronted with intimate care *with* real people that learning takes place. Nothing can prepare them for the shock of showering and inserting catheters for the first time:

> Jane: Like I think the first shower I gave to a patient was the biggest shock for me. I was only thinking of how I'd feel about it, and what I would do, and not how the patient would feel. I think that was the biggest shock for me and I guess that is like that for every new procedure for me.
>
> (Grealish and Trevitt 2005: 145. 'Developing a professional identity: student nurses in the workplace', *Contemporary Nurse*, 19(1–2): 137–50; www.contemporarynurse.com)

In this example, learning in the professional nursing workplace creates a climate necessary for the development of professional identity.

Practical knowledge is cued, used, developed and transmitted through immersion *in* the context. Learning in workplace contexts entails a higher element of psychosocial and physical risk for students as they participate in high levels of interaction with other people, technologies and unfamiliar circumstances. High risk and high stakes can be involved for students and other stakeholders. Juxtaposed for attention are workplace requirements, professional ethos, organizational goals, client needs and interests, workplace supervisor/guide work roles and responsibilities, student learning needs and work integrated learning outcome requirements. In workplaces, students are not the sole centres of concern but are required to participate in real, unique, unpredictable, ambiguous and sometimes high-risk learning experiences with other people, often in cultures and countries other than their own.

In workplaces, quick recall and prioritization of the most applicable theoretical and practical knowledge, time management and *just doing it* take precedence over long-term classroom discussion and writing about, and reflecting on, complex and contrasted theoretical explanations for ways of doing things. In the workplace, students need to learn to prioritize, problem solve, act like a professional and demonstrate civic commitment whilst being aware of their learner status and functioning accordingly (Billett 2009). Students first need to learn the skills and gain the insights that will enable them to function in this manner.

Constant communication (verbal, written, electronic, appearance, non-verbal behaviours), collaboration, cooperation, negotiation, collegiality and practice of specific skills are required for students and other stakeholders participating in work integrated learning in order to function effectively in workplaces. These interactions depend on developing trusting and respectful relationships. Students need positive personal dispositions towards seeking and accepting support from more experienced workers and peers, and the courage to interact and voice opinions with people they would be unlikely to meet in university or everyday life contexts. Developing these qualities in students is a critical aspect of the work integrated learning agenda. Some students may already possess these qualities, whilst others may need help in developing them. Thus, preparation for work integrated learning, as well as immersion in the workplace, becomes an important part of the curriculum.

The differences between learning in classroom and workplace contexts are illustrated metaphorically as contrasts between 'cold' and 'hot' learning in Table 3.3. The classroom is construed as engaging a type of learning that is cold, stable, safe and reflective, whereas learning in workplaces is construed as hot, transient, immediate and risky. The classroom situation places paramount emphasis on student learning, whereas the workplace must put its needs and those of its clients above all else. Some workplaces will place greater value on learning than others.

Table 3.3 Cold and hot learning

Cold learning	Hot learning
Predictable	Unpredictable
Replicable	Unique
Theoretical and simulated	Authentic
Low risk	High risk
Prolonged	Transient
Reflective	Action/interaction/performance
Planned	Spontaneous
Student-centred learning	Site of competing interests

Updated from Cooper *et al.* (2003: 4), Staff Development and Training Unit, Flinders University

Transfer of learning between classrooms and workplaces

Developing skills to make the two-way transfer of learning between classroom and workplace, and workplace and classroom, is not a student learning issue, although critical in the process. It is a curriculum issue and requires explicit attention in both teaching and learning. Strategies to facilitate this transfer of learning are described in Chapter 4.

Students face reverse challenges in making transitions between the classroom and workplace and the workplace and classroom learning environments. The differences between the classroom and workplace learning environments described in this chapter involve a two-way transfer of learning. In classrooms, students face the challenge of reflecting on the theoretical bases of their work. This can be difficult initially, especially for students who might have years of experience in the workforce and are used to making on-the-spot decisions to solve problems as they occur, or acting in accordance with new legislation and policy. These students are not experienced in consciously thinking about the theories behind their practice and theoretical alternatives. As these and other students perform the task of reflecting on classroom theory in light of what they do in practice they begin to reconceptualize theory, question the received wisdom of textbooks and, in some cases, question the assignments the university has given them.

In workplaces, the critical challenge for students is to notice what is important in a complex context and to make choices regarding interpretation, intervention and justification that comply with workplace culture and tacit procedural rules. These choices must also replicate those of more experienced members of that workplace community. It is a challenge for students to evaluate the choices of the more experienced workplace members, many of whom will have ritualized their practice and some of whom may have developed bad working habits over many years and become complacent. Student ability to notice what is important in the workplace environment and to question taken-for-granted practices is invaluable learning, but needs to be executed with professional tact. Students who are able to do this potentially benefit equally from both good and bad workplace practices.

Factors impacting on student learning in workplace environments

A wide range of environmental factors in workplaces can impact on student learning, including physical, cultural and managerial elements, the organization's ethos and the learning guides. One significant factor is diversity among workplace personnel, organizational cultures and students.

People in workplaces come from increasingly diverse cultural, social and ethnic backgrounds. Students represent the same or an even greater range of diversity. This diverse mix of people in the workplace environment has the potential to impact on the extent and type of student learning experiences. There may be positive, negative or ambivalent attitudes on the part of students and workplace personnel. An important element in understanding workplaces as learning environments is appreciation of the potential diversity of student profiles, as discussed in the previous section on students as learners in the workplace. There is considerable risk of social marginalization and emotional harm for some students without appreciation and anticipation of what might be required in terms of strategic planning and action. The goal should be to make success possible for all students. Achieving this goal requires attention to issues of diversity, inclusion and marginalization. As discussed in Chapter 4, achieving this goal also requires well-prepared students and workplace learning guides, whose characteristics play a critical part in creating a workplace environment that is conducive to student learning.

Summary

This chapter has described the work integrated learning agenda and considered characteristics of potential work integrated learning environments, making comparison between classroom and workplace learning contexts. One consistent feature is the often tacit qualities of many of the important elements of work integrated learning. These include what is to be learned, the roles and responsibilities of learners and supervisors/guides, and the knowledge that underpins the work of experts from whom students are expected to learn.

We have flagged factors and issues that need consideration when designing work integrated learning programmes, especially the diversity of human factors that can impact on achieving intended learning outcomes. Taking all of these issues into consideration, the ideal outcome of students undertaking learning in workplaces is work *integrated* learning. The integration of work and learning, of theory and practice, is central to the purpose of work integrated learning programmes. Integration sets out to develop students' contextual literacy through critical reflection on, and integration of, classroom, workplace and lived experiences. Chapter 4 focuses on teaching and teachers, and provides strategies to facilitate students' learning in work integrated learning experiences to help them attain contextual literacies.

Chapter 4

Teaching in Work Integrated Learning

Introduction

Teaching in work integrated learning takes place in the university as part of preparing students for the tasks, activities and responsibilities of the workplace. Teaching continues in the workplace with orientation to the workplace, and with direct and indirect guidance provided by more experienced practitioners and staff. Concepts of teaching differ between the university and the workplace. In the university the approach is frequently didactic, with the teacher being the sage on the stage. In the workplace teaching is a more indirect and nuanced approach with teachers being referred to as the guides on the side. We use the term 'learning guide' to refer to teachers in the workplace (Billett 2001): workers and peers who contribute to student learning in the workplace by providing students with direct and indirect guidance. Some sections of the university may refer to these learning guides as supervisors, field instructors, coordinators, practicum advisors or preceptors, whilst those in the workplace may call them coaches, mentors or supervisors.

Whatever the approach to teaching, the goal of teaching is to make learning possible (Ramsden 2003). Teaching does not just happen. Because it 'always involves attempts to alter students' understanding, so that they begin to conceptualise phenomena and ideas in the way scientists, mathematicians, historians, physicians or other subject experts conceptualise them' (Ramsden 2003: 7), it requires thought, care and planning before students enter the workplace, during the workplace experience and after the students return to the university. Educational support is a fundamental aspect of the functions of a university teacher and the workplace guide. In this chapter we examine teaching, including the responsibilities of university teachers in preparing students for learning and the task of workplaces to prepare students for learning in the workplace. The chapter concludes with a discussion of the teaching strategies that will enable learning to take place.

Teachers and teaching

Students have clear views about the quality of teaching in workplaces (Brandenburg and Ryan 2001; Fernandez 1998; Ingvarson *et al.* 2005). In one author's experience in managing and researching work integrated learning, students present consistent messages about quality teaching and learning experiences. Students regard good teachers in both environments as having the following characteristics:

- accept students in the workplace, enabling a sense of belonging;
- show concern for the student and their learning;
- are available for the learner with time for discussion, explaining, showing and demonstrating;
- respect and build on students' previous personal and work experiences;
- provide diverse learning opportunities with not too much work and not too little work;
- provide insight into their reasoning in problem solving;
- model good practice;
- integrate theory with practice;
- give students opportunities to practise new skills and allow students to learn from mistakes;
- provide regular constructive feedback;
- are non-judgemental about students' personal characteristics.

Paul Ramsden (2003: 111–14) outlined three concepts that underpin teaching: teaching as telling or transmission; teaching as organizing student activity; and teaching as making learning possible. Student views of teaching described above characterize an approach where the responsibility of the teacher is to make learning possible.

The standard view of teaching in the university is of a didactic method where propositional information is transmitted from teacher to student (Hager 2001: 2). A didactic approach is neither possible nor desirable in the context of work integrated learning. In the workplace students learn through participation in workplace practices, and purposeful engagement with people and processes. Through these processes, knowledge is constructed and reconstructed in an interactive and dynamic process that involves the learner interacting with workplace mentors and experts. Teachers in this context are learning guides whose task in teaching is facilitation, enabling student learning.

In the previous chapter, we made reference to the workplace as a site for learning and introduced the concepts of situated learning and communities of practice. In this section, we will draw on these ideas and continue with discussion of the workplace influences, paying particular attention to workplace attitudes to learners and learning and teachers and teaching. The workplace has a strong influence on how workers and students approach learning. Organizations, through internal policy initiatives, are able to take a strategic view of teaching and learning, developing a long-term commitment that extends across all work units. Learning can become explicit when organizations refer to themselves as learning organizations (Senge 1990) or when they encourage teaching and learning through a variety of work practices that include participation in learning circles or communities of practice

(Wenger 1998). Workplaces can support the activities of learning guides by recognizing the value of what they do. For example, this recognition may be manifested when managers reduce the normal workloads of learning guides to enable them to assist students or when practitioners are designated as learning coordinators.

A workplace may assign specific learning guides to students but there are many other employees in every workplace who provide students with opportunities for indirect learning. These more experienced workers may come from other professions and disciplines, and may be managers, administrative staff or co-workers. Whatever term is used to describe these people, they are experienced in the specialized vocational knowledge and practices of the workplace but not necessarily in facilitative teaching strategies. Despite this lack of pedagogical expertise, they are responsible for teaching. They guide, coach and mentor learners, structure learning experiences, provide insights and support, and model their practices. In some areas, clients or consumers can also provide guidance that contributes to student learning.

Guidance ideally is provided in the context of the workplace curriculum, 'a socially organized stock of knowledge in use in the particular environment as it is experienced by the participants, especially newcomers' (Moore 2004: 329). The workplace curriculum, rather than a written document, is a collective and tacit understanding of the sequences and steps to new knowledge, capabilities and values that shape practice. It incorporates the goals, tasks and activities needed to achieve competency. According to Billett (2001: 104–5) the workplace curriculum model includes:

- a pathway of sequenced learning from low to high accountability work;
- access to difficult to learn knowledge;
- direct guidance from experts;
- indirect guidance from the physical and social environment.

Although the workplace curriculum is intentional, its aims may not be realized or experienced in the workplace. There is no guarantee that the intended learning will occur. Guides can act in their own self-interest, and students and workers may learn inappropriate practices.

Whilst each workplace affords opportunities to learners, there are challenges for both learning guides and students in achieving desired outcomes. It is important when considering work integrated learning to remember that students are adults and agents of their own learning.

Teaching: the responsibility of the university

Quality preparation programmes cannot be stressed strongly enough. Teaching does not begin when students enter the workplace. It begins in the university with preparation for learning providing a foundation for positive experiences for learning guides, co-workers and students. Students require careful preparation to learn effectively in the workplace.

Many students beginning work integrated learning have experiences as volunteers or from previous employment. Despite these important events, a structured and organized learning experience with demands for particular outcomes can be uncharted territory for many. Some students may approach work integrated learning passively, assuming that this form of learning is similar to other work experiences, whilst other students may have many questions about learning in the workplace:

- What am I expected to learn?
- What is the best way to learn?
- What tasks or activities will assist learning?
- Who are the teachers in the workplace and what are their responsibilities?
- What are the expectations of teachers in the workplace?
- What feedback will be provided and how will this be delivered?

It is the responsibility of the university to prepare students for learning in the workplace. This has practical aspects but requires some discussion of learning itself.

Preparation for student learning: University responsibilities

Work integrated learning experiences are often regarded by students as the most critical part of their higher education. For some the experience may be decisive in determining a particular career choice or suitability for a profession. Students approach this learning with anticipation and anxiety about learning new skills and competencies. Student preparation in the university provides a foundation for positive learning experiences and facilitates a smooth transition to the workplace. If students are prepared for learning before they enter the workplace, they can immerse themselves in the learning context and feel confident confronting dilemmas and challenges. Without such preparation, students can easily become confused and discouraged.

In preparing students for learning, the university teachers need to draw attention to and elaborate particular attitudes and skills that are necessary in the workplace. These include workplace literacy, motivation, capacity to work and learn with others, and noticing (Cooper *et al.* 2003). These attitudes and skills can be elaborated in the classroom using a variety of instructional processes. Alternatively, students can be guided to achieve these outcomes with evidence provided in a portfolio. In the section that follows, we outline the skills and attitudes that could be discussed by a classroom teacher. Following this a portfolio approach is described.

Workplace literacy

We think of literacy as the basic skills of reading, writing and calculation. When university students are placed in organizations these basic skills are assumed. Workplace literacy refers to understanding of organizational issues that include the values, purpose, structure and function of the workplace, and the legal and ethical literacy that includes health and safety, equal opportunity and sexual harassment. Some workplaces have specific ethical stances that are essential for work performance. For example, in many English-speaking countries, governments use the concept of the Westminster principle for responsible government. This has particular relevance to government officials who are expected to be neutral and loyal to the government of the day. This principle applies to students learning in such workplaces. Professional literacy also refers to the ethical codes and practice standards of the particular profession (Cooper *et al.* 2003).

Motivation

Motivation refers to the learner's interest in participating in work integrated learning. Students are motivated if the challenges are not too hard and not too easy, if students can see the value in the learning activities and if they feel as if they are contributing something to other people (Bransford 2000). University teachers can help kindle student motivation in a variety of ways, including engaging and involving them in planning their learning in the workplace, removing or lessening anxieties, creating safe learning environments, exploring opportunities, using the experience of other students, being caring, providing resources and just having fun in the process (Caffarella 2002).

Learning to work with others

Learning to work with others is an essential part of student preparation before entering the workplace. Employers want students and workers to have the capacity and ability to work with others in teams, work groups and communities of practice. According to Lave and Wenger (1991), learning in the workplace takes place in a social context, where the student is immersed in a wide range of interactions with other people and everyday activities. Learning with others does not, however, happen spontaneously when new learners arrive in the workplace. It takes place through conversations, socialization and associations with others. This learning is shaped by the context, the cultural aspects of work and the nature of activities, and is thus strongly influenced by the way in which learners give of themselves and respond to more experienced people. Students begin at the periphery and by participating in work practices learn the knowledge and skills to fully engage in the complexity of these practices. Working and learning with others are simultaneous and mutually reinforcing processes that depend upon learners' active participation. It follows that learning with others depends on good communication skills, being prepared to give and take, an understanding of group processes and a capacity to participate in networks.

The university can assist the learning process by drawing attention to the need to learn with others and also through encouraging collaborative learning activities, such as group project work, in preparation for work integrated learning. Collaborative learning concepts include activities where there is positive interdependence between the participants, face-to-face interaction, individual accountability, the development of social skills and group processing (Johnson *et al.* 1991).

Noticing

Although noticing is part of the learning experience, it is also the university teacher's responsibility to alert students to the importance of noticing as a conscious process. Learning guides will expect students to notice and to use noticing as the basis for reflection and action.

Noticing is an active strategy to absorb the characteristics, actions and interactions in the work milieu. It is, according to David Boud (2001), an awareness of what is happening in and around us, and ascertaining what is important. Noticing involves not only noting what is happening in the external world around us but, just as importantly, also considering what is going on inside with our thoughts, feelings, motivations and intentions to engage. The habit of noticing is the keystone to self-awareness and reflection.

The university can assist students by helping them to understand this concept and the importance of using it proactively in the workplace. As an example, a School of Pharmacy may show their students video clips of interprofessional communication in a memory clinic setting, and then ask students to notice the dialogue and quality of interactions between participants. Quite often students' previous theoretical learning in the classroom will assist them to identify and notice important workplace cues for further consideration.

Self-awareness

Teachers can best prepare students for learning in workplaces by explaining the concept of self-awareness and modelling the ways it can be used in the workplace. Self-awareness is a helpful attribute and capacity as students approach work integrated learning. It means understanding what one is feeling and knowing, and understanding the limits of one's knowledge and competence to perform. It is important to understand one's emotions as they have the potential both to inhibit and enhance learning. Work integrated learning is stressful and anxiety-provoking because it is a new and assessable experience. During such learning experiences students may be exposed to harsh realities such as child abuse, violence, homelessness, fraud, loss, death and dying, and breaches of privacy. Dealing with these realities means discussing the powerful emotions they arouse and how to separate personal life from work experiences. For safety reasons, it is equally important to be willing to consider one's own limitations in the workplace.

Students often reflect on their new experiences to understand their practice. Such reflection allows consideration of thought processes, feelings, schemas, emotional and evaluative reactions to events in the workplace, and responses to clients, co-workers and experienced others. As students learn how to conduct this internal dialogue, the greater their orientation to, and understanding of, the complexities of practice becomes. Learning guides can assist this process through the use of questioning and seeking clarification, analysis and evaluation of activities.

Self-awareness is even more important in learning new skills and practices. Mistakes are made in learning; this is an inevitable part of human development. Students can react to these mistakes in many ways. Some can acknowledge the mistakes and the feelings associated with them and learn how to work differently, thus avoiding similar mistakes in the future. Some may make similar mistakes yet never learn how to rectify their practice errors. Unfortunately, some people are so traumatized by mistakes they have made that they may avoid similar situations in the future (Beard and Wilson 2006: 270). The work of a guide is critical in the reflective dialogue process. If learners are tuned in to their feelings, which can be an assisted process, they can better reflect positively on the emotional challenges in acknowledging errors and constructing other ways of working. When such situations are handled badly, students seek comfort by not changing and through avoidance. They then experience the debilitating consequences of failure to learn.

Portfolio preparation

Teachers can work actively with students in a variety of ways to prepare them for learning. Alternatively, they can use an educational portfolio, a collection of student work which demonstrates learning and reflection on that learning. Specifically, the portfolio is an effective learning tool that is generally kept in the form of a journal containing student narrative and reflections. It gives students autonomy and the ability to identify their learning needs and follow particular interests. It assists the teacher in knowing that learning has taken place. The following is an example of a portfolio preparation based on five domains. These are:

- getting to know more about the workplaces in which students are to learn;
- preparing themselves and organizing their lives for working experience;
- negotiating workplace and associated cultures;
- learning in workplace contexts;
- surviving the learning.

As students complete either selected or all activities for these domains, which map the stages of student preparation for entering the workplace, they build a preparation portfolio which can be used by university teachers to guide classroom discussion; by university work integrated learning coordinators in working with students and workplaces to negotiate students' work integrated learning experiences; by students as a ready reference guide to learning in the workplace; or as an assessable component of the preparation process. The five domains and some of the associated activities in the portfolio method of preparation are outlined in Table 4.1, drawing on a good practice web-based resource used by Flinders University (Orrell *et al.* 2003).

Table 4.1 Portfolio preparation for work integrated learning

Domains of student preparation	Suggested student-directed activities
Getting to know more about workplaces	• Explore a variety of workplaces, outlining opportunities, benefits and potential challenges • Investigate a specific workplace and specify goals, structure, mission, management, product or services, clients or customers, organizational history, position in macro-environment, accountability to stakeholders • Investigate the community in which the workplace is based, outlining demographic information and cultural make-up • Explore the impact of economic and political changes on workplaces
Preparing for work experience	• Create a personal preparation checklist (such as work life, family life, child care arrangements, transport to the workplace, finances and employment commitments)
Negotiating workplace and other cultures	• Reflect on the culture of the workplace, specify what is new or strange and consider some ways to respond to this environment • Analyse the specific workplace culture, including its distinctiveness and the difference to the academy and other workplaces, and then reflect on working with these differences • Discuss diversity dilemmas and consider the best way to respond (e.g. gender, disability, race or class) • Reflect on barriers to communication in your community or workplace and consider ways to improve cross-cultural communication
Learning in workplace contexts	• Outline what skills, knowledge and strengths you will bring to the work integrated learning experience • Reflect on your prior experiences and consider how you can build on these in this new location • Outline personal goals for learning and draft learning goals • Consider how you will work with co-workers and more experienced others, and specifically how you will work with learning guides • Contemplate your personal characteristics in relation to being prepared, being prompt, asking questions, volunteering, contributing to group efforts and caring about learning, and think about how these attributes can hinder or assist you in the work integrated learning experience • Ask yourself how you have dealt with uncertainty in previous work situations and what you can use in new situations

Domains of student preparation	Suggested student-directed activities
Surviving the learning	• Research the occupational health and safety issues in the workplace • Elaborate on privacy principles, ethics and intellectual property, and anticipate the issues that might arise as part of your learning • Discuss scenarios that specifically relate to risks in work integrated learning experiences including bullying, sexual harassment, too little or too much work, lack of support from learning guides • Outline how to end the learning experience on a positive note

Adapted from Orrell *et al.* (2003) *Working to Learn: Practicum Online*, Adelaide: Staff Development and Training Unit, Flinders University. Online: http://www.flinders.edu.au/teach/workingtolearn/index.htm

In preparing students for entry to workplaces it is important to anticipate the needs of students who will undertake their work integrated learning experiences in locations which are geographically remote and culturally distinct and multi-faceted. In such locations students will be without easily accessed direct support from the university. Preparation for these situations will therefore involve careful assessment of the student's capacity to manage learning, and finding supervisors and learning guides in the nominated workplace who can provide support. If this is not possible, technology such as Skype, Facebook, Twitter, chats, blogs, SMS and other similar resources can be used to maintain communication. Any such long-distance arrangements require that the university coordinator and student discuss supervisory arrangements before departure so that there is a shared and contractual understanding of teaching and learning arrangements.

Preparation for student learning: workplace responsibilities

There is nothing more discouraging for students than arriving at the workplace to find that no one knows about their arrival; the learning guide is absent for the day; the student does not have an assigned space or work; and new colleagues are not prepared. Orientation to the workplace provides the necessary framework for learning. Dependent upon the workplace, this may include practicalities; workplace mission and mandate; legislative and policy requirements; work safe practices; and supervisory and accountability requirements. If these are not covered, the learning outcome may be compromised. Details are elaborated in Table 4.2.

In anticipation of communication failure in the workplace where students might find, for example, that their workplace guides are unfamiliar with the aims of the placement and the students' learning requirements, a work integrated learning programme may provide students with CD-ROM discs containing the information that was assumed to have been given to the workplace guides. One of the

Table 4.2 Orientation for student learning in the workplace

Key areas	Examples
Introductions	Key practitioners and staff
Practicalities	Room/desk; lunch room and toilet facilities, computer arrangements, identification cards
Organizational background	History, mission, mandate, strategic plan, and organizational structure
Legislative and policy requirements	Significant act governing work practices, privacy requirements, intellectual property, internal policy manuals, standards of practice, behavioural standards
Health and safety practices	Legislative framework and internal policies with respect to clients, patients and staff in the workplace
Learning plans and contract	Student life experience, skills and attributes; learning goals, learning opportunities, proposed activities and expected outcomes, and forms for formative and summative assessment
Supervisory requirements	Time and length of meetings, required assignments, back up supervisor, expectations and supervisory approaches.

student's first tasks could then be to ascertain whether the learning guides had the necessary information and if not, seek permission to download the information to a workplace computer.

Teaching strategies in the workplace

Learning guides can provide a variety of facilitative strategies when assisting students. The strategies used will depend upon the individual student, the learning guide and the context in which the learning takes place. As a general rule these selected strategies are facilitative to encourage participation in the workplace and make learning possible.

Facilitation

The learning guide enables access to resources necessary for learning and creates, wherever possible, a climate for learning. Brookfield (1986: 63) regarded the role of facilitators as resource people for learners rather than as didactic teachers and instructors. Effective facilitators engage in a democratic, mutual process where the teacher and learner share responsibility for the direction and methods of learning. The relationship between facilitator and learner, which has its origins in humanistic psychotherapy, is often referred to as being helping, with warmth, respect and purposeful interactions as core attributes (see Brill 1985; Rogers 1995; Rogers and Freiberg 1994). These interactive dimensions are evident in coaching, mentoring and supervision.

Facilitation is a person-centred process derived from adult education. This process necessitates that the learning guide acknowledge individual differences in learning style, previous experiences and personal dimensions such as diversity and cultural differences. A person-centred approach builds on the strengths of individuals, but this should not be interpreted as an approach that yields to learners' ambivalence or negativity. It is purposeful, structured and planned. Facilitators have to balance personal support, the demand for work and, if necessary, change. Learning arouses intense feelings that need to be understood and interpreted. Learners need to understand and process their experiences and make sense of what is going on in the workplace. Finally, a learning-centred approach can be confronting and challenging so that learners may become aware of where resistance and avoidance are manifested in practice.

If workplace learning involves participating in social interactions and relationships with experienced others in the workplace, it follows that the responsibility of the guide is to facilitate opportunities for this participation. Facilitating learning in workplaces requires sophisticated enabling skills, which may be difficult to accomplish for learning guides. There can be active and passive resistance from other workers depending on the workplace and personnel. The following factors need to be considered if learning guides are to be successful facilitators. There is a need for:

- a strong emphasis in the workplace on providing a meaningful context for learning where problems are framed by the workplace context;
- 'hands-on', interactive and dynamic approaches to learning activities that allow students to apply and interact equally with the thinking and performing aspects of learning;
- learning outcomes that are clear in their intent regarding what is to be achieved;
- opportunities for students to collaborate and negotiate in determining their learning and assessment processes;
- recognition of learners as 'co-producers' of new knowledge and skills;
- recognition of students' previous learning and life experiences as valuable foundations for constructing new knowledge and skill sets (although they can also impose limitations);
- flexible teaching approaches that address the different learning styles, cultures and experiences of students;
- provision of opportunities for social interactions and learning in groups.

(Adapted from Smith and Blake 2005: 3)

Modelling

One way that learning occurs is through a process of observing the behaviour, interactions and thoughts of more experienced others in the workplace. Experienced staff or experts in workplace learning environments need to be aware that there are various approaches to modelling which will depend on the nature of the work. Some workplace learning requires developing a set of demanding technical skills. In teaching these skills, it is important to realize that skill acquisition requires practice (Anderson 1983). The guide may demonstrate the skills in context and then elaborate the specifics of using a particular skill before allowing the learner to try the task alone.

Social cognitive theorists (e.g. Bandura 1986) argue that social behaviour, attitudes and values can also be learned through a process of observation. Whilst this does not necessarily mean that a person has to imitate the behaviour to learn, it is important that individuals understand the consequences of learning or failure to learn the behaviour. The learning process here involves attention, retention and behavioural rehearsal, including thought processes and motivation. Attending to features of the learned social behaviour is a critical aspect of learning, with attention being influenced by the characteristics of both the person modelling the activities or interactions and those observing. Influential models are likely to be compelling, with both social power and status in the organization, competent in the skills used in the workplace, concerned for the learner and similar in personal characteristics to the learner. Similarly, the extent to which learners attend to the features of social behaviour can increase or decrease according to learner characteristics. Attention can be influenced by status, race and gender, and the incentive to learn (McInerney and McInerney 1998: 123).

Cognitive apprenticeships

Cognitive apprenticeships are a particular form of modelling and are useful in professional areas where access to the way professionals think about problems is important. Dennen (2004: 814) says that a cognitive apprenticeship is like a trade apprenticeship. It takes place in a work context where students and experts interact socially to complete work activities. Cognitive apprenticeship is a method of instruction that comes from concepts of social constructivist theories. As the name suggests, cognitive apprenticeship refers to the thinking processes that experts use when handling complex tasks and solving problems in their workplaces. This process allows the experienced practitioner's internalized thinking processes to be externalized through discussion shared with students. In sharing such information with students, the experienced practitioners are:

- sharing their work and the intellectual processes they use as experts undertaking complex tasks;
- allowing access to the conceptual and practice frameworks underpinning their practice;
- discussing the specific knowledge that contributes to problem solving;
- specifying the dilemmas, doubts and uncertainty in their practice;
- outlining problem-solving processes.

This sharing allows students the opportunity to consider and reflect on experts' thinking processes and to model the experts' practice.

Cognitive apprenticeship involves a number of phases, beginning with modelling and continuing with approximating, fading, self-directed learning and generalizing (Brandt *et al.* 1993: 71). Using a real-life experience the expert thinks aloud retrospectively about the complexity that lies behind their practice and then provides scaffolding, coaching, mentoring and supervision to the student to use as a guide to enable them to complete tasks. The student is expected to approximate the work activity of the expert. When the student can do this alone, the expert decreases their support.

Scaffolding

Scaffolding is a teaching strategy used to support learners, enabling them to do new tasks and activities which initially they are not able to do alone. The concept of scaffolding comes from the work of Vygotsky (1978) with his elaboration of the zone of proximal development, a term that refers to the difference between what a person can do alone and what they can do if provided with support and assistance. The process involves a number of steps, beginning with the expert doing the task alone and then inviting the student to assist in completing the work. The student then attempts to do the task alone but with direct assistance from the expert. The support of the expert fades until the student does the task alone. Throughout this process, assessment of the student's readiness to complete the task is essential so that task completion is not beyond the student's capacity or ability. In scaffolding learning, the guide discusses, uses 'thinking aloud' strategies, enables students to access intellectual processes, and allows observation, demonstration and the use of cues, hints and partial solutions.

The process of scaffolding can be enhanced where there is a clear understanding of the task and the reason for completing it. It requires that the expert practitioner model the activity while describing the intellectual processes upon which their practice is founded. Teachers can improve this learning by specifying the steps, structures and order needed for completion of activities, and by then discussing, providing prompts and reminders, and noting signs or indicators and signals where students are challenged to achieve the key outcomes. When the work processes and activities have been grasped, the guide can withdraw their support. Whilst generally we think of scaffolding as being provided by experts to novice learners, it can also be effective when more advanced students work with novice students in the workplace.

Coaching and mentoring

Hawkins and Smith (2006: 22) define coaching as 'the focused application of skills that deliver performance improvement to the individual's work in their organization, through robust support and challenge'. They argue that the main focus of coaching is on skills, performance, development and transformation achieved through its various phases, which include contracting, listening, exploring, taking action and reviewing. Whilst Hawkins and Smith (2006) address the issue of transformational coaching, they do so in the context of consultancy and coaching of senior administrators rather than students in the workplace. Transformational change can nevertheless occur with students.

Mentoring is a concept closely aligned with coaching. The aim of mentoring is to allow personal and professional career development through a respectful long-term learning relationship. Generally, the mentor is more experienced and shares with the mentee knowledge, practices and experiences that can assist in achieving the mentee's aims of personal growth and career development (Zachary 2000).

There is a great deal of overlap between mentoring and coaching. Hawkins and Smith (2006: 39) argue that both are based on a personal relationship where the learners are active participants and the guides are facilitative and responsible, enabling self-directed approaches. Mentoring and coaching use strategies that include modelling, scaffolding, cognitive apprenticeships, and enabling reflection and self-awareness. Differences are evident. The length of the relationships is different, with mentoring being ongoing and coaching time-limited. Coaching is more likely to be structured by the coach, with mentoring being more dependent on demands established by the mentee. Most importantly, whilst mentoring is provided by more experienced workers, a coach does not necessarily have direct experience of the work entailed.

Coaching, mentoring and supervision are closely related. In this chapter, we consider coaching and mentoring together as these concepts are most alike, but we need to draw attention to supervision. In Chapter 6, we specifically address the practice of supervision. In coaching the focus is on the performance at work and does not seek to resolve any underlying emotional problems. The agenda for coaching is established in the workplace, often in agreement with the requirements of that particular workplace. Mentoring focuses on long-term professional and career growth, and takes a broader view of the person and their learning (Hawkins and Smith 2006: 39). Supervision is an intense learning and teaching strategy based on a close and collaborative interpersonal relationship. The supervisory relationship is of critical importance as it is in, and through, this relationship that learning occurs. In many areas the supervisor not only has responsibility for learning but may also have responsibility for management, thus adding to the complexity of the relationship. In coaching and mentoring, the coach or the mentor rarely has any organizational responsibility for the student's work.

Reflection

Practice is messy. Students in the workplace are confronted with a lot of information about situations, interactions, procedures and people. Initially they may not be able to distinguish what is relevant and necessary from what is irrelevant and unnecessary. One of the demands made by learning guides is for students to undertake reflection, a process that takes this raw material and makes some sense and order out of the chaos (Boud 2001). In making sense, students will need to understand their thoughts and emotions. Moon makes a similar observation, saying that:

> reflection is a form of mental processing that we use to fulfill a purpose or to achieve some anticipated outcome. It is applied to gain a better understanding of relatively complicated or unstructured ideas and is largely based on the reprocessing of knowledge, understanding and possibly emotions that we already possess.

(Moon 2005: 1)

Learning guides facilitate student reflection on their learning by asking them a series of questions about their experience.

The concept of reflection has come from the work of educators such as Dewey (1938) and Brookfield (1986), and from the pioneering work of Schön (1983, 1987). Schön examined practice in a number of professional areas. He determined that practice problems cannot easily be resolved by merely applying classroom theory to complex and uncertain real-world issues. Schön (1983) presented two concepts: reflection-on-action, an analytical process of thinking about an experience after it has occurred; and reflection-in-action, the 'in the moment thinking' that gives rise to experimentation. Reflection is present in the work of Kolb (1984) and also Boud *et al.* (1985). These authors see reflection as an iterative process that involves returning to the experience, attending to feelings and re-evaluating the experience (Boud and Walker 1990: 67).

Reflection can be used for both academic and practical learning. In practical learning, students can use reflection to understand the practice wisdom. It is also important in integration of theory and practice because the reflection allows students to question the theoretical assumptions in the context of the practice realities. Reflection is an important aspect of transformational learning where it can be used to challenge our taken-for-granted assumptions about people and social problems. In particular, reflection is useful to examine discrimination that comes from cultural assumptions (Thompson 2006: 56).

Reflection on experiences in the workplace does not necessarily come naturally. It takes time and motivation to pause and reconsider taken-for-granted assumptions. It also arouses unanticipated emotions and feelings. Asking a student to write a paper on their reflections or to talk about their experiences does not mean that they understand what they are expected to do. Consider the following case study:

> A new social work student was asked by her supervisor to tell the supervisor what happened in the recent interview with the father of a sick child. In asking this question, the supervisor was expecting the student would tell a story

about the experience and then use this story to reflect on areas of uncertainty. The student, who was not familiar with the concept of reflection, responded by saying, 'A lot went on, what in particular do you want to know about?' This created an impasse where the supervisor did not know how to explain reflection and the student was not able to complete the required task.

Students have to learn that reaching quick solutions may imply certainty and efficiency but in reaching them they may not be seeing or imagining other possibilities. Reflection is potentially uncomfortable and destabilizing but does open the door to seeing practice in other ways, allowing students to think about their thinking, thus developing metacognition.

Learning reflection is achieved by a process involving dialogue, coaching, supervision and mentoring where the learning guide is thinking aloud about their reflective processes. John Smyth (1996) suggested using the exploratory questions:

- Describe: what do I do?
- Inform: what does this mean?
- Confront: how did I come to be like this?
- Reconstruct: how can I do things differently?

This can be supplemented by such things as learning logs, reports on critical incidents, reflective journals, use of critical friends, and activities such as mentoring and supervision.

Values

Exposing students to workplace values, and teaching students to perceive and understand them is challenging. Values and ethics are important components in workplaces and engaging with them in work integrated learning discussions can be contested. In professional programmes, ethical foundations and values are core to professional practice and identity. In service learning, appreciating the way organizations treat and value consumers and respond to social problems provides a basis for transformational learning. Understanding the core organization values and the way these ethics and values are enacted in strategies are major expected outcomes of cooperative learning.

Where values and ethics are taught in the classroom, students should rapidly grasp the necessary conceptual understanding. Values are part of the explicit and implicit curriculum. In practice, the teaching and assessing of values and ethics is a more complex process for a variety of reasons. First, even where workers share a common understanding of values and ethics, their interpretation in practice may be contested, with workers having diverse views on a common issue. There may be no such common understanding when dilemmas arise regarding values. Second, as discussed in Chapter 3, values are personal, and particular beliefs and attitudes are part of the legacy of family life, schooling, religious or cultural affiliations and community involvement, with expression of these values often undeclared and unsaid. Third, our values and ethics are evident in our practice, in how we treat people and respond to situations, and in what is included and omitted when we do these things. Thompson (2006: 46) refers to this as our 'invisible footsteps'.

Given this situation, teaching values involves an iterative process of dialogue and critical reflection. Assisting students to develop an ethical imagination so that they learn to identify potential ethical issues increases their critical perceptiveness and ethical literacy, and contributes to learning for the longer term (Boud 2001). The alternative is to develop formulaic approaches to solving ethical dilemmas where solutions to known problems are taught. The difficulty lies in the fact that no programme of teaching could ever anticipate every situational dilemma students will face.

There are many opportunities to discuss values and ethics, starting from the time students arrive in the workplace. When students ask how to identify themselves to clients and other workers, learning guides can link this question to professional ethics. Learning guides may model thinking as an expert practitioner and discuss how they see the connection of theory and practice. They can also prepare students for value clashes by helping them anticipate potential value conflicts. Consider the following example:

> An elderly care organization has adopted the concept of positive ageing as its fundamental value. This value is nuanced but its use is intended to liberate the way the organization thinks about its work with older people. The concept can be used to challenge ageism. Students may not be aware of their discriminatory attitudes towards older people. Discussion of this organizational value provides a way to reflect on work practices with older people and consider personal interactions with them. For students with an interest in policy, they can use this concept to reflect on existing policies and construct new ones. Learning guides might model how they use this concept in their practice.

As values are most frequently tacit, teaching involves examining the invisible footsteps evident in practice, in life experiences and in relationships with others, questioning what is taken for granted and making the implicit explicit. This process can be undertaken as an aspect of personal reflection or in consultation with learning guides, mentors, supervisors and coaches through enabling self-awareness. Exploring and challenging values allows students to make transitions from simple to more complex, nuanced understandings. It can be disruptive, but potentially it is transformative. Making personal changes to strongly held values engages students' affective, cognitive and behavioural dispositions (Mezirow 1996).

Responding to diversity and its companions – oppression and marginalization

– is a challenge in all workplaces. Some of the interpersonal teaching challenges arising from diversity discussed by Thompson (2006: 43) include:

- Students may respond to challenges of their personal values by agreeing with the importance of a value but not demonstrating a commitment in their practice.
- Students may also minimize the seriousness of their value stance, particularly when it relates to oppression and marginalization in the workplace.
- Students may not take ownership of their particular values and may dismiss their relevance to the work experience.

Students may view having to consider changes in their habitual ways of thinking and doing as a threatening and anxiety-provoking process. Knowing the value stances of practitioners and the learning guide, students may be frightened to raise questions in sensitive areas, fearing they will be judged harshly if they hold different opinions. If the learning guides openly portray the characteristics identified earlier in this chapter as those that make good teachers, this fear of judgement will be diminished in the students and they will feel comfortable asking questions or expressing opinions.

The effectiveness of the teaching strategies discussed in this section relies on good relationships between learning guides and students, and honest self-appraisal by students. The strategies themselves develop these relationships further as part of the teaching process in work integrated learning.

Student support

Student support is a function of teachers. It is a strategy that is necessary before the student begins learning, during the learning process and after the experience is completed, as outlined in Table 4.3. The support of students is the responsibility of all teachers, including those at university and those in the workplace. If work integrated learning is to be successful, the learning guides and others in the workplace also need particular support. This support is generally provided by university staff and occurs during the whole process.

One key support for students is emotional support. This takes time and sometimes requires assistance from specialist counsellors. The nature of work and incidents in the workplace can provoke memories of past experiences, causing a negative impact on learning, or can lead to trauma, as illustrated in the example following Table 4.3, highlighting the importance of emotional support as a key dimension of overall support for students in work integrated learning. It is a vital teaching strategy which, when used in conjunction with other strategies described in this section, helps facilitate productive work integrated learning experiences not only for students but for their university teachers and workplace learning guides.

Table 4.3 Work integrated learning support matrix

Support	Before starting work integrated learning experience	During work integrated learning experience	After work integrated learning experience
Student support	Explain expectations, goals, assessment, and institution and workplace protocols Outline and negotiate special accommodations for students with disabilities Prepare students for workplace learning and supervision of practice Resumé writing Work literacy skills Interviewing skills Career planning	Assist students in making sense of experiences Assist students to deal with tensions, difficulties and health issues Ensure student learning goals are specified and achieved Problem solve difficulties between students and practitioners in workplace Formative and summative assessment Guide and support students in ethical behaviour	Reflect on learning Manage positive and negative feelings associated with learning Evaluate the learning experience for future students Enable students to use these experiences in subsequent employment or work integrated learning experiences Provide access to complaint and appeal processes
Workplace support	Prepare workplace for students by providing relevant information about academy policies and procedures Provide orientation programmes for students in workplace Prepare organizations for students from diverse backgrounds	Manage contracts and learning Help workplaces work with students from diverse backgrounds to maximize learning Assist workplace coordinators in maximizing student learning Act as a sounding board for issues or difficulties in the workplace Connect workplace coordinators with other coordinators undertaking similar tasks	Debrief workplace supervisors and coordinators Connect workplace coordinators for support Resolve any difficulties as a result of student learning Encourage evaluation of student workplace experiences Prepare workplace for next group of students

A learning coordinator reported that her student was having difficulties in seeing particular clients. The need for emotional support and specialist counselling assistance became apparent when the student wrote a poem called 'Tears'. In this poem she wrote about her experiences as a young child coming home from school to find her single mother dead as a result of suicide. In the workplace, the student was refusing to see single mothers because of the overwhelming sadness associated with her past experiences. This situation could not be resolved with a quick chat and referral to the counsellor. Both the university and workplace staff had to provide ongoing emotional support over the course of the student's work integrated learning experience.

The above experience highlights the importance of emotional support as a key dimension of overall support for students in work integrated learning. It is a vital teaching strategy which, when used in conjunction with other strategies described in this section, helps facilitate productive work integrated learning experiences not only for students but also for their university teachers and workplace learning guides.

Summary

Teaching responsibly is an important activity in the workplace, a process beginning before the student arrives in the workplace and continuing throughout the learning experience. The teacher or learning guide enables the student to move from the periphery towards the centre of the organization, beginning with simple activities and graduating to learning more complex practices. Students achieve outcomes with the direct and indirect guidance of all people in the workplace. In undertaking guidance of students, learning guides use a diverse range of facilitative strategies, as described in this chapter. In using these strategies, learning guides balance tensions between the demands of the workplace, the needs of clients and the needs of students. Trust and acceptance are critical for students to develop a sense of belonging in the workplace. At the same time students need to be exposed to the unfamiliar to critically evaluate and question what they notice. In addition, learning guides should ensure students work beyond their comfort zone, meeting challenges whilst perceiving the limits of their competence and not working beyond these. These are not small challenges. Success in learning and teaching in work, and in integration of learning and work, is dependent on workplace environments and learning guides within them being well prepared for their roles, and giving them adequate respect and resources to carry out those roles effectively.

Having discussed the challenges inherent in teaching in classrooms and workplaces in work integrated learning programmes, and suggesting strategies for teachers, we now turn to assessing work integrated learning.

Chapter 5

Assessing Work Integrated Learning

Introduction

Assessing work integrated learning and beginning professional capabilities is a challenging and complex process imposing educational, ethical and moral responsibilities on workplace guides and their organizations. When workplace staff and leaders are supervising and assessing student learning, they are responsible for ensuring the integrity, functioning and success of their enterprises, and the safety and interests of their clients and communities. Students, on their part, may find assessment of their placement learning a high-risk aspect of their programme of study.

This chapter examines the distinctive features and challenges of assessing work integrated learning. There is also a focus on the multiple purposes of assessment, what is assessed, what can be assessed, how workplace practice might be conducted and interpreted, and how the resulting information might be reported. The chapter begins by outlining a set of guiding principles for work integrated learning assessment. It then addresses some of the challenges in designing and conducting work integrated learning assessment. Strategies are suggested to aid institutional policymakers, curriculum designers, leaders and work integrated learning experience providers to meet these challenges.

First order principles of work integrated learning assessment

Outlined here are first order principles for assessing work integrated learning. These principles are intended to guide the development of institutional policy regarding work integrated learning as well as everyday practice and interaction between students and their learning guides. Curriculum designers, work integrated learning programme coordinators and institutional managers might consider the following parameters in making provision for assessment of students' performances in workplace settings:

1 Work integrated learning is a formal component of the curriculum and therefore should be assessed formally.

2   Assessment should focus on the integration and application of theoretical knowledge into practice and 'real-world' matters.
3   Learning expectations should be articulated publicly as explicit learning outcomes that are aligned to core curricula and used consistently to guide students and their assessors in the assessment process.
4   All stakeholders in work integrated learning should have an active role in the assessment process after induction into the process.
5   Students should receive feedback on their progress while on their placement so they can make adjustments to their practice and improve.
6   Ultimately the educational institution must be responsible for determining the record of the work integrated learning outcome, although they might be guided by reports from the workplace.
7   Institutional policies should account for the distinctive characteristics of work integrated learning assessment and recognize the contextual difference of assessing practice.

Challenges for assessing work integrated learning

Assessing work integrated learning is possibly the most complex of all assessment modes because what is being assessed is student performance or workplace practice. Learning that occurs in the workplace is difficult to capture due to unpredictable environmental factors, the difficulty of isolating brief instances of performance, and the variability of capabilities assessed and workplace conditions. These factors challenge taken-for-granted assumptions about assessment processes, and require a high level of literacy about the nature of practice and its intersection with learning and assessment.

Designing assessment for work integrated learning requires consideration of three major challenges:

- assessing higher-order reasoning in practice;
- oversimplification of assessment; and
- recognition of work integrated learning assessment in institutional policies.

It is also important to consider the context in which student performance and assessment occurs. In assessing the student's application of knowledge and skills, both assessor and student need to be aware of the dynamic interaction between practice and its context. Student practice in the workplace will impact on the workplace milieu and be influenced by it, just as the workplace context will impact on the student's performance.

Assessing higher-order reasoning in practice

A major issue is to ensure that the expectations and requirements of assessment encourage higher-order thinking and not surface learning (Biggs 2003).

Higher-order thinking is typified by observations and practice that are supported by elaborated, evidence-based reasoning. Surface learning is typified by knowing what to do in a specific situation, but not necessarily why or how to modify practices to account for variable local conditions. In work integrated learning, some student performances that might seem acceptable on the surface may be based on imitation of the actions of expert models in the workplace rather than on professional evidence-based reasoning. Mimicking expert behaviours, while leading to efficient performance, fails to prepare students for understanding how to adapt their practice to account for prevailing conditions. Further issues arise when workplace supervisors give highly positive assessments to students whose practice choices lack evidence-based reasoning, but reflect accepted workplace values and practices. Inaccurate positive evaluations of workplace performance can lead students to develop false confidence in their capabilities. This lack of student awareness of their limitations can place the student, the client and the host organization at risk. The challenge is to find ways to ensure that students get access to expert reasoning wherein experts expose their thinking and publicly justify their practice decisions.

Oversimplification of assessment

Institutional fixation with validity and reliability in assessment has resulted in many professions-based university programmes oversimplifying assessments to pass/fail systems. Validity and reliability in assessment are problematic concepts in work integrated learning contexts. Their use is premised on an expectation that all students will be assessed under common conditions. It has already been discussed that this is not only unlikely in work integrated learning programmes but is also possibly undesirable. However, in light of the high variability of conditions, a common response has been to resort to work-required systems in which student performance is not assessed; merely, tasks are required to be completed. A work integrated learning audit in one institution found that a majority of programmes had defined the work placement assessment element of the curriculum as either a 'work-required' assessment or a 'non-graded pass'. Attending the placement and participating in the work was enough to pass. In none of these instances was it made clear what was required to pass or what would constitute a fail, or indeed whether a student could fail. The use of 'pass/fail', 'non-graded pass' and 'work-required' systems of assessment in work integrated learning is often symptomatic of a lack of articulation of learning outcomes, standards of performance and alignment between these and programme aims.

Recognition of work integrated learning assessment in institutional policies

While the standard requirements for on-campus programmes are clearly stated learning outcomes to which assessment and feedback processes are explicitly aligned, there can be an ad hoc attitude to what must be learned in work integrated learning and what performances are valid proxies for assessing that the particular learning has occurred. The primary goal for selecting work integrated learning assessment approaches is that they meet the following criteria. They should be:

- *aligned* with the learning objectives of the unit of study associated with the work integrated learning;
- focused on *integration* of theory and practice;
- *authentic* to the nature of real-world practice;
- *iterative* to give students the opportunity to practise complex skills and respond to feedback;
- designed to promote *transfer of learning* between contexts.

A survey of university assessment policies in Australia identified that many universities lack policies and processes that recognize the need for assessment approaches based on the above criteria (Orrell and Parry 2007). This policy deficit resulted in:

- assessment that was frequently guided by tacit 'wisdom of practice' or intuition and personal dispositions unrelated to expected learning outcomes and inaccessible to public scrutiny;
- students frequently receiving feedback on their progress on placement at the end of the placement or when they returned to their university;
- universities being reluctant to assess, grade and report student performance in work integrated learning as they do with other aspects of the curriculum.

Issues arising from the policy survey include the need for policies and guidelines that encourage:

- explicit learning outcomes for students to use as frameworks to communicate expectations and standards of performance;
- learning outcome assessments that are linked to the core curriculum or unit of study;
- processes or structures in place to ensure they are used consistently in the assessment process;
- requirement that students will receive formative feedback on their practices and an expectation that they will use the feedback to improve;
- adequate preparation of, and support for, all stakeholders in the assessment process.

This prevailing policy deficit situation stresses the need for improved institutional literacy about workplace performance assessment (Orrell 2005b, 2006). It can be expected that developing explicit clarity of intent as well as policies and processes to support best practice related to work integrated learning will enhance assessment literacy.

Having established the problematic nature of assessing work integrated learning, the following sections of this chapter will use Rowntree's (1977) five-dimensional framework of assessment as an organizing structure.

Dimensions of assessment

Rowntree (1977) proposed five questions to signify the broad dimensions of the assessment process in designing assessment and in determining the quality of students' performances:

1　Why assess?
2　What to assess?
3　How to assess?
4　How to interpret?
5　How to report?

These dimensions will be used in the remainder of this chapter to explore comprehensively the field of assessment of work integrated learning.

Why assess work integrated learning?

Assessment is a fundamental aspect of curriculum design and an inevitable process in education by which information is gathered to make evaluative judgements about the quality of a student's performance. Biggs (1992) argues that this judgement should be made in relation to an orderly scale of achievement levels. The feedback gained from this process by both student and learning guide can be used to determine future learning and teaching activity.

Everyday concepts of assessment often limit its scope to the assessment *of* learning, yet assessment, done well, has been found to encompass concepts of assessment *as* learning and *for* learning (Stiggins 2002). It has been found that the assessment process not only gauges what has been learnt, but also defines the learning agenda, shaping and determining what is to be learned, as well as how it is to be learned. Designing assessment is essentially designing the learning (Biggs 2003), and in work integrated learning it defines the work or the occupation (André 1999).

Assessment performs (1) a definitional function to clarify what is valued in learning, in this instance practice behaviour; (2) a formative function (assessment as learning) to enhance learning; and (3) a summative function (assessment of learning), which determines what learning has occurred.Whilst these three functions are clearly distinctive, a single assessment activity can fulfil all three (Table 5.1). The formative function can have a profound impact on student learning for the longer term, but the summative function often overshadows and complicates it (Scriven 1967; William 2006). The definitional function often goes unrecognized, and its tacit impact has unintended consequences, particularly in the form

Table 5.1 Educational functions of assessment

The Definitional Function

Students' understanding of what is expected and the nature of good performance in the profession or work at hand is determined by the stated learning outcomes, what is actually assessed and the focus of feedback provided.

The Formative Function

Feedback on performance indicates to students their progress towards professional competence, and, ideally, what future learning and performance efforts are required.

The Summative Function

Judgements are made and reported as a measure of students' attainment in relation to established expectations.

of misperceptions and conceptions about what is central to work and particular professions.

Definitional function

The definitional function in professional education programmes is often embodied in an agreed set of competencies that guide curriculum frameworks and are the focus of agreed standards for accreditation by professional regulatory bodies. For graduates, registration to gain employment within a profession or a sector may be dependent upon using their programme of study to produce a portfolio of evidence that attests to their ability to perform competently. Highlighted here is the significance of the posted, public definitional function of assessment. The assessment expectations should establish students' learning agenda and at the same time define for students what it means to work or practice in particular fields.

Formative function

The formative function of assessment is dependent on a learning climate that recognizes and rewards critical self-reflection and understands that professional practice is always a work in progress. The ultimate goal of formative assessment in education is for students to become effective critics of their own behaviour (Orrell 2006; Sadler 1989). It requires an explicit process for focusing on learning outcomes, and on giving feedback to, and engaging with, all stakeholders. The essentials of formative assessment are summarized in Table 5.2.

Summative function

In some professions summative assessment is essential to ensure that students meet professional requirements and expectations established by regulatory bodies

Table 5.2 Essential elements of feedback in formative assessment

- Clearly stated learning goals and behaviour expectations.
- A learning environment that values and rewards the acknowledgement of individual limitations and failure.
- Identification of performance indicators as reasonable proxies for demonstrating learning achievements.
- Opportunity to practise difficult skills and procedures with feedback.
- Clear, specific and explicit feedback in relation to the learning outcomes.
- Shared understanding of what must be done as a result of the feedback.
- An expectation that students will use the feedback to improve performance.

that certify graduates' 'ability to perform'. The rigour of summative assessment is highly variable and exists on a continuum. According to Bachor *et al.* (1994), sound summative assessment has three hallmarks: *representativeness*, namely that the attention of the assessor focuses on expected learning outcomes; *consistency*, namely that the assessment is consistent with the assessment of the student's capability over time; and *accuracy*, namely that two assessors observing the performance would arrive at a similar judgement of the student's capability and that the same assessor would arrive at the same judgement if they were to do it a number of times.

These three hallmarks are a useful alternative to the more scientistic notions of validity and reliability that confound classroom-based learning. They imply rigour and integrity, and have greater utility for the ill-defined situations of workplaces. Representativeness, consistency and accuracy should be present regardless of whether the summative assessment is graded or not.

What should be assessed in work integrated learning?

Work integrated learning assessment seeks evidence that the student is a reflective practitioner capable of self-development, understands the world of work, knows the rules of the profession or workplace setting, and acts in a professional way (Webber 1998: 9). These qualities can only be assessed where they are *integrated* in practice. This constitutes a challenge to teachers, mentors, guides and students to focus on the application of knowledge and skills in practice whilst recognizing that knowledge is the cornerstone of competent practice (Page 2000). The question of what might be assessed in work integrated learning is often confounded by a general reluctance to define precisely the purpose of work integrated learning. Page (2000) argues that a student's overall capacity to perform in a real-world context must be the focus of what is assessed in work integrated learning. Employers indicate that in selecting graduates for their first posts, they prefer to rely on assessments that have occurred in real-world contexts rather than on university abstract pen and paper examinations (Hart and Associates 2008; Holden and Hamblett 2007).

In order to produce sound summative assessments that are valid representations of graduates' capabilities there is a need to articulate specific learning outcomes within more broadly stated programme and curriculum intentions that satisfy first, institutional approval processes for a curriculum, and second, those professional bodies that accredit curricula or certify graduates. Representative, consistent and accurate self-assessment by students, and formative and summative assessment by workplace supervisors, teachers, coaches and mentors, is impossible without clearly explicated learning intentions. Yet developing learning outcomes is a contested process, as illustrated in the following case example.

After an external review of a professional work integrated learning programme, the reviewers recommended improvement of assessment standards. The professional programme director made a decision to develop competencies as learning outcomes and successfully sought external funding to achieve these outcomes. Academic staff were opposed to the concept of competencies, as they believed this meant a 'tick the box' assessment of student achievements. Their view was that practice knowledge was complex and not reducible to a list of outcomes. The professional association, including its academic membership, also opposed this approach. However, when employers and practitioners were consulted, they welcomed the attempt to differentiate standards of performance because it gave them a language to describe and acknowledge the actual practice and how it compared with the ideal performance. After the competency standards were implemented, the University Appeals Committee complimented the department on the changes because the introduction of standards had provided an explicit and transparent assessment process, and had reduced the number of student appeals.

The initial task in developing clearly specified learning outcomes is to map the work integrated learning curriculum and identify the points at which students are expected to integrate theoretical learning with practice learning. Figure 5.1 provides a map of elements that might constitute the range of capacities that could be addressed in a curriculum agenda. The curriculum elements include:

- the locus of practice where the work integrated learning assessment occurs;
- a knowledge base;
- a range of capabilities and specific workplace skills;
- general social and ethico-moral dispositions as well as those specific to the field of practice.

These elements are discrete but not exclusive. Knowledge and capability elements

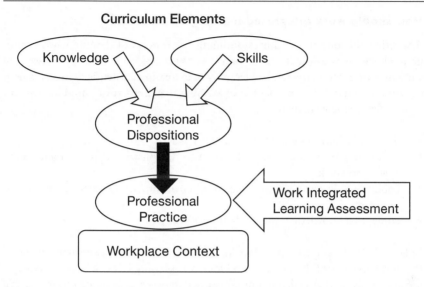

Figure 5.1 Map of elements addressed in a curriculum agenda (adapted from Newble 1992).

of the curriculum coalesce in an integrative process at the point of practice when students apply them in their performances.

Publicly agreed performance goals that are explicitly used in the assessment process reduce the risk of disjunction and contradiction between espoused expectations and everyday practice. Performance goals to be assessed in a real-world context might include:

- being an astute observer who is able to notice what is important in a real-world context;
- transfer and effective application of previous learning and knowledge bases to interpret what they observe;
- utilization of previous knowledge to make and justify decisions;
- select procedures that are appropriate to the context from a range of choices and carry them out;
- review of personal choices and actions, and evaluation of their appropriateness;
- seek feedback and advice, and negotiate areas for improvement;
- listen actively, and change and adapt plans in order to collaborate and cooperate with others;
- meet contractual obligations, such as report writing, planning and running projects, and conducting pieces of research/needs analysis.

Assessment that focuses on the point of *integration* of a student's previous knowledge, capabilities and dispositions with authentic practice fulfils the primary intentions of work integrated learning programmes.

How should work integrated learning be assessed?

Answering this question requires outlining the process of designing work integrated learning assessment. At the basis of this process is the concept of assessing students' progression through a hierarchy of increasing authenticity in assessment demands and the different qualities of learning that are best captured in different forms of assessment, namely:

- declarative knowledge: what a student *knows*;
- procedural knowledge: an explanation to demonstrate that a student *knows how* to proceed;
- conditional knowledge: in a simulated environment a student *shows how* to perform;
- contextual knowledge: the student performs – *does*.

Miller (1990) developed a model to illustrate this hierarchy of assessment. It shows the distinctiveness of the function and focus of assessing in work integrated learning in contrast to that which might be assessed in other parts of the programme of

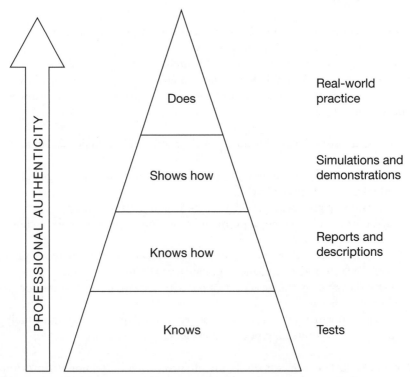

Figure 5.2 Assessment of professional competence (adapted from Miller 1990 and Page 2000).

study. We have adapted this model to include the assessment strategies that provide evidence of students' attainment of each of the levels of competence (Figure 5.2).

Designing work integrated learning assessment with the aim of assessing students' levels of professional competency requires consideration of subsets of questions, including:

- Timing: When should the assessment occur?
- Who should be the assessor?
- What methods, tasks or evidence should be used?

Timing of assessment

There is a strong case for assessment to occur at three different points in the process:

- before the work integrated learning experience for safety and duty of care reasons;
- during the work integrated learning experience to provide formative feedback and assess the application of knowledge and skills, and the ability to perform;
- post-work integrated learning experience to encourage reflective practice, self-evaluation and review.

Assessment before the work integrated learning experience

Assessing students' readiness for practice is an important element in work integrated learning. An essential step in the curriculum design process in work integrated learning is to undertake a rigorous needs and risk analysis to identify just what knowledge, skills, capabilities and professional dispositions students will need to demonstrate before entering the workplace. This process needs to be scaffolded in curriculum approval documentation, assessment regulations and guidelines, as well as training provided in professional development. Students will need some specific knowledge and skills before they enter the workplace, as discussed in Chapter 4. This is to ensure that students have the knowledge, capabilities and dispositions to understand the work environment, notice what is important and function safely. Students should be aware of the need for their behaviour to demonstrate values and dispositions that form the culture of particular professions, work environments and communities in order to function socially within the workplace. The following case example illustrates the need to ensure specific student competencies before students go into the workplace.

The essence of social work is the capacity to form relationships, begin an interview process with clients and understand the ethical practice foundations. A school of social work introduced a pre-placement module that included developing students' basic interviewing skills and foundational practice knowledge. Students were taught skills and knowledge in several laboratory simulation sessions. The pre-placement assessment required students to interview actors whose social problem was based on real practice examples, and to attend a viva to answer questions about practice fundamentals. The interview between the social work student and the actor was videotaped. The performance was assessed using feedback from the actor and the extent to which the student engaged with the actor. Students were then invited to view their videotape and provide reflective comments on their use of interviewing skills. The final aspect of the evaluation was feedback from the coordinator. Students were required to pass this assessment before undertaking their internship.

As part of preparing students for their work integrated learning experience, assessment of brief, pre-work integrated learning exercises can help establish a student's readiness to go into the workplace. The following example illustrates how students can self-assess readiness for work integrated learning experiences by completing a questionnaire, which is then assessed by their academic teachers to identify areas that need more preparation.

What are your learning goals in undertaking work integrated learning experience?

What skills and knowledge do you bring to the work integrated learning experience?

How do you plan to build on these during your time in the workplace?

What are you expecting to do in the workplace?

What professional practice responsibilities do you think you will be required to undertake?

Who will you work with and what do you imagine is important to them?

What values and principles will you take to the workplace that will influence the way you work?

What issues might arise because of your values?

What strategies could you use to address the issues you have just identified?

What communication issues are you aware of that you might find challenging?

What strategies could you use to enable better communication with the people with whom you will come in contact?

Source: Orrell et al. (2003).

Assessment during the work integrated learning experience

Assessment methods during the work integrated learning experience will vary according to workplace settings, what is to be assessed and who is doing the assessment. The diversity of methods used in the assessment process is inexhaustible. A number of possible approaches are outlined here, which suggest that variability is limited only by imagination and willingness to go beyond the recipe-like, ritualistic approaches often seen in traditional assessment of classroom-based learning, for example a word-limited essay or end of semester examination. As stated before, the guiding principle of assessment in the workplace setting is that it should be ongoing, formative, involve student reflection and utilization of feedback, and be focused on performance and the application of conceptual learning and integration of capabilities into everyday practice. We provide the following exemplars for curriculum designers to modify for their use.

WORK REQUIRED APPROACH

An agreed set of tasks and challenges is established. As students satisfactorily complete a set of tasks while in the workplace, these are checked off a list or evidence of completing the task is placed in a portfolio. In some instances this may be used in a limited competency-based approach where students may be required to demonstrate mastery of particular processes and capabilities. Students may have a protocol list where they observe one another and check off completion of tasks for a buddy learner.

COMPETENCY-BASED APPROACH

Each student is required to demonstrate achievement of competency standards using evidence or professional observation of their practice. The student passes and the experience ceases when they have demonstrated they have achieved all standards.

REFLECTIVE ASSESSMENT APPROACH

A student or group of students reviews an episode of work, and discusses the strengths and limitations of the decisions made and what has occurred. This discussion forms the basis for establishing new learning goals in an iterative process. This reflective process may be guided by a scaffold of questions, statements of qualities about work practices, personal learning goals or workplace protocols.

Alternatively, students maintain a reflexive practitioner diary or log of recordings that can be the basis of a larger review. Sometimes students are required to hand in reflective journals to their university supervisors as a record of their learning. This may be problematic because it restricts what students are prepared to write or expect to read; generates an excessive workload for assessors reading and responding to large numbers of students; and the journal may not represent an accurate account of events or may be biased. A solution to the workload issue is to require students to reflect on their journal entries and write an evidence-based personal learning statement based on the entries. Students then ask a learning guide or an expert to observe them in action as they exhibit their new learning in practice.

WORK/LEARNING CONTRACT APPROACH

The work/learning contract forms the basis of planned activities, reflective reviews, feedback and summative assessment. Each student negotiates a set of learning objectives and work responsibilities. These are specified as deliverables to be achieved within a time frame. Support from the workplace to achieve the learning objectives is also specified in the resulting contract.

PROJECT WORK APPROACH

The student is responsible for carrying out a project within a set time frame. A written project report resulting from work completed is assessed on the success of the project, effectiveness of the students' execution and completion of the project. In this instance the report is not assessed on the basis of knowledge or skills the student has acquired to carry out the project, but merely on the fitness of the project report. There may be an additional assessment component in which acquisition or improvement of some essential knowledge and skills might be assessed.

CRITICAL INCIDENT ANALYSIS APPROACH

A student generates a record of a critical incident in which they were involved. This incident may only constitute a brief moment or exchange. They report verbatim to their learning guide, and evaluate how they functioned within the incident and how they might have responded to, or managed, the incident more effectively.

CASE STUDY/HISTORY APPROACH

The student undertakes a detailed study of a person or a feature or an event utilizing multiple theoretical frameworks to give meaning. They present a plan for change or improvement.

PORTFOLIO OF EVIDENCE APPROACH

The student generates a portfolio of evidence that is grounded in the stated learning outcomes. Students must analyse and internalize the learning objectives of their work integrated learning experience in order to identify what kind of evidence they need to produce. They then undertake or seek challenges in the workplace that will provide them with opportunities to generate evidence regarding their competency or capability. Students collect evidence of their capability and may seek feedback from an expert. Once they are satisfied with the standard they have achieved they can then include the evidence in the portfolio. They may seek validation from an observer or participant in the work integrated learning experience. There may be evidence of a growth in capability across a number of pieces of evidence. The portfolio is characterized by a contents page commentary grounded in the learning objectives. The student uses the commentary to direct the assessor's attention to particular evidence. Portfolios are particularly useful in a developmental sense if students have to undertake multiple work integrated learning experiences. Students can reuse the portfolio over several work experiences to establish increasingly challenging personal learning outcomes and to demonstrate improvement over time. The other advantages of portfolios are that:

1　They can combine 'on the spot' assessment with a more reflective mentoring assessment.
2　They focus students' attention across all the learning outcomes, reducing the risk of avoidance of challenging responsibilities.
3　They support formative and summative assessment processes.

DIRECT OBSERVATION APPROACH

Students are observed over time in their placements and a record is kept of the observers' estimation of student competence in relation to learning outcomes. This information is presented to, and discussed with, the student in both formative and summative evaluations. This form of assessment works best when driven by clearly specified learning outcomes and descriptions of performance standards.

Assessment post-work integrated learning experience

Some programmes reserve either all or a substantial component of assessment until after the work integrated learning experience. This is particularly the case in programmes using graded assessments in an attempt to incorporate greater consistency and similarity for all students. These post-work integrated learning experience assessments include project reports, critical incident analysis, self-reflective evaluations, business analysis and case studies. Portfolios that are developed in the work integrated learning experience can also contribute to, or be the focus of, this assessment. While highly appropriate in some programmes, post-work integrated learning experience assessments are limited in their authenticity when it comes to assessment of ability to perform in professional practice. One danger in over-reliance on post-experience assessment is that it may be the first time some students are made aware of limitations in their performance, as illustrated in the following example.

It was the final day of the student's work experience. At 3.00 p.m. in the afternoon, the learning guide called the student to her office and told her that she was going to be failed. Up until that point, the student believed that she had been doing well. There had been no negative feedback to the student or university. When the student asked for further information, the learning guide said the student had breached some of the organization's protocols, which had been noticed by her colleagues. Her colleagues recommended a failing grade to the learning guide. Subsequently, the student appealed this recommendation. The appeal was upheld because the student had not been informed of poor performance at any stage and had not been given the opportunity to correct her mistakes.

This example raises the issue of who may be the most suitable assessor of student performance and learning in any particular situation.

Who should assess?

Assessors are drawn from the broad scope of all stakeholders including workplace staff, educational institution teachers, independent expert professionals, students and their peers. There is particular value in the perspective each assessor brings to providing students with an insight into their learning and their capacity to practice.

Significant tension lies between the domains of practice expertise and theoretical, conceptual expertise. There is a risk of setting up these domains as competing entities rather than as complementary parts of a whole. This dichotomous view can be overcome by creating a learning environment in which theory and practice are understood to have catalytic functions; an environment in which each enhances and evolves from interplay with the other. Multiple assessors are important in enhancing this integration of theory and practice in the assessment process.

Some work integrated learning programmes use only workplace assessors. Whilst assessment by on-the-ground supervisors possibly provides the most informed perspective about individual student capabilities, this approach is risky. The personal relationships, which are necessary to create safe, trusting environments in which the student can learn, often confound the summative assessment of the student's capability. It is important to ensure that there is a moderating influence on the final assessment made by the primary workplace supervisor to relieve them of the sole burden for this subjective judgement and also to ensure a representative, accurate appraisal of a student's capability. A further reason for moderation is that the educational institution is legally responsible for assuring the student's learning achievement. This means that the work integrated learning experience programme coordinator must ultimately determine the academic record or the outcome. The importance of the university's final responsibility is seen in the following example.

A student was placed in an organization where conflict and turmoil were evident. At the mid-point in the internship, a formal assessment was completed with the student reaching the recommended performance standards. In fact, the student was complimented on her high standards of work. After this point in time, the student's learning guide was replaced, which prompted a hostile response from the student due to a lack of consultation. The inter-organizational conflict resulting from the sudden change of learning guide and the antagonistic student reaction meant that a senior manager took over the supervisory arrangements. The university coordinator was asked to validate new supervisory arrangements. In the course of confirming these new arrangements, the coordinator discovered that this senior manager was also responsible for the organizational changes. As the internship was coming to an end, the new supervisor recommended that the student fail. This recommendation contradicted the previous recommendation. At this point in time, the university coordinator overturned the manager's recommendation because of the positive previous assessment and conflicted work environment.

Equally, workplace supervisors can find it difficult having sole responsibility for assessing students, as they are aware that the close personal relationships they develop with students can make it difficult to exercise objectivity in making evaluative judgements. They may also have insider information about challenges going on in students' lives, which may have undue influence over their final report on the student's progress.

Students and peers gain much from playing an active role in the assessment process. Self-assessment is a powerful tool for learning when adequately supported and developed. Successful students, and successful workers and members of society are those with the capacity to reflect on their own actions and recognize their strengths and limitations. Cognitive psychologists call this 'metacognition' – knowing what you know and what you don't know, and how to go about learning. Metacognitive ability is not an inherent personality attribute. It is learnt and, once learnt, remains. When students are required to review and critique their behaviour in the assessment process, they will, if guided appropriately, develop their metacognitive ability. This capacity for self-assessment must be learned and guided. Kerwin (1993), a philosopher, paid careful attention to 'knowing what you don't know' in a course called 'Medical Ignorance' she taught to medical students. The aim was to instil a belief that one of the most important things for a practitioner was to be aware of their own limitations and what was yet to be learnt. This is true of any profession or responsible role, and provides a strong argument for designing opportunities for students to be engaged in self-assessment. The capacity to self-critique is fundamental to developing a disposition for lifelong learning.

Peer assessment also contributes to metacognition because it is often easier to examine critically the behaviour of others and identify their strengths and limitations than to consider one's own behaviour. Once a peer's practice limitations are observed and noted, the transference is not too far to consider one's own practice in similar circumstances. Peer assessment can assist in developing student capacity for self-review. A further argument for including peer assessment in the design of work integrated learning assessment is that it can be an authentic learning opportunity which can teach students how to provide peers (or colleagues) with constructive critical feedback. This skill is a highly valued work-related capacity worthy of intentional development and assessment.

How to interpret students' performances

Practice performance is difficult to capture or replicate because no two workplaces are the same and no two situations in a single workplace are ever the same. Making judgements about how well students have performed in practice settings occurs in highly transient and variable contexts. It is a complex process and a 'wicked' problem (Rittel 1984), ill defined and where solutions to one problem are not easily transferred to another similar problem because conditions change. If a student mismanages a particular workplace event, it is difficult to recapture or recall all the important factors in a review process, or to replicate the precise contexts so that the particular process can be redone and relearned.

What is evaluated or appraised is often difficult to observe or articulate, as environmental and personal factors can distract and influence an observer. Assessment of complex professional behaviours is subject to unintended and tacit influences, including:

- Other students' performances. For example, if previous students have been rated poorly, currently satisfactory students may be rated over-highly and vice versa.
- The influence of initial student behaviours on the relationship between the assessor and the student.
- The assessor's previous experiences in guiding and assessing student achievement in work integrated learning experiences.
- The assessor's personality. Do they see themselves as learning enablers or guardians of professional standards?

(Orrell 2008)

Research indicates that even where assessors are trained to account for or ignore these factors, the impact on the assessment outcomes (grades or appraisals) is still evident (Sweedler-Brown 1992). The likelihood of these subjective influences on educational judgements does not mean we should not assess development and attainment of professional practice standards. It does suggest, however, that shared, clearly outlined guides are needed to assist in the more accurate and consistent observation of appropriately representative indicators of professional practice, and therefore assist in making more consistent, accurate judgements. Assessment rubrics provide the necessary guides.

Using rubrics to guide the interpretive process

Rubrics for assessing developing practice capability are invaluable developmental assessment aids for students engaged in self- and peer-assessment. They provide a scaffold for students to calculate their own and their peers' level of performance in an orderly sequence that is not solely reliant on peer comparison. Rubrics also provide concrete evidence of achievements and indications of further work to be done. The ultimate performance goal is not located in any comparison between student performances but in a carefully described ideal that enables students to identify and articulate concrete personal learning goals. Rubrics that can be used for scaffolding self- and peer-assessment are described here.

Assessors increasingly use two-dimensional rubrics to ensure that the interpretive process is accurate, consistent and focused on what is important. Rubrics are frameworks that direct assessors' attention to what must be assessed. They provide descriptions of the possible range of performances from low to high. Developing assessment rubrics requires the articulation of substantial tacit understandings related to expectations of good practice performance. An advantage of developing rubrics is that the actual development process can be a catalyst for experts to retrieve their tacit practice understandings. The value of rubrics is that they clarify for students what is expected of them. Rubrics address two assessment dimensions. Dimension one attends to *representativeness*. It identifies the precise capabilities and attributes that need to be assessed. Dimension two attends to the need for *consistency and accuracy* in the interpretation of the performance into levels of achievement (or '*How well?*'). In the model generic rubric shown in Table 5.3, the descriptions of *how well* are grounded in several theoretical frameworks. The general concepts of cognitive learning attainment are derived from Biggs' 'Solo Taxonomy' (2003) and influenced by Givens Fisher and Grant's (1983) 'Florida Taxonomy of Learning' attainment. Concepts of ethical and dispositional capabilities are derived from Perry's (1999) 'Taxonomy of Ethical Moral Reasoning' (discussed in Chapter 3). Important to note here is that the model generic rubric is a limited example focusing only on communication skills, cultural and global literacy, and professional and workplace literacy. Each profession and each field of work or community engagement will need to identify the attributes and indicators relevant for their particular field and use the conceptual frameworks of Perry (1999) and Biggs (2003) to describe the developmental nature of the desired capabilities. The following description of the four generic levels of standards of attainment may be used as a guide to this process.

The process of developing a theoretically grounded rubric translates the expected beginning professional competency standards into a developmental framework. In the model rubric, Biggs' (2003) and Perry's (1999) taxonomies have been synthesized into four levels of attainment to enable a shared understanding among students, the university and workplace supervisors, and to assist university coordinators and workplace supervisors to *assess, provide feedback* and enable the *development of workplace practice* to the standards required.

Table 5.3 Generic work integrated learning assessment rubric

Assessment Attributes	Levels of Attainment			
	Developing	Functional	Proficient	Advanced
Communication skills	Poor verbal communication and listening skills accompanied by a lack of self-awareness of impact on others.	Communicates ideas and relates sensitively to others. Can listen to the ideas of others and respond to them.	Communicates most effectively and explains ideas clearly. Actively listens to others and responds appropriately, reflecting a personal understanding of the viewpoint expressed.	Balances listening and responding. Synthesizes what has been heard, and responds and evaluates or elaborates on ideas, offering alternative perspectives.
Cultural and global literacy	Fails to recognize cultural differences in practice or personal bias in their own culturally embedded values. Takes a fairly 'black and white', ethnocentric view on most issues.	Understands that their own viewpoint is one of a number of competing views and that tacit personal biases influence their opinions and actions. Observes and recognizes cultural differences and competing interests.	Is mindful of cultural differences and how social and economic privilege are enacted in personal and political empowerment and marginalization. Interrogates their own interpretations and practice choices to identify personal bias and discriminatory behaviour.	Demonstrates a critical understanding of their own cultural history and its influences on their interpretation of privilege and oppression. Can articulate how social institutions perpetuate racialized practices and marginalization.

Assessment Attributes	Levels of Attainment			
	Developing	Functional	Proficient	Advanced
Professional and workplace literacy	Fails to notice important information and factors in the workplace. Is not safe, requiring constant supervision and is unable to make independent decisions. Does not relate appropriately to colleagues and clients. Does not seek guidance through sensible questioning. No attempt to integrate theory and practice.	Can practice safely. Carries out most procedures without direct supervision. Notices basic contextual cues and asks questions. Attempts to relate personally with colleagues and clients. Functions largely through imitation, and following protocols and rules rather than through problem posing, critical reasoning and effective problem solving strategies. Finds little relevance in the workplace for theoretical concepts.	Establishes personal learning goals. Practises safely, balances initiative and independence with seeking guidance and feedback. Uses/critiques theoretical learning in the workplace. Considers and prioritizes alternative practices. Relates professionally to colleagues and clients. Makes effective contributions to the workplace. Understands organizational structure, functions and contemporary social context and issues that impact on it.	Makes a major contribution to the organization through judicious use of theoretical learning. Notices important cues in the workplace environment. Can work independently and take initiative as well as co-operating effectively in a team. Investigates the organization and understands the social, political and economic factors that impact on it. Establishes personal learning goals and monitors their own learning.

Source: Orrell (2009)

The four generic levels of standards of attainment are:

- **Level 1 – Developing (or Unsatisfactory).** Performance that does not meet the basic level of expectations. Some expected features may be present, but are not sufficient to be determined as acceptable beginning practice. This level of practice is not considered safe and will require a high degree of supervision as well as further practice, exposure and re-evaluation. Students' communication and relationships with workplace staff and clients might be inappropriate and require monitoring. It is hoped that few, if any, students should exhibit this level of performance, which would be assessed as failure.
- **Level 2 – Functional (Acceptable).** Performance meets very basic requirements. Close supervision is still needed as the student will exhibit a high degree of reliance on authority and protocols for guidance in decision-making. Decisions made at this level of performance will be recipe-like and, although theoretically correct, often fail to account for contextual factors. Very little translation or integration of concepts, advice or transference of learning from one event, experience, task or responsibility to another is exhibited. Students' communication and relationships with workplace staff and clients still require some supervision and advice. Particular attributes assessed as 'functional' could be the focus of new learning goals and particular effort in achieving change and improvement.
- **Level 3 – Proficient.** This is the desired standard for all or most students. Such student performance exhibits independence of thought and initiative in planning and practice. Students at this level are capable of being left unsupervised for considerable periods of time. Their performances demonstrate translation, integration and application of core theoretical concepts into practice. They pose wise questions, and seek and utilize feedback and advice judiciously. They demonstrate an ability to transfer advice into new contexts, having an observable capacity for insightful analysis of an event, situation or case. They communicate and relate appropriately to workplace staff and clients. Student performances at this level demonstrate an awareness of social, psychological and economic influences on human and organizational behaviour, and use this to interpret their observations and make attempts to incorporate this awareness into their practice. They are able to evaluate and assess their own achievements, set new personal learning goals and are mindful of the limits of their own competence. They exhibit an enthusiasm and commitment to the work they are required to do and actively seek novel challenges.
- **Level 4 – Advanced.** This level represents professional practice that is beyond the basic expectations of the stated learning outcomes. The practice is highly independent, yet consultative, evidence-based, creative, critically reflective, generative and transformative. There is evidence of an ability to develop new approaches to routine practices. Students relate exceptionally well to workplace staff and clients. Student interactions are appropriate and respectful. Students at this level are mindful of diversity of opinion and approaches to

work, showing an ability to adapt to others while at the same time developing their own views of their preferred ways of working. They are active agents of their own learning, seeking opportunities to have new experiences that will expand their repertoire of capabilities. These students' performances are models of effective and engaged learners who promote a positive and professional image of themselves to their profession and the community

(Biggs 2003; Perry 1999).

The model generic rubric illustrates the process of assessing using these levels of standards in relation to communication skills, cultural and global literacy, and professional and workplace literacy.

Potential problems with student performance can be uncovered using rubrics. Rubrics also provide a reliable and consistent guide to measuring students' levels of competency attainment. Students' practice behaviour is not necessarily developed uniformly. Therefore, rubrics can be helpful for students and their learning guides to note what they have mastered and to identify those aspects of practice where they would be well advised to direct their attention. Areas where students fail to master critical elements or attributes of work-based practices need to be clearly identified and managed. The issue of failing students can create difficulties for students, assessors, the university and the workplace.

Indicators of unsatisfactory performance

Workplace supervisors, work integrated learning coordinators and students all have a duty of care to each other, to the university, to the workplace and its clients/consumers, and to themselves. Any unsatisfactory student behaviour or performance can have immediate consequences for all of these people and institutions. When a workplace supervisor or guide raises concerns with the university work integrated learning coordinator about a student's behaviour or level of performance, it is important to act on this immediately, and involve the supervisor, student and coordinator in discussion of the issues of concern to gain an early opportunity for change (Bogo and Vayda 1998: 253).

Indicators that a student is having problems in the practice area are diverse. They relate to the specific nature of the workplace and the model of work integrated learning. In general, a student who is unable to demonstrate growth towards achieving the intended learning objectives designated for their work integrated learning experience will be considered as having problems. Such a student may:

- display behaviours that are destructive to others;
- demonstrate untrustworthiness or dishonesty;
- be judgemental and critical of clients and/or staff;
- attempt to impose his/her own belief system;
- be harsh, angry, bullying or subtly deprecating;
- be overly authoritarian, directive and task-oriented;

- be overly passive, task avoidant and constantly seek guidance;
- be unreliable and fail to behave responsibly.

(List adapted from Cooper *et al.* 2003: 18)

Despite the best efforts by the university and the workplace to address a student's problems, it may be necessary to take the last resort strategy of failing the student and removing them from the workplace. This action inevitably creates tension in the relationship between the university and workplace. Reaching a suitable agreement among all stakeholders in the work integrated learning enterprise in the shortest possible time, while maintaining the required performance standards, is essential in such a difficult situation.

Discord or accord between the workplace supervisor and university work integrated learning coordinator about student performance can sometimes place students in invidious and risky situations, as the student is likely to disagree with any decision that precludes them from the workplace and gives them a fail grade. In such a situation, consideration must be given to the student's rights. To avoid unfair treatment of students the following are essential conditions:

- Ensure that students have been informed early of the criteria and standards in which they are judged to be deficient.
- Give students time and support to demonstrate that they can meet the criteria and standards and can maximize their own evidence to support their position.
- Allow students to include a 'gatekeeper' against discrimination if any is suspected.
- Ensure that students can find their own support. Keep students fully informed of the subsequent assessment process, including assessment methods and formal mechanisms.

(Evans 1990: 36)

It is wise to remember that if students' rights are not considered, the worst case scenario may ensue, with the student taking legal proceedings against the university. Knowing how to report and provide regular feedback can, in most cases, avoid problems of this nature.

Providing and reporting feedback

Students expect regular feedback on their progress to give them the best opportunities to reach expected performance and behaviour standards. Feedback needs to be analytical and constructive in relation to student progress and performance. One of the most important functions of feedback is to increase students' metacognitive awareness and their capacity to evaluate their own performance. Feedback from the workplace supervisor during the student's workplace practice can be verbal and/or written in report form.

Feedback to students to avoid major interpersonal dilemmas or unsatisfactory work integrated learning performance is critical to the assessment process. It is essential to (1) make the student aware that what the workplace supervisor and university work integrated learning coordinator say or record is 'feedback'; and (2) stress to the student the expectation that they will act on the feedback received. This expectation of further action closes the formative assessment loop; without it, providing feedback is futile. Workplace supervisors and guides, mentors, coaches and university coordinators do well to encourage the student to evaluate their own performance before they themselves provide feedback. The supervisory process, discussed in Chapter 6, involves regular feedback to students.

Summary

Underlying work integrated learning assessment is protection of the workplace's core business and its clients' needs. As such, the principles and challenges of work integrated learning assessment, compared with those of classroom-based assessment, must be taken into account when designing the assessment component of the work integrated learning curriculum. Clearly identifying the need for assessment, what to assess, how to assess it, who should do the assessment, and how to interpret and report the assessment provides a framework for designing work integrated learning assessment. A useful tool in interpreting students' performance in the workplace is the work integrated learning assessment rubric. This provides a guide to levels of competence attainment that can be used to provide feedback to students to enable them to improve their performance, and for the purpose of final assessment. The variable nature of the workplace means there is no guarantee that all students will be assessed as meeting the same challenges and undertaking the same performance requirements.

There is often a strong personal relationship between assessor and assessed, which can influence assessment. Chapter 6 describes the supervisory relationships that develop in work integrated learning, and the purpose and processes of supervision – an essential strategy in ensuring students gain the greatest amount of learning they can during their work integrated learning experiences.

Chapter 6

Supervision

Introduction

The intention of this chapter is to describe key elements of supervision; outline useful strategies for supervisors to assist their students to learn effectively; and to present case studies and think pieces to assist those new to supervision to understand the diversity and complexity of supervision in the workplace.

Supervision is a deceptively simple term that has multiple meanings depending on the context in and profession by which it is used. For the purposes of this book, supervision is an intense learning and teaching strategy primarily based on a close and collaborative interpersonal relationship between supervisor and supervisee. Supervision is a purposeful activity providing guidance to students in the workplace, enabling them to practise their professional skills and knowledge confidently, safely and 'as effectively as possible' (Brown and Bourne 1996: 9) in the 'real world' of the workplace, while maintaining professional standards and commitment to clients. Students are enabled to reflect on their practice, describe and analyse observations in the workplace and achieve learning outcomes as agreed in their supervision contract. It is through this purposeful activity that students develop an understanding of themselves and others, begin to form a professional identity and situate their learning in a specific workplace practice culture. In short, the purpose of supervision is for an experienced practitioner to support and enable a student to develop a level of competence that will allow them to function in a safe and effective manner.

The core elements of supervision include:

- Supervision is an intense learning and teaching strategy.
- It is based on a close and collaborative interpersonal relationship.
- The process of supervision enables students to develop their professional practice skills in the real world of the workplace.
- Supervision is an important management and educational responsibility as students are learners working in an organization for formal course recognition in a degree course.

Supervision is a training strategy spanning many disciplines in which experienced professionals interact with students to provide workplace education, skill development and an understanding of the parameters of professional practice. The strategy is primarily used in settings where students undertake various forms of interpersonal practice with clients and project activities. These settings will, for example, include such professions as nursing (Bond and Holland 1998; Butterworth and Faugier 1992), psychology (Bernard and Goodyear 1992), social work (Bogo and Vayda 1998), occupational therapy (College of Occupational Therapy 1997), physiotherapy (Chartered Society of Physiotherapy 2005), dietetics and pharmacy (Cooper and Anglem 2003), family therapy (Todd and Storm 2002) and speech pathology (Ho and Whitehill 2009). The supervisory relationship is of critical importance as it is in and through this relationship that learning occurs. Both teacher and learner are active participants in a complex process, with both parties taking mutual responsibility for the relationship's success and resolution of any difficulties that may arise.

In Chapter 5, we spoke about the role of the learning guide and outlined some teaching strategies used to assist learners, including the importance of noticing, modelling, scaffolding, coaching and mentoring. These strategies are also used in supervision. There is one important difference between teaching in the workplace and supervisory practice. Supervisors are responsible for the management of practice, the allocation of work and the standards of care. Many workplace learning guides who are responsible for teaching do not necessarily have that level of management responsibility. Brown and Bourne (1996) argue that supervision is a process by which a designated practitioner in the workplace takes responsibility for practice and for the standards of practice.

Supervision is an important management and educational responsibility in the learning process. In many organizations, students are not only learning but are also undertaking work for, and on behalf of, an organization. There is, therefore, a need to ensure that work is performed at a satisfactory level to the professional standards of care. In a management context, supervision assures the organization that new learners are maintaining organizational practice standards; adhering to the law, policy and protocols; seeking support in difficult situations; and ensuring that the organization's reputation is not compromised through poor practice. As student learning is the educational institution's responsibility, the quality of supervision and learning is of particular concern. Work integrated learning involves a shared assessment of student performance and formal recognition as part of courses and degrees. It is this array of interests that has led writers in the field of supervision to describe its key functions, and these are discussed in the next section.

Functions of supervision

Specification of supervisory functions is part of the history of supervision as scholars have attempted to conceptualize the complexity of practice. In recent years, Kadushin (1992) has referred to three key supervisory functions: administrative or managerial, educative and supportive. Other writers have expanded these functions (Hawkins and Shohet 1989; Proctor 1986). Explanation of these functions assists in understanding the elements of teaching and learning in many professional contexts.

The administrative or managerial function acknowledges the importance of the hierarchical relationship between supervisor and supervisee; nominates the person responsible for decision-making; and ensures the implementation of policy and procedures in the organization. The supervisor is responsible to the organization for delivery of services, to meet the needs of clients or patients, and to ensure professional standards are maintained in the interest of those served.

The educational function is to enable the learner to develop the skills, competencies and knowledge necessary to undertake workplace practice. The strategies used are similar to those described in Chapter 4 but there is an emphasis on reflection in a one-on-one relationship between the supervisor and supervisee.

Supportive supervision focuses on the stresses associated with work and learning. The supervisor facilitates the discussion of emotionally charged situations, and attempts to reduce and manage the stress. Throughout this process, the supervisor supports the learner, instils confidence, maintains functioning and enables them to provide the necessary services to clients.

There is disquiet about Kadushin's specification of functions because it has been perceived negatively. It is assumed that a focus on the administrative or managerial function gives too much emphasis to a directive approach to learners. The three functions should be seen as equally important in working with students. One function does not take priority over any other.

Some writers, including Proctor (1986) and Hawkins and Shohet (1989), have developed similar approaches to the primary focus. Proctor, for example, referred to formative, restorative and normative functions. Formative refers to learning skills and competencies through reflective practice and corresponds to an educative function; restorative addresses support and the supportive function; and normative is the accountability dimension and the alternative term for the administrative function. Hawkins and Shohet (1989) prefer to outline the multiple foci which enable us to see the intricacies of functions, content, process, pedagogical strategies and supervisory relationships. In their approach, supervision provides for:

- Reflection on the content and process of learner practice.
- Development of skills, competencies and understanding of practice and context.
- Discussion of an alternative perspective on practice.
- Provision of feedback from a more experienced worker on the content and process of practice.
- Confirmation of practice capacities and support of the learner as a person and worker.
- Collaborative opportunities for learners so that they are not left to practice in

new and or difficult situations without guidance and support.

- Regular, weekly time to explore the personal dimension of practice and resolve issues that arise in relation to the learner's practice.
- Opportunities to plan, organize and use personal, supervisory and workplace resources more effectively.
- Possibilities for learners to be pro-active and not reactive.
- Quality of practice.

(Hawkins and Shohet 1989: 43)

There are many theories, types and models of supervision in the context of student learning in the workplace. Each supervisory approach depends on:

- the professional practice knowledge specified by the educational institution;
- the supervisor's professional background, preferences and practice orientation;
- the student's professional education and level of experience;
- workplace expectations.

In some professional areas, different preferences for supervisory models may exist between the educational institution, workplace, student and supervisor, whereas in others they may not exist. In psychology, for example, some academic clinicians require that a particular psychotherapy taught in the classroom is also used in practice. Clinicians may then use the same psychotherapy model as a framework for student supervision, thereby mirroring theory, practice and supervision. For example, a practitioner with a cognitive behavioural approach to practice with clients may prefer this orientation in work with students. In the classroom, however, a range of models are taught and one model does not always have preference over others.

Whatever the supervisory approach, all involve extensive use of questioning and take place in the context of a close interpersonal relationship. This relationship is an essential component for effective learning. The factors impacting on the type of supervision are shown in Figure 6.1.

The supervisory relationship

Supervision takes place in organizational, professional and policy contexts. These contextual factors have important influences on the learning relationship. In addition, both the student and supervisor bring their personal and professional history to the relationship. This may include a variety of work and life experiences, personal qualities, values, ideologies and world views. Both students and supervisors have previous experiences of teaching and learning, risk-taking and meeting challenges, differences and diversity, trauma and crisis, success and failure, experiences of organizing time and priorities, and experiences of teams and groups (Doel *et al.* 1996). All these factors impact on this relationship positively and negatively.

Learning involves changing the way students think. Supervisors in the workplace

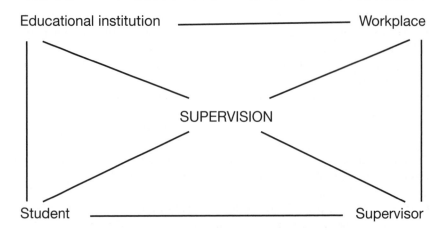

Figure 6.1 Supervision impact factors.

are also attempting to make the learning of complex practices possible for students by shifting their ways of thinking and doing. Whilst this learning can be achieved by observation and modelling of practice, generally it is achieved through a process of supervision and a close relationship between the supervisor and supervisee. It is only through this intense and close relationship that student understanding and insights can be continually considered, challenged and changed through a reflective and insightful conversation. Understanding the emotional climate of work in the supervisory relationship is important. Scaife and Walsh (2001) argue that the emotional climate of work and the development of self-awareness are important aspects of supervision. In addressing the emotional climate of work, the supervisor and student may consider the psychological morale of the organization and its impact on the learner, the unique cultural dimensions, relationships with colleagues, and the positive and negative emotions generated in the supervisory relationship. When the student is aware of the impact of organizational issues on them and their practice, they are better prepared for their professional responsibilities.

The personal aspects of supervision also include the personal impact on the professional work of helping others. In many professional areas the student is required to communicate with people about intensely emotional issues. This may entail breaking bad news or listening to stories about the lives of clients. A speech and language therapist may need to tell an older woman who has had a stroke that she will need assistance with feeding; a nurse may be present when a patient is given bad news; or a family therapist may listen to stories about family violence, trauma and dysfunction. Dealing with these realities of the human condition can be challenging for newcomers to the profession.

Learners in workplaces are influenced by relationships, circumstances and activities outside the workplace that impact on their functioning in the workplace. For example, concurrent academic demands for assessment may create stress for the learner and affect the time and thought given to workplace activities. Similarly, personal experiences, values, attitudes and beliefs can impact on how professional practice is conducted. Although professionals are meant to act empathically towards others, this does not always occur. Students may react with a variety of negative and potentially harmful emotions, and may not be able to keep a professional distance in many situations. Supervision can address these challenges by exploring the meaning of these issues in the students' relationship with their clients and their ways of working. These discussions enable awareness of the professional self.

These intense discussions are facilitated within the supervisory relationship, which does not happen immediately. The close working relationship between supervisor and supervisee, the core of supervision, goes through a number of developmental stages and takes time to evolve. This can be an anxiety-provoking time for both parties.

The supervisory stages

A key way in which supervision has been conceptualized is as a series of developmental stages in which the supervisor and student are learners developing new sets of cognitive, emotional, interactional and ethical skills. While Stoltenberg (1981) and Gardiner (1989) have particularized a development approach, Hawkins and Shohet's (1989: 49–52) later model is used here to describe the developmental stages of supervision, despite these authors not addressing the simultaneous ethical and emotional development of students that occurs.

Stage 1: High dependence

In the beginning stages of supervision, the relationship is characterized by dependence on the supervisor. The student is both self-centred and anxious. This anxiety comes from evaluation apprehension, the new learning and objective self-awareness. The supervisor assists this process by providing a clearly structured environment, encouragement and feedback, thus minimizing but not removing the apprehension.

Stage 2: Fluctuation between dependence and autonomy

In the second stage, one compared to adolescence, the student has overcome this initial anxiety and begins to fluctuate between autonomy and dependence. The capacity to focus on client or project needs in a more complex way is developing. This stage of supervision is less structured but there is evidence of emotional support.

Stage 3: Confidence and collegiality

Being able to meet individual client needs or understanding the complexity of activities and tasks, and seeing them in a wider context, is apparent at stage three. Students have greater confidence, less dependence on their supervisors and a more collegial supervisory relationship.

Stage 4: Integration of work and practice wisdom

In the final stage of development, the supervisee is ready to become a fully fledged worker. Work is integrated and practice wisdom is evident. Some students, especially beginning students, may not progress past stage one or two, but students with more maturity and participation in more than one work integrated learning experience would be expected to reach the last stage before graduation.

Complexities in the supervisory relationship

The supervisory relationship develops over time, with a number of phases being described in the literature. Holloway (1995), for example, refers to the 'developing' phase, the 'mature' phase and the 'terminating' phase, regardless of the period of time the student–supervisor relationship has existed. Whilst the amount of time students spend in the supervisory relationship is determined by their university, the reality of workplace practice is that supervision may extend over a much longer period of time. Supervision may take place daily and most often weekly, extending over periods of weeks or months. Although the developing supervisory relationship may not reach the levels of maturity expected of experienced workers, it is an intense, complex interpersonal relationship that addresses the emotional climate in the work, the workplace and the relationship. This emotional climate brings its own complexities to the relationship.

Students come to supervision with a range of feelings, including anxiety, confused/contradictory expectations and uncertainties. Supervisors, whether new or experienced, may also encounter a similar range of feelings about supervision. Supervisors deal with these emotional issues by exhibiting trust, honesty, respect, commitment, integrity, a non-judgemental approach, emotional openness, a willingness to ask questions, and the capacity to enable and empower.

Initially, students may be self-centred and dependent on the supervisor for direction. As the relationship develops students fluctuate between dependence and a desire to make autonomous practice decisions. With reduction in their anxiety, students are better able to focus on the process of working and can begin to work in a professional capacity. Over time, the balance between dependence and autonomy changes, with increasing self-confidence and capacity to appreciate the complexity of practice. The relationship brings with it particular challenges, including a demand for work. This is an expectation that the students will get on and do the work; they are expected to perform. Some students may see this as threatening, and react with ambivalence and resistance. Students may address the trivial issues rather than the difficult issues. It is anticipated that over time there will be a deepening of trust, better management of difficulties, exploration of boundaries and developing worker competence. Once this position has been reached, it is possible to evaluate the supervisory relationship and review the learning outcomes.

Any intensely interpersonal supervisory relationship, where the feelings, behaviour and competence of an individual are at the core, raises complex issues of privacy and confidentiality. Whilst some students and supervisors believe that the content of this relationship is private, with all information discussed being absolutely confidential, the situation is not so clear-cut in the reality of the workplace and university learning contexts. Issues of student competence can be the subject of discussion, and from a host organization viewpoint any issues of risk discussed by the supervisor are a matter for broader host organization management and also for the university which certifies the practice competence of the student. Consider the situation in the following case study, which illustrates the importance of sharing information about a student's competence in a particular work integrated learning context, and seeking a way forward for all parties involved.

A young autistic student with good academic skills was undertaking a work integrated learning experience working with young people with disabilities. The university coordinator was aware there may be some problems with the placement and had talked with the supervisor before the student entered the workplace to ensure adequate supervision. It became clear early in their placement that the student was not safe working in a hands-on position, and that the learning experience would need to be terminated. The supervisor and course coordinator assessed the student, provided extensive feedback on learning achievements, and worked to counsel the student out of that particular practice specialization and into one that better suited the student's abilities. Student counselling worked specifically with the student. The student was channelled into the area of project management, where he was very successful.

Given the likelihood that personal issues may impact on learning, it is not surprising that the supervisory relationship has the potential to move from a focus on learning how to practise, to an examination of the student's intrapersonal concerns and capabilities. The line between what is personal and what is educative and professional is blurred. This is referred to as a 'boundary issue'. When a supervisor intervenes in matters that are strictly personal, they are said to have crossed the boundary. Although there appears to be a clear distinction between the educative and personal, in practice this is not so clear. It is always important for the educator to ask, 'Is this what an educator/supervisor does?' When personal issues are raised in supervision, students might also question themselves and their supervisor about whether these personal matters are appropriate for discussion.

These questions serve as a device to avoid the danger of harming students (Gutheil and Gabbard 2008).

The impact of the personal and professional dimensions is revealed in the following example from mental health nursing, adapted from Cooper and Anglem (2003: 31).

> A patient interrupted a team meeting and was immediately asked to leave. When the patient refused to leave, the student left the meeting and called two other students to assist them move the patient to a quiet area. In supervision, the student raised the parenting role she was playing in this team. This parenting role was a source of anxiety, with the student commenting that this directive role did not allow her to work with patients in a caring manner. During supervision, the student learned that she was adopting this role for several reasons. The patient was on a behaviour modification schedule that involved withdrawal of privileges and as this was administered by nurses, this function covertly encouraged them to adopt a paternalistic, police-like role. Other reasons were more personal and included family relationships and dynamics. Discussion of these system problems, the interpersonal issues and transference between the student and patient were all part of the supervision session.

Some of the complexities of the student–supervisor relationship can be addressed during the early work of its development. Clarifying expectations and developing an understanding of each other can be facilitated through either the initial verbal or written supervisory or learning contract. A contract is useful for establishing purposes and processes for working together, as well as intended outcomes. Developing the contract requires active participation of students and supervisors, an essential part of which is the establishment of the ground rules and basic conditions under which supervision will proceed (Cooper and Anglem 2003: 48). Discussion may cover:

- frequency of supervision;
- purpose of supervision;
- confidentiality;
- safety of practice issues;
- setting agendas;
- review of contract;
- accountability for client work;
- relationships with other staff;
- preparation for supervision;
- interruptions and cancellations;
- management of personal issues;
- resolution of conflict;

- boundary issues;
- recording of session;
- cultural issues;
- feedback to manager;
- group norms.

Contracting done well can avoid difficulties as the relationship progresses. A written contract can provide a useful resource to turn to if difficulties arise.

Supervision arrangements

One-on-one supervision is generally the most common form of supervisory arrangement, but group supervision and sometimes peer supervision are also utilized. In this section we focus on one-on-one supervision and group supervision.

One-on-one supervision

Many students have a preference for the one-on-one approach in areas of practice that involve personal disclosure about their performance. As outlined in Table 6.1, there are many advantages to the one-on-one arrangement, as well as several disadvantages.

As the name implies, one-on-one supervision means that the supervisor and the student meet on a one-on-one basis to discuss the student's work. It is done in private with the time protected from other intrusions. One challenge in this intense relationship is the issue of professional and organizational authority, and its place in supervision (Munson 2002). Supervisors come to supervision with an authority to supervise granted by the host organization, and recognized by the educational institution and profession. Some supervisors will hold management or senior practice positions as line managers or clinical specialists within the organization. They have status, and both formal and informal power. It is not surprising that the student–supervisor relationship may be difficult, as power issues add to the complexity. From a student viewpoint, the most important authority held by the supervisor is their technical and professional expertise.

Although generally accepted by students, this authority is sometimes challenged, raising tensions in the learning relationship. Similarly, the supervisor's authority arising from their administrative and clinical positions means assisting students to understand professional and organizational responsibilities. This can include discussion of how to record material in case files or ensure compliance with policies and procedures. There are many ways in which the supervisor can manage the issue of structure and authority, but also a variety of ways in which students can undermine the supervisor's intentions and authority. It is helpful for the supervisor to be clear with the student about the learning contract, including the structure, purpose, content, frequency of supervision, agenda for the sessions and decision-making about practice issues. The student, on the other hand, can

Table 6.1 Advantages and disadvantages of one-on-one supervision

Advantages

- Both student and supervisor can arrange their own agenda and supervisors are able to respond to emergencies or crisis situations in the student's work.
- There is time available to discuss every case and students value this learning time.
- The student's work can be examined closely, thus allowing greater depth to the work and the learning.
- The one-on-one supervision models practice, as it duplicates and mirrors the practice relationship.
- The supervisor gets an overview of the student's total workload, and the organizational arrangements and relationships providing background to the student work.
- There is a high degree of trust, and whilst not completely confidential for reasons described later, many issues around the learning are private and respected.

Disadvantages

- It is a time intensive-approach and if learning difficulties occur, it can take supervisors away from the organization's work, thus creating resentment.
- The learning relationship is hidden – not open to scrutiny from other practitioners – and this may result in the student being subjected to abuse and bias.
- The learning relationship may be collusive if the student and supervisor share similar views. This collusive behaviour is experienced by university coordinators who collaborate with supervisors and students on mid-term and final assessments.

Adapted from Feltham and Dryden (1994: 44–5)

subvert the supervisory process by bringing questions previously addressed to the supervision session, raising administrative issues instead of discussing case material, or simply discussing office gossip or politics.

Contractual requirements from funding bodies about the number of therapeutic sessions per client or family and type of work, or external policy demands, can intrude into, and complicate, the student–supervisor relationship and learning. Inevitably problems arise for the student as they struggle with the demands of the external environment, including the higher education institution, and their own desire for personal and professional autonomy. It is the supervisor's responsibility to assist the learner to reconcile these differences. During supervision sessions, the supervisor can assist by acting as a mediator between the student and other professional staff in the organization, and between the demands of the organization and the university. Consider the following case studies where the supervisor had to mediate relationships in very different ways.

Case study 1

The student brought a number of cases to supervision for discussion. These cases had been transferred to the student for follow-up. In the discussion with the supervisor the student raised concerns about inadequate documentation of case material. Privately, the supervisor made a mental note of the poor clinical performance of her colleague.

In the supervision session, the student indicated that she was not confident about her ability to manage the cases referred by another worker. She said the process was piecemeal and she had no sense of the previous worker's intervention, and that she did not know how to respond to the clients. Clear patterns emerged through discussion. Most files were in disarray. Files did not contain psychometric results and there was no contact with the General Practitioners. The previous worker provided a limited diagnosis only. The supervisor drew attention to the student's clearly documented process for transfer and then assisted the student to develop a strategy to manage the transfer of cases. The strategy included involving the previous worker, client and student in the handover process.

The supervisor, a practitioner in a senior clinical position, took steps to rectify the situation with the transfer of cases to the student and worked actively with the clinical manager, previous worker and student to ensure an effective and smooth transfer for all stakeholders. The supervisor mediated effectively with all parties to ensure a positive outcome for the student.

Adapted from Cooper and Anglem (2003: 45)

Case study 2

Frequently, the supervisor is the mediator between the requirements of practice and the demands of the higher education system. In this case, the supervisor has been working with a student whose first language is not English. In a supervisory session, the student asked the supervisor about his report writing and whether he was writing enough in the case files and reports. When the supervisor asked the student about his particular concerns, the student said that the university faculty had told him that his writing skills were poor because they were not detailed enough. The student was informed by the university that his writing needed to be more descriptive and analytical. The supervisor explained that writing reports for an organization required a different set of skills. Reports and notes were to be factual with a brief account. She provided the SOAPIE acronym as a framework for the student. SOAPIE stands for subjective information, objective information, assessment of the situation, the planned approach, actual intervention and evaluation.

Group supervision

Group supervision can be a satisfying and rewarding process for students and supervisors but the structure, process and preparation of students need to be considered carefully. It involves a similar process to that of one-on-one supervision, except that the membership contains three or more people. Group dynamics provide an additional and complex layer, but students can derive learning about groups by participating in these groups. The facilitator and group members address complex practice issues, and participants ask questions of each other, seek clarification and provide support. As is the case with one-on-one supervision, authority is also a concern in group supervision. The advantages and disadvantages of group supervision are outlined in Table 6.2.

Modelling and dialogue at the heart of supervision

In Chapter 4 we discussed modelling and its importance in teaching and learning. The supervisor is a practice expert. Through the process of supervision, the supervisor has at their disposal their practice experience, knowledge and skills.

Table 6.2 Advantages and disadvantages of group supervision

Advantages

- The contribution of experiences from all group members provides variety, allowing breadth and depth of experiences.
- Each student can provide different experiences as well as theoretical and professional approaches.
- The variety of views from students may prevent collusion, prejudice and bias.
- The approach is efficient.

Disadvantages

- There may be insufficient time to discuss the work of all students in the one session.
- Some students are able to hide, and minimize their work to avoid difficulties.
- There is competition between students for attention and some may withdraw from the group process.
- In discussing cases, too many viewpoints may create difficulties for learning.
- There is the danger of 'group think'.
- Group interaction may take precedence over discussion of case material and issues.
- There may be little privacy for students where learning issues and personal issues are the focus of the discussion.

Adapted from Feltham and Dryden (1994: 46–7)

The complex processes for attending to, and resolving, practice issues are done automatically: practitioners *just do it*. While this expertise can be shared with students through a demonstration of practice, there is a more important way of sharing this knowledge. Supervisors who are practice experts can model their ways of problem solving through a process of *verbalizing their practice thinking*. In doing this, the supervisor expresses their thoughts, feelings, concepts, dilemmas and ways of thinking about a particular situation. Supervisors can talk to students about the processes they go through automatically. They demonstrate their mental processes so that through this elaboration students have at their disposal a complex and detailed understanding of practice. With access to the supervisor's strategies, students can then approximate practice skills in new activities whilst articulating their thought processes. Ongoing practice should enable students to begin constructing their own practice knowledge.

Supervisors talking to students about the processes they go through automatically in practising their expertise forms an important part of the supervisor–student dialogue that lies at the heart of supervision, which is a conversation with the specific intention of enabling students to learn. This conversation is similar to other learning conversations except that it is done in private and on a one-on-one basis. In this conversation, supervisors ask students to describe events occurring in their practice, and throughout this process, supervisors:

- ask questions;
- seek clarification in particular areas;
- demand analysis of interactions;
- request an evaluation of effectiveness in work;
- explore affective and interpersonal skills used;
- ascertain knowledge and understanding of the student;
- connect practice knowledge with theoretical constructs.

In summary, the supervisor, through questioning and discussion, is helping the student to develop practice knowledge, competence, and the awareness and insight necessary for practice. Although dialogue is at the heart of supervision, the practice teacher has at their disposal a range of methods to enrich the dialogue and deepen the discussion, including Interpersonal Process Recall, process recording and critical incident analysis.

Interpersonal Process Recall

Anxiety associated with learning in a workplace may result in some students attending to, and focusing on, their anxiety at the expense of tuning in to the interactions between themselves and other people. In other words they act diplomatically towards others but do not become involved at a level that is helpful to those others. Students may miss or avoid important cues, making it necessary to assist them to appreciate and understand those cues' importance. Interpersonal Process Recall

(IPR), a strategy developed by Norman Kagan (1977), is used as a supervisory approach to address the above issue. This strategy was originally based solely on the student's memory of the interaction. Audio and video tapes are now used to assist students to attend to their perceptions and the subtle interactions occurring in human relationships, as many organizations now have access to this technology.

How to use IPR for student learning

- IPR is learning that takes place in a private conversation between the supervisor and student. Ensure privacy and time to do this thoroughly.
- It is usual to use an audio or video tape of the student's work. Beginning students often prefer an audio tape.
- Suggest the student review all or part of the tape privately before the supervision session and request that they take notes of their observations, reflections and interactions.
- Ask the student to select a part of the tape for discussion. Generally, the part selected should include the interactions that were most significant for learning.
- Create a non-threatening atmosphere to enable discussion and learning. The critical aspect is to allow the student to discover the complexity of human interactions for themselves.
- Ask the student to play the tape. The student can determine a point in the tape where they want to stop and talk about particular thoughts, feelings or interactions. Alternatively, the supervisor can do this.
- The supervisor uses a variety of open-ended questions to inquire into the blocked or hidden interactions, thus facilitating a discovery process that enables greater awareness. Some suggested questions include:
  — What thoughts were going through your mind at this point?
  — What would you like to have said?
  — What would you like to have done differently?
  — Why did you or the other person react or respond in the way you or they did?
- The process of watching and discussion continues, with the supervisor continuing with open-ended questions.
- Allow the focus of these sessions to be on discovery rather than telling students how to do better in practice.

Process recordings

Process recording is an old approach to learning tool that is being replaced by an increased use of video and audio tapes. The ideas embedded in this method can, nevertheless, be used with other electronic technologies. A process recording is a specific written account of the interaction between the student and clients or other significant people, and is based on the student's accurate recollection of events.

The purpose of a process recording is to recall the dialogue, describe the subjective feelings and responses arising in the interaction, and reflect on the interaction. These reflections include interpretation of feelings, behaviours, issues and interactions. The process of writing, with feedback from the supervisor, facilitates learning from experience. The emphasis is on the quality and depth of reflection rather than on rights and wrongs or quality of practice. It is essential for the student to present an accurate account of the process rather than replacing the actual dialogue with a more polished account of that dialogue. Students can use process recording in working with clients, in groups, with families and in other interactions where there is a need to reflect on the interactions. The method does have limitations, being dependent on an accurate memory and the recording being done as soon as possible after the interaction. Table 6.3 outlines how to write a process recording.

Critical incident analysis

Critical incident analysis is a useful learning tool for students. The learner perceives the critical incident as an event or turning point in their practice that enables them to learn and reflect on their activities, and on the applicability of their theoretical frameworks.

Table 6.3 How to write a process recording

Steps

- The process begins with a summary of background and explanatory information.
- The actual interaction is then recorded in four columns as indicated below.
- The process recording is complete when the student writes a summary of the learning from the overall experience. It can also include a statement of future work.
- Whilst the focus of process recording is on reflection, feedback and learning, by adding an additional column this process recording framework can be adapted for programmes that require demonstration of professional standards.

Dialogue between the student and significant others	Subjective feelings and responses	Reflective analysis	Comments from the supervisor
Include in this column a word-for-word account of the interview including verbal and observations of non-verbal communications	Subjective feelings refer to what the student was thinking and feeling about the interactions with others	Reflective analysis is the student's interpretation of feelings, behaviour, issues, interactions and their use of self	Here the supervisor poses questions that enable the student to discover new possibilities; clarify meanings; and provide feedback.

This event becomes a critical incident because of the student's views about how the event occurred and was resolved, the way it was perceived by any party or stakeholder, or through the value or significance attached to it. Generally, a critical incident is a piece of work that has a beginning, middle and end, and is sufficiently comprehensive to allow analysis. Critical incidents can be any of the following:

- an activity or task that went well;
- an activity or task that was difficult for the learner;
- practice where an error or mistake occurred and was recognized by the leaner;
- work that was demanding in terms of skill, knowledge or competence;
- any work where the student's views about practice were challenged;
- areas of conflict, hostility or aggression in the organization/workplace.

A critical incident analysis can be used in the following ways:

- to provide a brief background description to orient the supervisor or reader;
- to state the action that began the incident;
- to specify the person or persons to whom the statement or action was directed (students should use aliases and not the real names of clients or colleagues);
- to outline the stimulus precipitating the action;
- to describe the hoped-for response;
- to state what actually happened;
- to outline your understanding of the skills, concepts and standards of practice that underpinned your actions;
- to finish with an analysis of the situation. This can include theoretical understanding or integration, workplace activities, the law and its application in the workplace, values, new knowledge or skills, interprofessional practice, or the student's self-awareness and insights.

Consider the following case example of a student's critical incident analysis.

I had an issue where I went into the office one day in shorts and the clients were most impressed. The staff were not at all impressed. It was simply an oversight on my behalf. I knew it was going to be very hot and I would not be in contact with many clients as I had tasks to complete. As soon as I entered the office, I felt hot with embarrassment as I realized my mistake. I took my work into the office kitchen hoping the floor would open up and swallow me, but it didn't. Instead, staff came in, initially grim, then supportive, and now they still laugh good-naturedly at the day I came into the office in shorts and hid in the kitchen.

It was an important lesson for me and taught me professionalism is not just about attitudes and ideas, positions, ideals or policy; it is about an entire mindset. It is about understanding the way you affect others on a broad scale and not only is what you wear important but also the way you move, personal habits such as fingernail chewing and hair adjustment, the little things you do without thinking (also about awareness of mindsets of other people).

The critical incident allowed the student to appreciate the norms of professional behaviour and provided an opportunity for the student and supervisor to discuss such issues in greater depth.

This example clearly illustrates the important reflective element of critical incident analysis. Getting the student to talk about a critical incident, their feelings during the incident and their analysis of it in hindsight, during a supervision session, is a strategy that can open dialogue about other issues for the student that have arisen in the workplace, or that may arise in the future. This strategy, and others described here, can be used at any time during the supervision process depending on the concerns and issues raised by the student and their supervisor.

Summary

Supervision is a specific form of teaching and learning that is particularly important in professional learning. It may be used in service learning situations where there is an orientation to client or patient work. The defining feature of supervision is that the supervisor not only has teaching responsibilities but also managerial responsibilities for the student's work, especially the maintenance of practice standards. Supervision is a complex interpersonal activity which has particular functions, stages, characteristics and complexities. The success of supervision depends on the quality of the contract between the student and the supervisor or learning guide. The predominant strategy is dialogue and discussion focusing on work with clients as well as the emotional content and responses to the work. Supervisors can act as models, sharing their practice wisdom and approaches with students. In addition, particularly in student education, there are some specific tools that facilitate access to the nuanced aspects of practice. These include Interpersonal Process Recall, a variation titled 'process recordings' and analysis of critical incidents.

This chapter has flagged some of the complexities that arise specifically in the supervisory relationship and the ways of addressing them. Chapter 7 focuses on managing risk and difficult situations that may arise in work integrated learning due to its overall complexity.

Section 3

Managing work integrated learning

Managing Difficult Situations

Introduction

Work integrated learning is expanding and taking many more students off campus into various workplaces. The learning and work combined make for complexity. It can be challenging for students, universities, host organizations and their workplaces, and it is inevitable that some problems will arise. Many workplaces are local but some are in remote and international locations, thus making it difficult to assist students should issues arise. With the expansion of work integrated learning it is likely there will be a greater frequency and opportunity for injury and risk to students, clients, patients or consumers, and workplaces. It is therefore important for the university to know the students and the university's capacity (or incapacity) to protect them, understand the nature and severity of risk in work integrated learning environments, and foresee situations when students and their clients, patients or consumers might be harmed. Work integrated learning involves understanding particular frameworks as background knowledge to ensure programmes operate within a managed risk environment.

Whilst work integrated learning provides remarkable opportunities for students to learn new knowledge and practice, these opportunities come with risk for students, the university, learning guides, and workplaces and their clients, consumers or patients. The following examples illustrate a spectrum of learning experiences in which students may encounter risk:

- driving the organization's car as part of work activities;
- sexual harassment or abuse of students by work colleagues;
- white-water rafting as part of an eco tourism programme;
- delivering babies as part of a midwifery course;
- trauma experienced by listening to a client's stories of torture or abuse.

Risk is part of everyday life and work experiences. It may not be possible to remove risk but it is necessary to understand the extent, probability and nature of risk, and to ameliorate and manage it as part of work integrated learning. If students or service recipients were harmed in any of the above situations, those responsible for managing work integrated learning would be required to manage and resolve the resultant difficult situations.

This chapter discusses the concept of risk management, some of the many identified risks in work integrated learning, the legal frameworks within which risk management operates, the importance of extensive and sustained support for all stakeholders when managing difficult situations, and risk management strategies to minimize and reduce harm to all parties when difficult situations arise.

Risk management

Understanding and knowing that risk exists does not mean that administrators should be fearful of work integrated learning activities and their management. Risk is a normal and necessary part of many human activities. Fear, uncertainty, ambiguity and anxiety are normal emotions associated with risk and its management. When students learn new skills or when workplace guides provide support and guidance for students, errors and mistakes are highly probable. Consider the German who constructed the first hang-glider in the early nineteenth century. Whilst his early flights were not successful, the risks and dangers he faced allowed later designers to test their ideas and designs, and then test and retest prototypes until the modern hang-glider was created. Learning, innovating and improving practice bring potential risk. It may not be possible or even desirable to remove risk but it is possible to understand it and prepare for, and manage, situations through a risk management process.

Risk management is a set of well-established processes used by organizations to minimize and reduce harm. These processes encompass:

- identifying activities likely to create risk for any and all stakeholders;
- assessing the impact and probability of risk;
- analysing and quantifying exposure to, and the impact of, risk;
- developing strategies that will best manage risk, including policies and procedures incorporating insurance, safety measures and stakeholder education;
- continually reassessing risk and improving practices to ensure risk is avoided or minimized.

Risk and difficulties

All partners in work integrated learning have complex responsibilities to clients, consumers, patients, students, their profession or discipline, their own institution or workplace, and to any contractual or partnership arrangements. Collegiality and cooperation are features of university–workplace relationships, but despite such understanding, commitments and goodwill there are times when tension and conflict arise around different expectations and perceptions held by the various stakeholders in relation to the behaviours, performance and competence of the student and the workplace guide. Contradictory expectations are exacerbated when parties become entrenched in a particular view, emotions are high, communication is difficult or when dynamics between all stakeholders are nuanced or fraught. Multiple stakeholders with different interests may leave students vulnerable because students lack the intellectual and practice background to make sophisticated decisions. Complexities arise between the educational institution and the workplace, and within workplaces and institutions. This may become exacerbated when their competing needs and expectations are not clearly stated or understood. It is within this context that difficulties arise which must be recognized, acknowledged and managed.

The following example illustrates how different parties involved in a common situation may have quite different expectations and understandings of that situation, and how this may impact on the most vulnerable party – the student.

A foundation whose goal is to further citizenship and involvement in community life through service learning has funded a university to provide service learning for a fixed time. The foundation expects that the university, the faculty and the student body will actively contribute to the common good of the broader community through active engagement, volunteering and participation.

The university administration wants students to have a broad liberal education. Students are diverse and have a variety of expectations and interests in learning but are ultimately driven by the assessment requirements in their women's studies course, which addresses specific, well-defined issues and questions.

A faculty member in women's studies negotiated for her students to gain a deeper understanding of both theoretical and practical matters through first-hand experience of domestic violence in a women's crisis centre but does not expect that these students will become engaged long term in the community.

The service learning centre responsible for managing the university's service learning programme wants the foundation to continue supporting it and to demonstrate that service learning can further citizenship. Towards this end the centre has formed a community advisory group representing those community agencies most closely linked to it and is demanding greater engagement of the university in education and research initiatives. The advisory group appears to have unrealistic expectations of the student behaviour and educational goals of the institution, which do not fit well with the goals of the service learning centre.

Difficulties arise when the students from the women's studies programme finish their time-limited observation at the women's crisis centre and complete their course assessment requirements. The crisis centre accuses the university of taking advantage of their generosity and complains about the students' lack of involvement in the life of the centre, suggesting that the students should fail their assignments. The women's crisis centre threatens to withdraw from the service learning arrangements. The students believe their grades and career in the human services are threatened by these actions.

The parties in this case include the philanthropic foundation, the faculty member in women's studies, the university administration, the service learning centre with its advisory group and the students. Their disparate expectations of the work integrated learning experience require clarification and negotiation, as discussed later in this chapter in the section that provides strategies to respond to risk and difficulties. In short, in this example initial clarification of all parties' expectations and agreement about the outcomes for each party could have ameliorated the risk to students.

General and specific risks to students

The work integrated learning literature outlines a range of general and specific risks to students. These are elaborated in Table 7.1 and repeated in Appendix 2 with references provided. Whilst it is not possible to discuss every type of risk, some concerns, including harassment, injuries, stress, discrimination, standards of care or service, individual dispositions of students and learning guides, and learning guide workloads are common to all areas of work integrated learning. This suggests a high degree of probability that these risks may occur. Some risks, such as harm to clients, consumers or patients, may be less likely to occur but may have a greater impact because the resulting harm or damage may result in legal action, with associated negative publicity for the student, the organization, the particular workplace and the university.

Harassment

Harassment of students by co-workers, other students, learning guides or clients, consumers or patients and service providers is a common issue in work integrated learning. Harassment refers to behaviour that is intimidating or threatening in some manner. Harassment is generally confined to bullying or psychological intimidation but may extend to sexual harassment and abuse. Concepts of reasonable and unreasonable behaviour are difficult to define and highly contestable in cases of sexual harassment. Women are particularly vulnerable to sexual harassment. In the most extreme situation, learning guides may take advantage of their power and status to sexually harass students, threatening them with negative reports if they refuse to participate. Such harassment has damaging consequences for the student victims, including anxiety, depression, learning difficulties and self-destructive behaviours. These consequences may result in students losing interest in the area of work, discipline or profession. Harassment may well be under-reported by students because they fear retaliation and a backlash associated with incident reporting. Students fear that senior colleagues can ruin their reputations and career opportunities.

Injuries and stress

Injuries occur despite workplace attempts to minimize and prevent them. Health care work environments provide many examples, such as risk of infection, musculoskeletal injuries from lifting, needle stick wounds or physical violence resulting from dealing with people who are mentally ill or under the influence of drugs or alcohol. Workplace stresses arising from relationship tensions and learning new activities occur frequently, resulting in emotional impacts on students. Whilst some workplaces may not present such dramatic examples of injuries, even simple activities such as using computers or having to communicate with people from different cultures may result in injury or emotional stress respectively. Traffic accidents are possible because many workplaces allow students to drive clients or service recipients in workplace vehicles. Students making home visits may encounter aggressive dogs or obstacles such as mats, resulting in injuries such as bites, falls, sprains and fractures. Students working with people who have experienced significant trauma are themselves at risk of secondary trauma when these clients retell and relive traumatic experiences. Difficulty in concentration, tiredness, anxiety, depression and changes in sleeping or eating habits are some consequences of this secondary trauma. In many situations students may not have any form of legal redress or protection, such as workers' compensation, for any harm they may suffer.

Discrimination

Discrimination in all its manifestations is common in workplaces and under-reported by students. Students from visible minority groups complain about racism in many organizations, with this leading to similar psychological effects to those associated with secondary trauma. Racism is often manifested in complaints about the student's lack of understanding of English speaking and writing in record keeping. Some gay, lesbian, bisexual, transvestite and queer (GLBTQ) students complain about their treatment, citing in particular normative heterosexual assumptions about interpersonal relationships.

Standards of care

Students' previous personal experiences may create difficulties in the workplace, especially in relation to the standard of care provided to clients, consumers or patients. Consider the following examples where a student may be:

- recently released from jail because they murdered their wife;
- on day release from prison after embezzling money from older people;
- on a good behaviour bond as a result of aggravated assault;

- undergoing a gender change;
- lacking day-to-day colloquial language skills but able to speak and write well in the formal academic language.

If university work integrated learning coordinators are made aware of such issues ahead of time, they can manage to set up more suitable learning experiences that pose minimal risk to all parties.

Risk and harm to clients, consumers or patients is a serious issue in work integrated learning. Potential liability begins as soon as a student commences work with a service recipient. Service recipients expect to receive the same service standards from students as those provided by other workers. At times students may harm clients, consumers or patients through provision of inaccurate information, failure to act on reports of neglect or abuse, not foreseeing harm, breach of privacy or confidentiality, specific injuries such as providing the wrong medication, or failing to use the most efficacious intervention. In some more serious situations, students may take advantage of a client's, consumer's or patient's vulnerability and enter into personal relationships with them. There are, fortunately, very few instances of situations where students or their supervisors have been taken to court for damages as a result of injuries.

Student learning in the workplace

Students are a disparate group. They come to higher education with wide-ranging cognitive, ethical and emotional attributes, and previous learning, personal and work experiences. Their particular backgrounds and personal characteristics present universities and workplaces with challenges in finding suitable learning experiences. Whilst students' personal experiences before university may expand or restrict their options, in this chapter we draw attention mainly to restrictive issues such as some student disabilities that impact on the ability or willingness of workplaces to accept them for work integrated learning experiences. Student attributes or experiences can be linked to difficulties that arise in work integrated learning situations. They may manifest as lack of motivation, attitudinal problems such as learned helplessness, 'don't blame me if I get it wrong' or refusal to work with particular people, and behavioural problems such as absenteeism, flippant comments or disruptive behaviour. Irrespective of presentation, these attitudes and behaviours suggest tension in expectations and values between workplace learning guides and students. These situations may also create tensions and resentment between the university and the host organization and its workplace, with the workplace arguing that they should have been advised about such behaviours. Time is needed to address these concerns and learning guides may need support.

Table 7.1 Risks and difficulties: General and specific concerns and issues (see also Appendix 2)

General concerns	Specific issues
Safety of student	• Harassment or bullying of a student by workers, other students, clients, consumers or learning guides. • Sexual harassment by workers and learning guides (comments, behaviours, and intimidation). • Physical violence. • Verbal abuse from clients. • Threats of violence.
Personal injuries and work-related stress	• Musculoskeletal injuries. • Low back pain. • Infections, especially blood borne pathogens from needle stick and other communicable diseases. • Lack of sleep. • Emotional, physiological and psychological turmoil as a result of vicarious traumatization (witnessing death, hearing stories of torture, violence). • Dormant personal issues awakened by situations in the workplace (e.g. alcoholism).
Discrimination	• Experiences of racism by workers, clients, consumers, patients or learning guides in the placement process and in the workplace. • Discrimination of students with disabilities by workers or learning guides, preventing students from maximizing learning experiences. • Discrimination based on gender, religious beliefs, cultural orientation, sexual orientation or age.
Other student concerns	• Lack of financial support for students with a lengthy work integrated learning experience. • Distance from student's home to workplace and associated costs. • Disclosure of personal information to the agency and learning guides (e.g. dyslexia).
Standards of care to clients, consumers and patients	• Failure to disclose student status or provide name. • Students breach client confidentiality or privacy, or fail to seek informed consent. • Failure of mandated notifier to report. • Student errors (wrongful advice, medication errors). • Students under the influence of drugs while working with clients. • Students who do not work with the level of competence determined by the profession or workplace.
Learning in the workplace	• Lack of clear expectations by learning guide and workplace. • Conflict between academic and workplace priorities.

(continued)

Table 7.1 (cont.)

General concerns	Specific issues
Learning in the workplace (*cont.*)	• Student's competence or behaviour poses unacceptable level of risk to clients or workplace. • Inadequate information on safety policies and procedures provided to students. • Quality of learning experiences. • Heavy workloads with little time for reflection. • Conflict between students and others in workplace. • General conflict and politics in workplace. • Unfriendly and unsupportive atmosphere in workplace. • Driving workplace vehicles with clients. • Fear of making mistakes.
Learning guides	• Learning guide is not available for assisting with learning. • Lack of feedback on student work. • Lack of integration of theory and practice. • Learning guide's work performance and skills perceived as weak by any or all stakeholders. • Inappropriate relationships between student and learning guide that compromise learning. • Interpersonal difficulties between learning guide and student. • Conflict between the learning guide and student.
Preparation for learning in the workplace	• Students are not oriented and are ill prepared for learning in the workplace. • Expectations, policies and procedures are not adequate.
University policies and procedures	• Inequities in programme policies that cause risk to students. • University policies and procedures are not followed.

Learning guides

Many work integrated learning experiences are provided by organizations without payment from the institution. Providing guidance to students is carried out on top of existing workloads. Learning guides may often be stressed because of this additional burden and may not be well prepared for their responsibilities. It is not surprising that a range of student complaints arise, including a lack of orientation to learning in the workplace, quality of the learning experiences, and either insufficient work or an excessive student workload. Inadequate support from learning guides is a common student complaint to university coordinators; a complaint accompanied by a desire to find an alternative work integrated learning experience.

The illustration in Table 7.1 of the number of risks to students undertaking work integrated learning highlights the need to recognize the necessity for, and take steps to implement, effective management of difficulties.

Management of difficulties

Management of difficulties should be understood in the context of statutory and common law, and those legislative frameworks that apply to the university, profession, host organization and workplace. Work integrated learning necessarily involves managing any difficulties that arise through the differing expectations, organizational mandates, and legal and professional responsibilities held by students, university academics, workplace learning guides, organizations and their workplaces, clients, consumers and patients. Universities and workplaces can deal with difficulties by taking a *reactive approach*, responding only to issues as they arise. Alternatively, they can be strategic, taking a *proactive approach* that includes naming risks, foreseeing difficulties and developing effective strategies to manage them.

A reactive approach is understandable. Priorities, responsibilities and expectations may be tacit, nuanced and possibly in conflict. In this situation, not every party has the same level of understanding of the challenges associated with resolving these issues. Blaming other parties can readily occur. This polarization can create adversarial approaches and resultant problem-solving difficulties. Resolution of these concerns takes place in a set of complex interlocking and frequently well-established personal and professional relationships. Whilst some parties, especially university personnel and workplace learning guides, may have long-standing personal and professional relationships, these are not necessarily friendly, supportive or positive. The students are also connected to both university- and work-based people, further complicating already complex learning relationships.

A proactive approach – effective management of risks and difficulties – is based on the following principles:

- an agreed rationale of the purpose of work integrated learning;
- recognition and acknowledgement of differences and similarities between the classroom and workplace contexts and cultures;
- clear university and workplace expectations of what is provided, by whom and for how long;
- reciprocal respect through open regular communication of each other's professional, legal and organizational frameworks and cultures;
- university and workplace partnership agreements;
- sustained support for students and workplace guides;
- working within the conceptual frameworks, practicalities and budgets imposed by both university and workplace whilst striving for an ideal.

These principles operate within, and recognize, external frameworks, which include broader legal frameworks. Significant considerations here include negligence and duty of care as they impact on organizational, workplace, university and professional responsibilities.

The legal framework

In order to understand and resolve difficulties that arise in work integrated learning, it is necessary to understand the legal frameworks in which rights and responsibilities are established and decisions determined. Every nation has a different system of law rooted in its customs, historical and religious traditions, with many originating from the civil law traditions of ancient Rome. It is imperative that all parties engaged in work integrated learning arrangements understand the principles underpinning their national legal system. The following section is written from the perspective of the English legal system based on statutory and common law and associated concepts of duty of care, negligence and vicarious liability. Whilst universities, professions and workplaces are all subject to the same legal framework, each stakeholder's responsibilities within the law will be addressed separately here.

Statutory law

Workplaces and universities operate within the legislative frameworks of their national and lower levels of government. Laws or Acts of Parliament are referred to as 'statutory law' and are written and enacted in response to societal needs, to improve government functioning or to protect the rights of individuals. Statutory law specifies rights and obligations, but can also authorize the making of other provisions which are referred to as 'regulations'. The law outlines the general principles, whilst the regulations, which are managed by a government agency or department, specify the finer details. Many statutes provide a framework for the way in which institutions, workplaces and people should act, and provide penalties such as fines, imprisonment or compensation to others for breaches of the law.

Legal problems arising in work integrated learning are frequently reported to the university or workplace as a serious student or supervisor concern. These problems commonly include sexual harassment; discrimination based on race or other personal characteristics, including mental illness and language skills; breaches of privacy and/or freedom of information; an unsafe work environment; relationship difficulties in workplaces; and situations where a disability impacts on learning. As these issues appear common to all areas of work integrated learning, it is important that all associated with work integrated learning are familiar with legislation and the rights and responsibilities associated with each problem. It is worth noting that where students may not be covered by legislation in some situations, it can be extremely challenging to determine the boundaries of some matters such as the meaning of sexual harassment.

Common law

Common law has its origins in the English legal system and is based on principles that have evolved from decisions made by English judges over the centuries. These common law principles are used to decide cases where no written law applies. One area where common law still operates is in torts or civil wrongs, an area of particular relevance to work integrated learning as difficulties in these areas can create liabilities for the university or workplace. For this reason universities should ensure their students are covered for public liability insurance, professional indemnity and personal injury before engaging in work integrated learning activities.

Negligence and duty of care

The common sense view is that negligence is carelessness. Professionals, service providers and all citizens have a responsibility to act with care towards others. It is important that solicitors provide accurate information to their clients, just as it is important for general practitioners to provide accurate information that will allow patients to give informed consent for medical interventions. Road users have a responsibility to ensure that other road users do not come to harm. Students undertaking work integrated learning experiences and practitioners in workplaces have responsibilities to act with care towards others, especially their clients, patients or customers. Workplace supervisors have a clear responsibility for the safety and well-being of students, and universities have similar responsibilities towards students, host organizations and their workplaces. In other words, a special relationship exists between the parties.

When a duty of care exists towards another person, a subsequent failure to provide care of an appropriate standard or carrying out an action that results in loss, suffering or injury to a second party may be deemed as negligence. The loss, suffering or injury may impact on a person's health, emotional well-being, finances or psychological capacities. Where a person has a responsibility to act with care towards others, any breach of a duty of care is determined by what 'a reasonable person' would have done in the same circumstances. Where that person is a professional, these standards are seen as consistent with the concept of practice standards held by the profession; they are what a skilful and careful professional would do.

In particular, practitioners and their students have an obligation to avoid actions that are foreseeable and likely to cause harm. The concept of duty of care is complicated because students are beginners and supervised in their practice by more experienced practitioners. The standard applied to beginning practitioners may not be the same as that applied to more experienced professionals because a beginner would not be expected to do the complex tasks performed by a more experienced professional. A number of factors are considered in assessing whether a breach of duty has occurred, including likelihood and foreseeability of harm, the gravity of the injury, and the effort taken and/or required to remove the risk. It is the responsibility of all parties to take reasonable steps to ensure that any student engaged in work integrated learning is able to fulfil safely the requirements of the position, thus fulfilling their, and the workplace's, duty of care to the client or patient. The failure of duty of care, the litigation that follows and the implementation of strategies to minimize and prevent risk are significant issues across many professional programmes and in institutions providing such programmes.

Important here is the concept of vicarious liability. Under this common law principle, a workplace employing any person who has failed to carry out their duty of care to a sufficient standard, thereby causing harm to another, may be found similarly guilty of negligence; that is, the employer is vicariously guilty. An important factor here is to establish whether or not the negligent party was acting in accord with workplace policy and practice standards, or was acting on a 'folly of their own'. This area has the potential to become extremely contentious in workplace learning situations because both the university and the workplace may readily become embroiled.

University responsibilities

Modern universities have been established by governments under specific Acts of Parliament governing the way in which each university is to operate, and outlining their powers and responsibilities. Universities, in most cases, have the power to enter into contractual arrangements, and to make statutes and policies about matters that relate to their governance and the education of students. Given the wide range of educational institutions and approaches to learning arrangements, there is a broad diversity of contracts, statutes, regulations and specific policies. Regulations concerning educational policy, student conduct on campus and in the workplace, and assessment practices are of particular relevance here. These regulations provide the framework for resolution of the educational aspects of difficulties that arise. It is clearly important that institutions have specific regulations to cover students engaged in work integrated learning situations. It is not sufficient to rely on regulations formulated around classroom work on campus because these may not cover the multiple issues and complexities arising through work integrated learning programmes.

Universities generally provide insurance for students and faculty engaged in activities relating to university business, including work integrated learning. Each university will have its own set of policies. Ideally, these will include public liability insurance covering loss or injury to persons on or off campus resulting from negligent acts carried out by, or on behalf of, the university. These policies should cover actions of students engaged in 'approved' work integrated learning experiences; those experiences in which the university is aware of the multiple learning arrangements in workplaces. Insurance policies also include professional indemnity for harm, loss or injury (on or off campus) resulting from a breach of professional duty. This is particularly relevant for staff in professional programmes. Student associations may provide enrolled students with personal injury cover for injuries sustained during university activities, including work integrated learning experiences.

Insurance policies may not, however, cover injury or loss resulting from activities unrelated to university business. This may include actions that breach policy coverage (criminal conduct, breach of statutory obligations, unauthorized actions) or actions taken by outside staff, host organization workplaces or contractors (unless this is specified in the policy). A good example of the complexities that may arise is the use of private vehicles in connection with work integrated learning. There is a broad range of possibilities, for example: Who is driving the vehicle (student, workplace supervisor, university staff member)? Who is travelling in the vehicle (student, workplace supervisor or university staff member)? Who owns the vehicle (student, student's family, student's friend, the workplace, the university)? These complications precede any consideration of matters such as who has suffered harm and which party may have been negligent. These examples highlight how essential it is to have clear insurance guidelines.

Professional responsibilities

Many professional programmes require a work integrated learning component as part of training to become a fully fledged practitioner. Professional programmes are strongly influenced by the various professional and regulatory bodies that determine such things as course requirements, competency standards and learning outcomes. Professional bodies have clearly defined professional practice standards and codes of ethics which determine how students and practitioners should behave towards employers, clients and other professionals. Such codes of ethics or conduct are not restricted to the professions. Many occupational groups, for example human resource professionals, financial businesses, software developers and home builders, have their own ethical standards, as do universities that have codes of conduct for students, and governments.

Organizational practice standards and codes of ethics or behaviour are important public statements informing the community of the principles on which an organization operates and how it controls its members' conduct. These codes can be used to guide learning behaviour in the workplace: how to protect the health and welfare of people; how to promote competence and do no harm; and clearly setting out confidentiality and privacy protection. Associated with these codes are policies and mechanisms by which the public, consumers, clients, patients and students can raise concerns about behaviour and understand the ways in which these concerns will be heard. In many professions, serious ethical breaches can result in removal of practising rights and public disclosure of the professional's name.

It is clearly essential to become familiar with legal, organizational and professional responsibilities, and to understand and apply these frameworks in the context of the complex relationships that emerge when students learn off campus in host organization workplaces.

Workplace responsibilities

Each workplace is unique, with its own professional and disciplinary practices, but many statutory provisions, such as privacy, discrimination, harassment and workplace safety, apply to all workplaces. Many workplaces will operate under specific statutes governing their work because of the particular business they conduct.

Laws relating to child protection and safety apply in family and child welfare services; in health settings health-related Acts provide the practice and operational framework; in information technology settings, information technology and business-related Acts provide the framework; and in financial settings, fiscal-related Acts guide professional operations. In government organizations, administrative law and specific Acts relating to the organization's role are relevant. Practitioners in service delivery organizations have a duty of care to their clients or patients, and issues of negligence are a cause for concern. These concerns must be considered within the context of the statutory framework that applies to the organization as well as its operational policies and practices, and any professional and organizational codes of conduct and behaviour that may apply. In many work integrated learning arrangements, students are not paid employees. They have a different status to the organization's employees, meaning they may not have the same industrial and workplace rights as other employees and are subject to the educational policies of their university. It is important that work integrated learning arrangements recognize this complexity and protect students from 'falling between the cracks'.

Legal operational frameworks require students to meet specific conditions such as having police checks to determine if their background is suitable for working with particular client populations or in particular organizations. A police check may reveal a history that is not acceptable in particular settings. For example, a history of aggravated assault, fraud, child abuse or homicide may preclude students from working with clients in particular workplaces. In some jurisdictions, for example, students have an obligation to report any incidences of suspected child abuse. Therefore, part of student preparation is providing teaching in the university and the workplace about the nature and types of child abuse and legal reporting responsibilities. Health care settings may require students to undergo screening and update vaccinations as part of their preparation.

Community and business organizations have particular mandates to provide services or products, or make a profit for their shareholders. Student education is not their first priority, with some exceptions such as teaching hospitals. In many instances, organizations are providing this student education without compensation from the university and students are learning without payment from employers. The organization's clients, patients or consumers are dependent on the services provided to them, and students assist in working with these groups, guided in their learning by an experienced practitioner to ensure an efficacious service. There are times, however, when workplace demands result in students being overlooked and their learning needs neglected. Thus, while work integrated learning potentially results in a 'win-win' situation for all stakeholders, this does not always occur. When students are not provided with learning opportunities or when the university disregards organizational needs, difficulties are likely to arise. Difficulties can also arise because workplaces may not appreciate fully the university's legal responsibilities for student education and safety. Students lack the power, status, experience and expertise of university and workplace personnel, and may be vulnerable in the learning environment for a variety of reasons, including the workplace learning guides not having time to teach them.

Many risks can be reduced through the careful management and preparation of students before learning, although risks may not be avoided totally. Management of difficulties is a common occurrence in work integrated learning. Problem solving means that all stakeholders appreciate each other's needs and perspectives. Appreciating that students and workplace learning guides need support during students' work integrated learning experiences, and incorporating support as a management strategy to avert, minimize or deal with risk, is an essential element in managing difficult situations.

Support of students and learning guides

There are cultural differences between the workplace and the university that present challenges for students and learning guides. The workplace has been referred to as a complex environment where there are messy problems to solve in dynamic interpersonal relationships (Schön 1983). When students move from the protected university environment to the rough and tumble of the practice world, they are expected to perform and undertake learning activities that they may not want to do or know how to do. The reality of learning in workplaces can be very confronting, creating personal, learning and relationship difficulties, particularly for students who are different from the mainstream in any way. Whilst this does not apply to all students in every situation, many students are vulnerable and need support.

Student support

Student support refers to academic support but more importantly social and emotional support to scaffold learning. Academic support consists of the activities and structures that allow remedial activities and encourage the development of new skills. Social and personal support strengthens the capacity to sustain social relationships, thus enabling students to take advantage of academic support services. The concept of support takes on a different meaning and greater complexity when many students participate in work integrated learning activities. Learning in the workplace is not easy, especially for students with little or no experience in such contexts. It requires an understanding of the differing expectations of the university and workplace; the capacity to negotiate unspoken tasks; the ability to appreciate and work with subtle social dynamics operating in relationships with workers, supervisors and management; and understanding the depth of emotions expressed when particular issues are identified. Supporting students as they experience this learning can be demanding for those most closely connected to them.

Student support begins as soon as a student makes contact with the university coordinator, who is the first to respond to the student's learning needs. Workplace supervisors, as well as coordinators, continue this process. In many countries, students have a right to higher education without discrimination based on their personal, cultural and racial attributes. Finding appropriate learning experiences where students can be supported to grow intellectually, practically and emotionally is important. Planning learning experiences with students can alleviate later difficulties, as illustrated in the following case study.

Barry's personal situation came to the attention of the coordinator as she was discussing the preliminary planning for the learning experience. Barry was very open with the coordinator and revealed that he was currently undergoing a sexual reorientation from a woman to a man. Although he was undergoing these changes, he dressed as a man and wanted to work with young men. Medical advisors had told the student that his current medications would create mood swings and impact on personal and work relationships. The coordinator noticed his voice was high pitched, a feature that would be obvious to people in the workplace. It was apparent that he was entering his learning experiences at a point in time when he was undergoing massive personal and life-changing events, and required support for his learning. The coordinator believed the student was vulnerable and should the learning be too stressful, he may withdraw from the programme. Some workplaces may subtly humiliate this student by making negative comments about his personal decisions. After discussing Barry's situation, the coordinator wanted to find a workplace where he would not be humiliated or derided because of his personal decisions. Respect for the student was paramount.

The university coordinator used her understanding of the student's situation to plan carefully for a learning experience where the student could focus on the learning without having to battle the politics of the workplace as a result of his identity. She also referred the student to student counselling to provide the additional personal support required throughout the learning process.

Particular challenges may arise for some students because of the demands of regular attendance at the workplace. Attendance may be compromised when students have competing personal, family, employment and study demands. The learning environment can also be challenging because of the nature of the work and the learning, students' unique previous experiences, their attitudes and values, level of work literacy skills, and capacity and willingness to participate. Many students will require individualized attention to help them understand their behavioural responses to events and people. Consider the following case study in which the student's workplace supervisor takes her aside in a supportive manner and orients her to the particular workplace and profession.

Young students often dress in ways which fit their cultural norms and this includes tattoos, piercings and clothing that is too revealing. Although the university prepares students for learning, including the need for appropriate dress, Emily did not think this applied to her as her peer group thought her dress highly fashionable. She arrived at the workplace to begin her learning only to have the supervisor talk to her gently about the need for a different sort of dress. The supervisor thought Emily's dress would compromise her learning and make learning professional practice a fraught process. The supervisor, also young and fashionable outside the workplace, then provided Emily with some suggestions about how to manage in the workplace.

STUDENTS WITH DISABILITIES

Students with disabilities are entitled to higher education. In many cases these rights are protected by statutes, resulting in an increase in the number of students with disability attending higher education institutions in many countries. Mental illness is one disability that is prevalent in the student community, with 7.8 per cent of the student population having a mental illness (Shaddock n.d.). Students with mental illness present potentially challenging behaviour which may include physical assaults, verbal threats, evidence of paranoid thoughts, and provocative and demanding behaviours that can pose difficulties in the workplace and threaten the student's capacity to complete their course of study successfully. In some cases, students with mental illness do not realize they have such an illness or do not disclose their illness, which makes supporting them very difficult. Encouraging students to disclose they have a mental illness is one risk management strategy that can enable required support to be provided in both the university and the workplace. If the university coordinator is aware of the student's disability, they can try to match the student with an organization or particular workplace in which they know the student will receive the support they need. However, some students are wary of disclosing any disability for fear of being precluded from work integrated learning experiences and treated overtly as different from other students. When students have not disclosed such a disability, workplace learning guides may pick up that something is not quite right, but require confirmation from the university coordinator about their concerns. If the coordinator is not aware of any issues with the particular student, the work integrated learning experience may be unsuccessful for all stakeholders. In such a situation, the learning guide requires support from the university coordinator to help them assist the student's learning.

LEARNING GUIDE SUPPORT

Workplace learning guides also need support. Whilst some workplaces are able to select the students coming to their worksite, this is not always possible. Guides often find themselves working with students who may not want to be there, or who have personal or behavioural characteristics that challenge their capacity to learn. Even when workplaces can select students, changes in student circumstances can create unexpected difficulties. Open and regular communication between university coordinators and workplace learning guides enables identification and management of difficulties. During learning, personal situations arise that require support from the learning guide and the academic support services at the university, as well as referral to appropriate resources. Some situations require the learning guide to seek support not only for the student but also for themself due to having to deal with the impact on the workplace environment of the student's issues. The following case study illustrates the unexpectedness of novel situations and their impact on the work integrated learning experience for both student and guide.

A mature international Muslim student was undertaking a service learning experience as an educational mentor for young adolescents and formed close relationships with personnel within the workplace. During the time in the workplace she discovered that she was pregnant but she was concerned because her common law partner was also Muslim and had episodes of violence. She was unable to tell her parents, who were overseas, about her pregnancy because a pregnancy outside of marriage was taboo. The woman did not know what to do or where to go for help. She knew nothing of rape crisis centres, domestic violence agencies or pregnancy help lines. After the student received advice from the university counselling centre, she decided on a termination and told her partner. This enraged her partner and he kept calling her at the service learning centre threatening to kill her if she did not have the baby and give him custody of the child. The student needed personal support from the learning guide to enable her to continue with her learning, whilst the learning guide requested assistance from the university coordinator in helping the student.

Whilst support for students and learning guides focuses mainly on students' learning needs, several strategies can be used to respond to the diversity of risk and difficulties that inevitably arise in work integrated learning. Some of these strategies are now discussed.

Strategies for responding to risk and difficulties

There is no recipe or list of 'dos' and 'don'ts' to follow in responding to risk and difficulties because each situation will be unique and specific to the context in which the work integrated learning experience is taking place. Solutions must be consistent with the legal, ethical and cultural frameworks. Different situations in different contexts call for different strategies. When any stakeholder is faced with a difficulty, the first thing that needs to happen is the awkward and challenging conversation with other stakeholders about the issues and concerns. Understanding organizational policy and procedures is a basic requirement but the most important principle is open and regular communication with all stakeholders. Communicate, communicate, communicate is fundamental to the management of all difficulties. The reciprocal dimension of communication is to listen, listen, listen! This communication process begins when partners in the work integrated learning enterprise get to know each other during the initial setting up of the partnership, on the initial and subsequent site visits, and on a continuing regular, cyclical basis. Perkins (n.d.: 20–1) outlines a range of clarifications to be made in discussions during the first 'get to know you' visit. Some of these include:

- the nature of the work integrated learning experience;
- logistics such as parking, reimbursements and hours of work;
- risk identification;
- tour of organizations;
- evaluations of the experience;
- privacy issues;
- agreements and learning plans.

Although these issues are addressed, the most important consideration is development of an effective partnership, an essential element of which is recognition and acknowledgement of possible risk and how to manage this.

Practical management of risk and difficulties

In many larger universities, a risk manager can provide important advice on the establishment of policies and procedures. Risk management is an important strategy for determining and evaluating specific risks in work integrated learning and minimizing the risk to all stakeholders. A proposed starting point is conducting a risk audit as part of a getting-to-know-you visit with host organizations. Other strategies include using learning contracts, preparation of all stakeholders for participating in work integrated learning, getting to know the students, orientation to the workplace and strategic problem-solving procedures.

Risk audit

Conducting a risk audit needs to be done in a sensitive way, strengthening the relationships between the university and host organization. Some of the questions asked might include:

- What is the location of the workplace? In some larger cities, community organizations and health centres are to be found in unsafe communities where students could potentially be at risk in travelling to and from their homes and to the university.

- What work activities are students expected to do as part of their learning and what are the risks associated with these activities?
- Are any of the student activities likely to be dangerous and who might be harmed? For example, students may be required to drive vehicles, make visits to clients' homes, operate machinery in fields such as aquaculture or work with chemicals in laboratories, collect samples associated with food handling or sanitation, or participate in outdoor tourism activities such as caving. Clients, colleagues and other students could, potentially, be harmed.
- What are the risks when students work with clients, service recipients or customers of the organization?
- What supervisory strategies are in place to minimize risks and ensure that the student works within the professional and organization's standards?
- What is the likelihood of property damage?
- What are the liability and general insurance covers for students on work integrated learning experiences?
- What are the processes and procedures for the protection of privacy and confidentiality of students, colleagues and clients?
- What is the legal status of the organization? This is particularly important for small community organizations where there is an expectation that they would have legal incorporation.

Learning contracts

In work integrated learning a contract between the university and the workplace demonstrates the stakeholders' intentions, rights and obligations; creates certainty; and reduces the risk of confusion or disagreement about terms and the relationship. It provides for prudent behaviour by identifying where liability rests, and clarifies indemnity and insurance arrangements. The contract should be written in a way that supports quality education. The contents should include:

- names and addresses of all parties;
- the purpose and objectives of the work integrated learning;
- a summary of programme activities;
- a statement of services to be provided by the parties to the contract, including a safe working environment;
- responsibilities of the stakeholders: university, coordinator, workplace, learning guide and student;
- financial and insurance arrangements;
- dispute resolution procedures when conflicts arise;
- length of the agreement and the renewal process.

Schedules specifically relating to professional or discipline arrangements can be added to the basic contract. A more comprehensive example of the contract contents is provided in Table 8.4 as part of the overall work integrated learning process (see Chapter 8).

Another type of learning contract is a student learning plan prepared by the student as part of their learning. This plan outlines learning objectives and outcomes, type and amount of work, and supervisory arrangements. Negotiation of learning objectives can be achieved by students when they know what they want to get from the experience; when they are clear about their personal goals and existing knowledge and skills; and are open to new experiences.

Preparation for learning

In Chapter 4 we discussed preparation for learning, with an emphasis on the coordinators' and learning guides' responsibilities. This discussion is continued here with a proactive stance focusing on strategies to prevent difficulties. In this situation, preparation for learning entails provision of a student manual outlining in writing the expectations and responsibilities of all parties in terms of length of placement, absenteeism, behaviour, dress, learning assignments, codes of conduct and codes of ethics, and supervisory arrangements, and reinforcing these expectations in special orientation sessions. To ensure the best possible learning environment, university coordinators and workplace supervisors need to recognize students' previous learning, and respond to student issues such as work, family commitments and cultural issues.

Preparation may require specific orientations and prerequisite courses to enable safe and effective work skills (interviewing skills, working with people who are different, or medication management). Young and novice students may be assisted with work literacy skills to enable them to maximize learning. As stated earlier in this chapter, some organizations require specific police checks, especially when students work with vulnerable populations. In some jurisdictions such as in the USA, fingerprinting is also necessary in order to attend some workplaces. When these checks are in place it is essential that policies and procedures respect student privacy in the event that a check reveals previous convictions. Also, in health care settings, vaccinations and screening for diseases may be necessary, and these are done at a cost to the student. Whatever the requirements, students need to be briefed fully so they can make an informed choice about where they undertake their work integrated learning experience. Students must be aware that some risks and difficulties will arise. Preparation means informing them about how best to manage some of the difficulties they might encounter, such as harassment or discrimination.

Learning guides based in host organization workplaces also need preparation for teaching students in the workplace. Learning guides appreciate an orientation to the university academic courses that students have taken before beginning their work integrated learning experience, as this can help guides to make links between the theory and practice and so assist students with the integration of theory with practice.

Getting to know the students

Many difficulties can be alleviated when the university coordinator understands the student's background, previous learning, interests and individual needs. In many situations, coordinators' knowledge of learning guides and the activities in particular workplaces enables them to match students with workplaces and learning guides. When large numbers of students require work integrated learning experiences, this level of assessment and matching may not be possible. Trust between the students, the university coordinators and workplace learning guides facilitates addressing and resolving difficulties that may arise.

Orientation to the workplace

Orientation to the host organization workplace is necessary for a quality learning experience and can prevent misunderstandings, conflict and unsafe practices. Students need to know the names of their supervisors and alternative support people in the workplace. Orientation should include seeing the physical workspace, the legal framework for practice, safe work practices, standards of professional behaviour, and the etiquette and unique work culture of a particular workplace.

Problem-solving procedures

When conflicts and disputes arise, they are best resolved using agreed written procedures. As a general rule, difficulties fall into three discrete categories. First, students may have a range of personal issues such as ill health or personal crises. It is the student's responsibility to advise the workplace learning guide and the university coordinator of these issues. After consultation with the learning guide in the workplace, difficulties are handled by the university as part of the general university procedures and services.

Second, students may have complaints about the workplace. Such complaints may include harassment and discrimination, the quality and nature of the work, or the performance of the learning guides. These issues are more challenging to resolve than the first category because the perceptions of each stakeholder often differ. Some learning guides may become defensive and angry when students complain. When this occurs, resolution requires working with the coordinator's need to deal with both the learning guide's resentment and the threat of the host organization withdrawing its services. Some students, too, may feel resentment because they believe their rights to a quality education have been infringed. Depending on the nature of the complaint, legal action may be necessary. If there are disputes about the lack of work, students may have to find another work integrated learning experience.

The third category of problems relates to the behaviour and unsatisfactory performance or competence of the student. In this situation, the learning guide reports this to the university. The student's learning contract with the host organization and the university policies are used to resolve the problem. If unsatisfactory performance is evident early in the learning, formative assessment, with feedback about how to improve performance, can assist. This may be accompanied by increased levels of supervision. The management of these difficulties is the responsibility of the university coordinator and depends on good communication, clarity about the responsibilities of all stakeholders and discussion of issues with all stakeholders – student, learning guide and university coordinator – often as part of a conference. In some cases, as illustrated in the example of the autistic student in Chapter 6, communication and collaboration with others who have a close relationship with the student, as well as the initial stakeholders, may help resolve the issue.

Most often, complaints are not so neatly packaged and the point at which the university needs to intervene is not clear. Consider the following case study.

> Not long after placing students in an organization it became apparent to the university coordinator that the workplace was having a number of management issues that included a high turnover of staff. At the same time, the students complained to the university about the quality of their learning, the sudden and unexpected changes to the supervisory arrangements in the middle of their learning experiences and the quality of their new learning guide. They were concerned that change was made without previous discussion with them and that this was in breach of their learning contract. While this was going on, the new learning guide phoned the university coordinator about a particular student's behaviour, suggesting that it was unprofessional and should constitute a failure. This behaviour consisted of unwanted advances to a member of staff. When the student was confronted, she said her behaviour was normal heterosexual behaviour and this did not constitute a lack of professionalism. She gave other examples of blossoming relationships in the workplace where no action had been taken. The response from the university coordinator was to stall any decision until the complaint had been thoroughly investigated. Clearly, the coordinator did not want to find another learning guide and alternative learning experience. Before this was resolved, the agency head complained to the head of school about the student and the university coordinator. The student's work integrated learning experience was to be terminated immediately.

It is apparent that every person in this scenario has a unique perception of the problem. This makes it difficult to resolve. All parties are part of the problem and cannot resolve issues satisfactorily among themselves. Having reached an impasse, the strategy of calling in a neutral mediator might have resulted in negotiating a resolution. Resolution might also have occurred if all parties had communicated openly at the outset, were clear about the contractual arrangements between the university and organization, and were willing to engage in problem-solving processes.

Summary

Risk is a normal part of the work integrated learning process. It follows that the university and workplaces commit to risk management strategies to assess and reduce risk, and, in the event of difficulties, to reduce harm to stakeholders. It is evident that students, clients and learning guides are exposed to risk during the course of work integrated learning experiences. Students may face harassment, personal injuries, stress and discrimination. Organizations, their workplaces and learning guides are concerned about the risk to their clients, patients or consumers if care or service does not reach the necessary standards. Universities are also troubled when students and clients are harmed. In addition, they are disturbed when organizations fail to provide learning opportunities for students. In managing difficulties, stakeholders benefit from understanding the statutory and common law frameworks particular to the workplace and/or profession, and the particular responsibilities of the profession, the workplace and the university. When difficulties arise, as they so often do, students and learning guides will need support to understand the problems and to work through the complex issues as they arise. Managing difficult situations is an essential part of the work integrated learning process, which is described in detail in Chapter 8.

The Work Integrated Learning Process

Introduction

This chapter is the culmination of previous chapters that have explored discrete elements of work integrated learning extensively and theoretically. By contrast this chapter is essentially practical, providing a comprehensive guide for those who are responsible for designing, resourcing and managing work integrated learning programmes.

Previous chapters have described the academic and workplace environments, models of work integrated learning, teaching and assessment, and the management of difficult situations. These chapters highlight the many complexities of work integrated learning. Throughout, stakeholder collaboration, cooperation and participation as partners in the work integrated learning process have been stressed as essential to successful outcomes for the university, the workplace, community and learners. In this chapter we begin with a checklist of factors to consider in making decisions about the type and purpose of a work integrated learning programme, design of the programme, and the setting up and implementation of the programme. Once the programme is established, other imperatives emerge including ongoing management of the programme and ongoing innovation and research. Discussion of these issues will follow the checklist. This chapter, like those preceding it, operates within the conceptual framework of work integrated learning laid out for this book in Chapter 2, thus focusing on the three models of work integrated learning described therein: professional learning, service learning and cooperative learning.

The checklist outlines five key stages in the work integrated learning process:

Purpose

- What does the university want to achieve?
- What sort of programme will deliver these goals:
  - Professional learning?
  - Service learning?
  - Cooperative learning?

Designing the programme

- What is the fit between degree structures and programme requirements?
- Is the learning to be optional or mandatory?
- What is the timing of the programme in the academic year?
- Where will the learning take place?
- What partnerships are possible?
- What is the point of entry into the work integrated learning programme?
- How long should students be in the workplace?
- Should the programme provide for concurrent or block work integrated learning experiences?
- What specific policies will guide the learning process?
- What is the location of the work integrated learning programme within the university?

Setting up the programme

- Involve workplace and community representatives, academic colleagues and students.
- Recruit the programme coordinator.
- Build relationships with workplaces.
- Specify systems of privileges and rewards from the university.
- Design the educational and practical framework.
- Develop the work integrated learning contract.
- Conduct a risk audit of workplaces.
- Establish stakeholders' tasks and responsibilities.

Implementing and managing the programme

- Manage students, learning guides and organizations.
- Manage the resources for the programme:
  — travel
  — technological infrastructure, communication software and management information systems
  — public relations.

Improving the quality of work integrated learning programmes

- Use databases for monitoring and research.
- Use benchmarking for quality improvement.

Purpose

What does the university want to achieve?

Every university has a particular vision, mission and strategic plans. In many institutions work integrated learning is part of their identity, character and branding. In previous chapters, we acknowledged that work integrated learning can incorporate social and personal responsibility of students, civic engagement, preparation of work-ready graduates and professional preparation.

What sort of programme will deliver these goals?

Delivery of work integrated learning takes place through professional learning programmes, service learning and cooperative learning. Each of these programmes has unique features, particular values and approaches. Universities will need to consider the purpose and characteristics of work integrated learning that best fit with their mission, vision, goals and plans, and determine the best way to achieve these ends.

Designing the programme

As work integrated learning is an umbrella term covering service learning, cooperative learning, practicum programmes, fieldwork and clinical education, each work integrated learning programme will have its own particular aims and outcomes unique to a discipline or programme of study and the individual workplace. Whichever model is best for your programme, it will be based around the seven key domains inherent in the construction of work integrated learning programmes: the purpose, the context, the integration, the curriculum, the learning, the partnerships and support.

Some early decisions about what work integrated learning will look like will involve the university at the school, departmental or faculty level, or other administrative units serving students' needs. Representatives from workplaces, industry and communities will also need to be involved in the design phase. Some logistical issues for consideration are outlined and discussed here.

What is the fit between degree structures and programme requirements?

Work integrated learning fits within an existing degree structure. Any changes to degree structures involve consultation with the academic faculty and navigation through the governance processes in the university. In some faculties, work integrated learning may not have been part of the culture. Academics may have to be convinced of its value to students and their learning. The points elaborated below will assist discussions between the university and academics about work integrated learning and new structures needed to enable it.

Is this learning to be optional or mandatory?

In considering whether work integrated learning should be optional or mandatory, take account of the professional and vocational requirements, the university's branding and, importantly, the diverse learning needs of students. In many professional and vocational programmes, work integrated learning is a compulsory part of the course. Some universities, as part of their branding and strategic directions, are establishing targets requiring that all courses have a work integrated learning component.

If work integrated learning is part of degree requirements, there will be constraints and limitations imposed on students. One limitation is diversity of the student population. Students are a heterogeneous group in terms of age, abilities, family responsibilities, health and well-being, social histories, previous educational and work experiences, and where they live. With electronic course delivery students can study in many different locations including prison, health care institutions, remote farming communities, even the Antarctic. Whilst students can access study programmes remotely, participating in work integrated learning experiences may pose logistical difficulties. If they are delivered remotely, this will add to the cost of the programme. As an example, a Canadian professional programme is delivering courses to China. Part of the delivery cost requires finding, compensating and monitoring a learning guide to assist student learning.

When thinking about student learning needs, a compulsory workplace learning component may not be necessary or even desirable. For example, mature students with previous working experience in a particular profession or industry may not need additional work-related skills. Younger students, on the other hand, may benefit from these experiences. Previous learning could be formally acknowledged in such situations. Mothers who are breastfeeding or caring for infants or young children may have the family support to take one or two subjects per semester but not sufficient time to spend in a workplace for one or more days per week. Similarly, students with severe disabilities want the opportunity to learn but may not have the financial resources or physical capacity to complete particular forms of learning in workplaces. Getting to and from their homes to workplaces may be a financial burden for students. International students may or may not gain value from workplace experience in their host country. Flexibility in assessing and recognizing learning needs should be considered.

If work integrated learning is compulsory, it is necessary to find learning experiences for all the above mentioned students. This requires creativity and more time to negotiate with workplaces for suitable student learning experiences. This issue needs to be considered when looking at resourcing the programme.

What is the timing of the programme in the academic year?

The timing of learning in workplaces needs negotiation and flexibility. The following issues need consideration when trying to work out the best time for students to undertake work integrated learning experiences:

- In most universities the academic year is structured into semesters followed by several weeks' break for students.
- This university schedule, with semesterized course delivery followed by marking, grading and confirmation of results before commencement of the next semester, provides a structure that does not fit with the realities of life and work in the outside community.
- What suits the university and students may not suit workplaces.
- What suits the needs of one student may not suit the needs of all students. Some students will struggle with the timing.

As with the question about mandatory work integrated learning experiences, the timing of the programme necessitates consideration of equity issues. Mothers may find that school holidays do not fit with their family responsibilities. Students supporting themselves financially during their studies want employment at the time of peak employment demand. In a recent USA commentary, business internships were described as a racket because they are only open to affluent students, making them irreducibly unequal (Paletta 2008).

Workplaces have high and low work demands. They may have a skeleton staff during the peak holiday time when some students are available or have busy periods when they are unable to accept students on placement. Allowing maximum flexibility for all parties is highly desirable. Advisory committees may assist here by commenting on proposed arrangements.

Where will the learning take place?

Work integrated learning can take place wherever workplaces are willing to accept students and students are willing to be accepted. Local workplaces generally suit students and the university, but there are also opportunities within the region, nationally and internationally. As a rule the process is easier to manage the closer the workplace is to the university. More remote locations mean that strategies need to be put in place to manage any challenges that arise. For example, students completing work integrated learning experiences with tourist operators may find themselves in remote areas during holiday periods. In these situations, satellite phones can assist but coordinators need to be readily available in case of student emergencies. With increasing numbers of students travelling to overseas locations to complete work integrated learning experiences, computer-aided communication helps maintain links between the university and student.

What partnerships are possible?

Work integrated learning is best achieved when the university and workplace collaborate in programme delivery. Although learning experiences can be found in a variety of different workplaces, partnerships provide value-added opportunities for enhancing student learning in the workplace. When the university and the workplace cooperate they combine their respective strengths for mutual benefit. Partnerships may also provide a way for the university to engage in joint research on common initiatives or on improving service delivery.

What is the point of entry into the work integrated learning programme?

There is no right time for students to complete work integrated learning programmes. Students who undertake learning in the first year of their course may lack sufficient appreciation of theory and the capacity to transfer ideas to the work setting. They may only have developed preliminary competencies and have a poor understanding of workplace challenges. Further work integrated learning programmes may need to follow in later years to enable consolidation between theory and practice. Later-year students transfer knowledge more effectively from classroom to the workplace and vice versa. Students are thus better able to use work integrated learning as the basis for employment.

Students may also gain value from an incrementally developed programme in which learning is a developmental process, with the amount of workplace learning increasing in length and intensity over the years. In their first year, students may make workplace visits where they are exposed to different workplace environments. In later years they will engage in more extended workplace learning experiences.

How long should students be in the workplace?

Many factors influence the length of time of learning in the workplace. Universities may specify particular learning outcomes with or without a timeline for completion. These learning outcomes may be stated generally or more specifically, designating sets of skills and competencies to be achieved.

Some learning outcomes take longer to achieve than others. A student wanting to complete a placement with an American senator may take some time to understand the intricacies of the American system of government before developing the administrative and social change skills required to complete project work in that office. A student studying elderly care may take a short period of time to learn how to assist an older person with their daily living skills but much longer to develop the counselling skills necessary to assist that same person.

Professional and vocational requirements frequently determine the exact length of workplace learning, either with or without stated learning outcomes. Some workplaces may define a discrete task or project for completion, or provide a learning experience for a particular time period only. In defining a particular project, the size and scope of the project need consideration. Many such projects may take longer to complete than anticipated at the outset, posing significant challenges to students.

Should the programme provide for concurrent or block work integrated learning experiences?

The strengths and weaknesses of concurrent or block work integrated learning experiences are debated universally. In concurrent work integrated learning experiences students attend both the university and the workplace simultaneously. Concurrent work integrated learning experiences allow students to integrate classroom and workplace learning. The quality of the integration is determined by the ability of supervisors in the workplace and the faculty in the university.

Block work integrated learning experiences involve students completing a certain period of time, for example 4.5 days per week over a half or full semester in the workplace. Students in concurrent work integrated learning experiences may not fully appreciate the cycle of daily and weekly activities and processes, thus missing some valuable learning experiences. Nor do these students experience the continuity of work. In block work integrated learning experiences the focus is more on workplace learning rather than integration of theory and practice.

Students have strong views about concurrent and block work integrated learning experiences. Some students prefer concurrent work integrated learning experiences because these enable them to retain part-time employment. Block work integrated learning experiences mean that students give up their jobs. Whatever arrangements are being discussed, it is important to consult with workplaces and students about optimal arrangements, as these decisions can increase or decrease opportunities. A flexible approach allows the programme to meet the needs of all.

What specific policies will guide the learning process?

Many university policies were conceived at a time when all students were on campus for their learning. With new arrangements, some university and faculty policies may need redrafting to take account of emerging forms of learning and assessment. Some policy examples include management of student behaviour in the workplace, student fitness to undertake work integrated learning experiences, and policy related to the use of electronic communication forms such as blogging on university websites or the use of social networking websites set up by the university so students can maintain contact with university coordinators. New policy may need to be created in relation to how work integrated learning will fit in the university's organizational structure.

What is the location of the work integrated learning programme within the university?

Some work integrated learning programmes fit neatly within the professional area. In these situations the goals are closely linked to specific professional outcomes. Where work integrated learning programmes have a more generic focus and cover a variety of disciplines and subject areas, they may be located in different areas within the university. For example, the programme could be part of a faculty or divisional structure, as part of student services or careers services. Whatever the location, it is important for the principles of work integrated learning to be followed.

Setting up the programme

Involve workplace and community representatives, academic colleagues and students

Successful work integrated learning programmes work closely with their local and professional communities. Therefore, the first step in setting up the planned programme is to involve workplace and community representatives in an advisory capacity.

It is essential to bring together an advisory committee at the outset of each work integrated learning activity. This advisory committee ideally should comprise members with experience in, and understanding of, work integrated learning in the community; representatives of professional bodies; workplace mentors and supervisors; and academics from within the university. Students with an interest in work integrated learning should also form part of this group. The aim of the advisory committee is to advise about the programme's directions, and provide feedback on policy, curriculum, timing of developments and strategic issues in working with the local community and workplaces. At a later stage of development, such committees can be formally constituted to include particular representation and structures. No matter how sophisticated work integrated learning programmes are, the advice and support of such committees adds to their value. The committees can provide timely advice about implementation, make referrals to key employers and industry groups, or advise about overloading particular workplaces with requests for learning opportunities. Committee members become ambassadors for the programme in the broader community, can assist when difficult situations arise and can help lower the risk of attrition of workplace involvement.

Once the advisory committee is in place, the next step is to recruit a work integrated learning coordinator to lead and manage programme implementation. The coordinator is the key person in the whole process. Therefore it is critical to recruit this person early in the implementation process.

Recruit the programme coordinator

When recruiting a programme coordinator, consideration should be given to whether this recruit comes with an academic or administrative orientation, noting that benefits and limitations are associated with both backgrounds. An academic recruit will bring a deeper understanding of curriculum and the university's educational mission. They may be better placed to provide integration between theory and practice. However, the demanding workload associated with coordination may compromise research and teaching components of the academic mandate to the detriment of coordinators seeking a longer-term academic career.

An administrative or professional recruit may have higher-level knowledge and experience of the workplace. They may not experience conflict between devoting time to coordination and collaboration with industry partners, and building an academic career. Whilst some professional staff may seek to engage in aspects of teaching and research, their prime skills lie in coordination, which may remain their primary responsibility. A disadvantage here is that administrators from this background may not begin the coordinator's role with a full academic appreciation of the curriculum dimensions. The challenge is to establish the optimum balance between focusing on curriculum management as an administrative task and collaborating closely with academic colleagues. Clearly defining the coordinator's activities can help achieve this balance. These are outlined in Table 8.1.

An essential element in the work integrated learning process is the work integrated learning coordinator's ongoing contact with workplaces. This plays a major role in building and maintaining relationships.

Build relationships with workplaces

Without strong and effective relationships between the university and workplaces there can be no work integrated learning, as this type of learning involves complex and intense purposeful interpersonal and administrative activity. Relationship development is important beyond the programme's initial stage; it is a continuous process needed to sustain, maintain and renew relationships. Core to creating and maintaining these relationships is regular, open communication between the university and the workplace. Universities will need to seek out workplaces with an active interest in providing learning experiences. In many cases, initial work integrated learning experiences are built on the basis of personal relationships and an established network of people. Alumni can play a role in building workplace contacts. Vital relationship building and maintenance strategies include:

- face-to-face connections;
- knowing the workplace, its products and learning opportunities. This demonstrates an interest in the workplace and facilitates matching learning experiences to the students;
- building a common agenda.

Table 8.1 Work integrated learning coordinator's activities

- Identify, negotiate and coordinate learning opportunities with workplaces.
- Induct students, mentors, supervisors and others in the workplace with orientation programmes.
- Work with students and workplaces to provide quality learning experiences for all parties.
- Provide educational support for students, and for mentors and supervisors in workplaces.
- Monitor, assess and review student learning to ensure that students are achieving the agreed learning outcomes.
- Resolve difficulties that arise between students and the workplace, taking account of the competing interests of the university, the workplace, students, clients and consumers.
- Manage the academic administration associated with the programme.
- Promote the programme to potential students and employers.

Specify system of privileges and rewards from the university

Recruitment and retention of work integrated learning workplace partners can be increased by offering privileges and rewards from the university as incentives. These incentives aim to make workplaces and their personnel feel they are valued contributors to student education and the university's mission. Some of these privileges and rewards are outlined in Table 8.2.

Relationships can be strengthened further by acknowledging the work done by workplace personnel. Some strategies to achieve this are outlined in Table 8.3.

Despite the goodwill of the university and their workplace partners, tensions inevitably arise between university and workplace contacts. Reasons for these

Table 8.2 Privileges and rewards from the university

- Recruiting workplace personnel to advisory committees and other relevant committees.
- Using workplace personnel for lectures and part-time teaching positions.
- Publicly recognizing the achievements of workplaces and their personnel.
- Awarding workplace mentors and guides adjunct professorial status.
- Giving personnel university library borrowing privileges.
- Providing free or discounted access to university sports facilities to workplace personnel.
- Providing staff development and training to workplaces.
- Paying for transport to relevant events.
- Free or specially designated parking.
- Reduced costs to university events, such as concerts.

Table 8.3 Strategies for recognition of workplace personnel

- Thank you letters.
- Recognition events (breakfasts or lunches).
- Framed certificates.
- Listing the names of participating workplaces and personnel, as well as writing articles about them in faculty and university publications.
- Publishing a newsletter on work integrated learning events and activities.
- Showcasing the workplace partners' work and practices for students and other workplaces.
- Providing discounted or free access to continuing education events.
- Inviting workplace personnel to staff training and development as trainers or participants.
- Hosting a fair where students and the university community can appreciate the breadth and depth of workplace activities.

tensions include changes in personnel and management structures, work practice changes in universities or workplaces and student behaviour. The critical issue is how these matters are resolved in an open, transparent manner. Good conflict resolution procedures can assist this process. The following case study illustrates how maintaining strong and effective relationships is so important to survive the tensions created when changes are made within workplaces. In this case, what appeared to be changes that limited work integrated learning opportunities led to other changes that opened up new opportunities.

During the nineties, one author experienced the downsizing of a large organization with amalgamation of regional offices. Downsizing meant lack of space for students and a destabilization of supervisory arrangements due to new organizational structures. Despite this, university-based coordinators maintained relationships with core organizational staff. Some staff sought employment in other workplaces, thus opening up unexpected student learning opportunities. In the longer term, the agency stabilized and returned to accepting students.

Having established the university–workplace relationships, the next step in setting up the work integrated learning programme is to design the programme's educational and practical framework.

Design the educational and practical framework

Again, the importance of good relationships and good decision-making processes cannot be stressed enough. Key parties to the learning relationship include the university and its work integrated learning coordinator, the workplace and the workplace personnel supervising students' learning in the workplace, and the students themselves. The educational framework requires specification of the programme aims, learning outcomes and assessment methods. Details of these have been discussed in chapters 2, 3, 4 and 5.

Integration of learning lies at the heart of work integrated learning. In establishing the programme, it is important to consider the ways in which integration can be achieved in the classroom and workplace, in the learning goals and assessment practices, and in the incentives provided to students, learning supervisors/guides and workplaces.

Practical aspects are very important. These include professional requirements, such as codes of ethics and registration requirements, and the expectations of students, workplaces and learning supervisors/guides. Developing a contract addresses some of these practical aspects.

Develop the work integrated learning contract

Establishing a contract between the university and the workplace outlining requirements for all parties provides a clear guide for the university, the workplace and the students. This contract may be implied and unwritten, but needs to be explicit and formalized. It is essential to keep in mind that the university and workplace partners are two very separate administrative systems with very different goals, motivations, products and outcomes. Whilst there may be some common interests, they do not share the same governance structures, policy influences, constituents, clients, consumers or opportunities. Thus the contract between university and workplace partners provides clarity and transparency, with documentation allowing for negotiation and communication. It formalizes the partnership. It is important to check that both parties have a common understanding of the contract provisions.

Many small work integrated learning programmes may not see the necessity for a formal contract, but for larger programmes and for workplaces a written contract is desirable. It provides a written record of agreements made between the university and workplace that may facilitate sustainability of the placement conditions for all parties in the event of changes in management or in personnel on the ground such as workplace supervisors/guides. A list of key elements that may be included in a contract appears in Table 8.4.

Schedules may be added to the contract. These may specify competencies, timelines for completing specified tasks, assessment requirements, problem-solving procedures between all parties and period of agreement. It is wise to add definitions of terminology, as these are helpful for addressing confusion in complex agreements.

Table 8.4 Elements of a contract between the university and the workplace

- Name of the university.
- Name of the host workplace.
- Name of student (if the student is part of the specific contract).
- Aims of the work integrated learning, assessment requirements and intended learning outcomes (e.g. application of theory to practice, development of competencies) – general goals and goals specific to individual students.
- Length and timing of placement.
- Insurance information.
- Police checks (if required).
- Vaccinations or health checks required prior to attendance in workplace.
- Remuneration (if applicable; not available in all work integrated learning experiences).
- Seminar attendance and written reports.
- Confidentiality and privacy issues.
- Other legal requirements such as intellectual property regulations.
- Unsatisfactory performance and how this is to be managed.
- Communication between parties.
- Conflict resolution process.
- Roles and responsibilities of all parties: university placement coordinator, the student, and the workplace supervisor and guides.
- Length of time this agreement is valid.
- Signatures of all parties to the contract.

Ensure contract validity

A contract, whether implied or explicit, requires that all parties indicate their intention to enter into an agreement, and a willingness to discuss the terms and conditions of that agreement. In preparing a contract there needs to be an offer made by one party and acceptance of that offer by the other party. This offer may be verbal but can also be formalized and in writing. In preparing a contract for work integrated learning the interests of all parties to the contract should be considered. At a minimum, the two key parties are the university and the workplace. This contract can be extended to include the students. Alternatively, some programmes prefer a specific learning contract between the student and the workplace.

The content and terms of the contract must be realistic for all parties, made with consideration by, and for, all parties and within their powers to agree to. If it is *ultra vires* (beyond the legal powers of one or both parties to enter into it), vague or illusory (e.g. conditional on a future contract), contains mistakes or has been agreed to under duress, it will not be valid.

Conduct a risk audit of workplaces

An important area for discussion between the parties is risk management. It is critical for the workplace and the university to consider issues of risk to students, the workplace, clients, consumers and the university. It is advisable to have a thorough knowledge of the workplace and the parties involved so you can identify as many risk factors as possible and indemnify against these in the contract. Some matters to consider as part of risk include: potential financial hazards; privacy matters; accessing secure databases; intellectual property; human resources management; and health and safety risks to students, clients and consumers. Carrying out a risk audit is an important step in minimizing and managing risk. Making all parties familiar with insurance policies and indemnity clauses in the work integrated learning contract, and ensuring awareness of compliance with occupational health and safety regulations, is also important. The case study below provides an illustration of what may occur with inadequate risk assessment in the absence of an explicit contract.

A student in his final year of an Information Technology degree was given a project in a company developing software for supply-chain management. There was no written contract between the university and the company; between the company and the student; or between the university and the student. By the end of his placement, the student had completed a substantial amount of work on the software programme. On graduation, the student established his own company and continued developing the software programme and was finally able to sell it to industry. When the company discovered the loss, they sued the student for theft of intellectual property. While the company did not take the university to court, the student's behaviour seriously harmed relationships between the company and the university. This episode prompted the university to develop, in conjunction with workplaces and students, written contracts for work integrated learning programmes, to be signed by the university, the workplace and the student, clearly outlining each stakeholder's roles and responsibilities, and expected behaviours in relation to ethical matters including intellectual property, privacy and confidentiality.

Having developed the university–workplace contract and undertaken a risk audit, the next step is to establish the tasks and responsibilities of the university, the workplace and the students to facilitate the best possible outcomes for all stakeholders in the work integrated learning experience.

Establish stakeholders' tasks and responsibilities

Key stakeholders in the work integrated learning process are the university coordinators, students and the host workplaces. Other interested parties include professional and vocational training bodies. Each stakeholder has particular tasks and responsibilities in creating and maintaining effective partnerships.

The university will need to:

- develop a database of workplace contacts. This will contain the interest in, and availability of, workplaces willing to accept students;
- provide information about work integrated learning experiences to students and recruit students to the programme;
- outline the educational framework (learning aims, assessment and integration) and the university's expectations to students and workplaces;
- orient and prepare students for learning in the workplace;
- work with faculty on integration of classroom work with workplace learning experiences;
- publish requirements, policies and procedures;
- determine availability of qualified supervisors and guides within each workplace;
- assess the quality of workplaces and supervisors for teaching and learning, and their readiness to accept students;
- prepare workplaces and supervisors to take students;
- develop internal mechanisms to assure the programme's quality at every stage of the learning process.

In considering and accepting students as learners, workplaces will need to:

- clearly describe the job or tasks that students are expected to undertake and communicate this information to the university's work integrated learning unit or programme coordinator;
- communicate clear expectations about the work activities to the students;
- recruit mentors, coaches, guides or supervisors from within the workplace to assist students with their learning;
- ensure the workplace learning environment is invitational, with all staff contributing to student learning;
- oversee the whole workplace experience, including provision of orientation programmes;
- provide feedback to students on their learning in the workplace;
- meet with the university coordinator to assess and review students' work;
- complete any required evaluation forms in a timely manner.

Like the university and workplace, students are expected to adopt and perform certain responsibilities as partners in work integrated learning. Student attitudes, preferences, values and previous experiences make an important contribution to the learning process. Students need to be prepared to:

- discuss their learning preferences and previous workplace experiences;
- understand and research the opportunities provided by workplaces;
- consider a range of practical issues such as transportation, drivers' licences and child care that can impact on their learning;
- provide an up-to-date CV;
- discuss any factors that impinge on learning (health concerns, financial considerations, cultural issues, disabilities, previous life experiences);
- attend orientation workshops.

Clear management strategies are needed to ensure all stakeholders uphold their responsibilities to achieve successful partnerships and student learning outcomes.

Considering what is needed to implement steps 1–5 in setting up the programme provides the guidelines for establishing management processes and identifying the resources required to enable these.

Implementing and managing the programme

Manage students, learning guides and organizations

Management processes in work integrated learning programmes are continuous. Once a programme begins, basic management strategies are repeated ad infinitum, with innovations introduced as a result of continuous programme evaluation to meet changing policy, economic and social structures, resourcing issues and changes in specified learning outcomes. Table 8.5 outlines this iterative process in working with students, learning guides and workplaces.

Manage programme resources

Management processes require resources, and resources require budgeting. Having established the steps needed to plan, set up and manage the work integrated learning programme, it is now possible to identify the infrastructure and other resources required to implement the programme successfully. The next section describes some of the issues that need to be addressed in this regard.

Developing a work integrated learning programme cannot be based on a creative idea, partnerships and goodwill alone. Any new programme needs infrastructure, resourcing and a budget. Although a plan for work integrated learning is outlined through university processes, resourcing the programme remains a task specific to each professional or disciplinary domain. Staff will require office space and associated equipment, and supplies including computer, phone and internet access, and access to a car or transport. Realistic budgeting is essential to successful programme management.

Table 8.5 Work integrated learning management process

- Establishing and maintaining relationships with workplaces.
- Finding work integrated learning experience opportunities (continuous).
- Preparing students for learning (what and how to learn, who are the teachers in the workplace, hot learning).
- Providing workshops for host workplaces to prepare them to take students.
- Establishing and updating contracts for learning (content).
- Implementing risk management strategies (updating and ongoing with every workplace).
- Helping students with the learning process (to use supervision, problem solve, guide, connect, support, question, reflect).
- Helping students to maintain and achieve competencies.
- Assessing student performance.
- Evaluating the programme.

Develop a realistic budget

Funds will need to be set aside for a number of contingencies. Budget items should include travel, technological infrastructure, communication software and information management systems, public relations events, and systematic and evaluative research.

Travel

Travelling to visit workplaces and students to provide supportive supervision in places located at a distance from the university is an important part of the work integrated learning process. Funds need to be allocated for this. If the programme is run in partnership with workplaces in other nations, funds may need to be set aside for international travel and for publicity material that profiles the programme. In the same vein, if the competitive edge of the university is to be maintained, staff will need access to membership fees to national and international organizations, conferences and staff training and development.

Technological infrastructure, communication software and information management systems

Technology is an important element in managing work integrated learning programmes. Resourcing technology (hardware and software) and its efficient use (staff development) are beneficial in several key areas. It provides a management information system or specifically designed software programmes, use of websites for providing information to students and workplaces, and other forms of technology such as webcasting. Computer-based communication serves multiple purposes: support for students and workplaces; assessment of learning; resolution of difficulties; and supervision of learning. Adequate resourcing of this is essential.

The most important element for managing the work integrated learning process is the management information system. This database system, at a minimum, contains information about students, workplaces who accept students, contacts in workplaces and information about supervisors in workplaces. In large programmes it can be used as a tool to match students with workplaces, although not all programmes use matching; some prefer an interview and selection process.

Some commercially available software programmes allow the creation of files on the student and the workplace as the basic components, which students and workplaces can access to update their own information. In these systems, files on the students contain personal, demographic and educational information including contact details, learning interests, previous work and work integrated learning experiences in industry. Workplaces will hopefully also have an electronic file listing learning opportunities and contact information. The range of information collected depends on the specific work integrated learning programme's requirements. Attachments such as letters, reports, learning evaluations, learning contracts and other forms of documents such as police checks can be incorporated as part of these software systems. Inclusion of attachments is a time-saving strategy as it allows fast electronic communication to students and workplaces. Manual creation of student files and stuffing envelopes for communication to students and workplaces are no longer required. Some software can also be used for performance monitoring of the work integrated learning programme and as the basis of more formal programme evaluation.

Communicating information to students quickly and transparently is a necessary element of the work integrated learning process. Email and university websites are important tools. These need to be accessible, up to date, well structured and designed to include information about learning opportunities, policies and programmes. With more work integrated learning programmes extending outside local areas to regional, national and international locations, computer technology such as VOIP or webcasting inside WebCT and Blackboard can be, and are being, used effectively.

Public relations events

It is important to consider future activities that acknowledge the contribution of workplaces to student learning. This may require special events and awards such as certificates. These occasions are valued by the university's workplace partners. Therefore, a budget item for these events needs to be factored in to programme resourcing.

Improving the quality of work integrated learning programmes

Improvement in the quality of programme delivery, teaching and learning is one of the goals of work integrated learning. In higher education systems across the world, there is an expectation that universities will monitor and improve the quality of programmes on an ongoing basis.

Research into the programme's effectiveness is part of the ongoing management process that requires human and technological resources. Research and evaluation requires development of valid methods of data collection from multiple sources, not just from students, to determine what has been achieved and what needs to be done to improve outcomes for all stakeholders. This component of the programme is sometimes forgotten when budgeting for overall planning, set-up and ongoing management.

Use databases for monitoring and research

Use of management information systems such as the Microsoft Access database or case management software such as Penelope™ by Athena can enhance administrative efficiency and enable evaluation of work integrated learning programmes. Management information systems incorporate the following information:

- personal information about students (name, gender, contact information);
- educational information (course, majors, learning interests, competencies achieved in previous work integrated learning experiences);
- features of workplaces (location, contact information, website);
- details of learning guides (name, level of experience, work interests);
- attachments:
  - reports from workplaces and students including the mid-term report and final report
  - workplace audits
  - notes from the programme coordinator on specific issues facing students
  - university and workplace contracts
  - student learning contracts
  - correspondence
  - student evaluation of programme.

Such databases can be used in a variety of ways that enable the university to monitor programme administration and evaluate student learning outcomes. As an example, the database could be used to determine the turnover rate of learning supervisors/guides, thus providing information on administrative and management issues. Alternatively, it could be used as a research tool to determine learning outcomes and the risks to which students are exposed, or to compare current and various programmes. Databases can provide a rich source of both qualitative and quantitative data.

Use benchmarking for quality improvement

Benchmarking, with its origins in the private sector, provides a method for comparing educational programmes and enabling continuous improvement, greater productivity and innovation. Using benchmarking as a quality improvement tool in work integrated learning programmes arises from the desire to improve and do better than other programmes. Whilst there are many difficulties associated with benchmarking (see Schofield 1998), Alstete (1997) claims that benchmarking can be reduced to simple questions which are applied specifically to work integrated learning programmes. For example:

- How well is the work integrated learning programme doing compared with other similar programmes?
- Do we know which is the best work integrated learning programme in the nation?
- Can we understand why it is regarded as the best and what is done to achieve quality?
- How can we use an understanding of other programmes to improve the quality of our programme?

Generally, at a university level, benchmarking assumes comparative use of statistical data. The value of benchmarking goes beyond statistical data to compare policies, processes and practices to enable continual improvement. There is great value in comparison of the programmes, whether this is with regard to statistics, programme design, learning outcomes, community partnerships or support provided to students.

Evaluative research can provide important data for implementing quality assurance and quality improvement processes – the final step in the work integrated learning process. As stressed before, these processes are part of the continuous cycle of planning, setting up and managing a work integrated learning programme.

Summary

The five-step work integrated learning process described in this chapter illustrates that work integrated learning programmes are not stand-alone processes but involve many interlinking processes and address diverse, and at times competing, concerns. To accomplish this, a clear purpose and mandate is essential. The programme design is complex as it must accommodate the needs of the university, the realities of workplaces, the interests of the community and, above all, the learning needs of students. All parties require an understanding of their particular responsibilities and the educational and practical frameworks underpinning the programme. Simultaneously, all parties need to attend to their particular primary responsibilities and be aware of their rights in this context and the rights of the other stakeholders.

Establishing and maintaining these programmes requires financial and human resources, clear policies and ongoing attention to partnerships. These are the responsibility of the university and the workplace. If work integrated learning is to thrive as a strategy in higher education systems, then the monitoring of performance and attention to quality improvement are essential.

Work integrated learning provides universities with the opportunity to graduate students with the capacity to integrate the theory learned in the classroom and the practice learned in the workplace to problem-solve difficult and complex matters in their lives and as part of their work. Work integrated learning also provides universities with authentic opportunities to forge strategic alliances with related industries, professions and communities that will enrich their public mission and their distinctiveness.

Engaging fully in work integrated learning opportunities provides industries, professions and communities with opportunities to enhance the capabilities of their workforce and membership. Through their engagement they will gain access to resources that will enable them to become effective learning organizations that support lifelong learning amongst their existing membership and, at the same time, make a valuable contribution to the education of the next generation of workers and citizens.

These benefits are predicated on student recognition of the worth of the opportunities for work integrated learning and, as a result, engaging fully in the opportunities as they arise. Such students are at a distinct advantage upon graduation and are excellent ambassadors for their institutions. Higher education institutions and their leaders are well advised to recognize this potential. In doing so they must ensure that their programmes are well resourced, the students well prepared, the staff sufficiently inducted into their roles, and their external partnerships genuine and comprehensive in outlook.

To achieve these outcomes much has to be accomplished at the university level. Baseline data are needed regarding the extent and nature of work placement programmes across the institution. Institutions need to develop appropriate policies pertaining to student work-placement learning, assessment and safety, which take into account the particular nature of learning in the workplace and account for the diverse legal, ethical and duty-of-care requirements. There is a need for public awareness of the risks involved in work integrated learning programmes and the development of a set of risk management policies and procedures. Such policies and procedures would include a requirement that all work integrated learning programme coordinators undergo an induction to their role, with ongoing maintenance of the knowledge through an institutional virtual and face-to-face 'practicum forum'.

Reformation of academic profiles and promotion policies is also needed. These must account for the effort and effectiveness of establishing high-quality work integrated learning programmes that forge authentic and robust relationships with associated professional and industry bodies and community organizations. Finally, universities need to celebrate and acknowledge publicly the valuable contribution of workplace and community partners who provide venues and support for their students' education.

Workplace Literacies – Knowledge, Skills and Attributes

Following is workplace literacy in detail for the six literacy domains described in Chapter 3: organizational; legal and ethical; profession specific; career; social; and cultural.

Organizational

Understand workplace organizational values, priorities, structures and culture:

- Adaptability
  - Be prepared for uncertainty
  - Demonstrate flexibility – understand workplace dynamics and work with these
  - Recognize and understand different learning pathways and affordances – why has the workplace offered the placement?
  - Recognize the learning value of good and bad experiences in the organizational context – think outside the square; demonstrate initiative and creativity
  - Respect for, and work within, the organizational culture, whether this is competitive or collaborative, whether its values are at odds or congruent with personal values.

Legal and ethical

Knowledge of, and behaviours related to:

- Universal Declaration of Human Rights; Occupational Health and Safety; Equal Opportunity, Anti-Discrimination and Sexual Harassment legislation; region-, nation- or religion-specific law; policies and procedures related to these in the workplace
- Legal and ethical requirements in areas such as:
  - client confidentiality and privacy
  - copyright

— trade secrets and intellectual property (IP – patents, new inventions or ways of doing things); understanding the difference between experience gained in the workplace and stealing a trade secret; understanding who has the legal right to ownership of IP
— duty of care (to those you work with, to yourself, to the workplace organization, to the university, to the wider community)
— risks and risk management.

Profession-specific

Understand specific profession's or specialization's expectations, standards and competency requirements:

• Willing to learn and practise profession-specific skills and attitudes to develop specific competencies
• Draw on knowledge from practising in laboratories or virtual simulations to practise in the real world context
• Develop procedural knowledge (rules and procedures), routine knowledge (situation-specific), conceptual knowledge (transferable between situations) and practical knowledge (tacit).

Career

Identify areas of interest and research these – ask other people in the workplace, seek career guidance, use the internet to gain greater understanding of possibilities:

• Reflect on your current knowledge, skills, attributes and values:
— How do they fit with your intended career?
— How much work will you need to do to attain necessary competencies (professional and generic; skills, attributes and values)?
— Evaluate realities of identified career path.

Social

Capacity to work with others:

• Communication:
— Verbal and written language and numerical literacy; Information and Communication Technology literacy
• Diplomacy, power and etiquette:
— recognize hierarchies and power relationships; understand where you fit – your status in the workplace context
— be respectful of others' status and roles, rights and responsibilities
• Responsible, safe self-management and concern for others' safety:
— Value self as a learner

- — Awareness of personal attributes, knowledge and limitations
- — Ability to manage own behaviour for the particular context and tasks
- — Project management
- — Time management
- Effective team work and partnerships
  - — Demonstrate adult behaviour in teams, including conflict resolution and mediation
  - — Be capable of adopting leadership and follower roles – create, collaborate and cooperate; follow instructions or work autonomously
  - — Learn with others – listen, respond, collaborate, seek and attend to feedback, offer feedback, contribute to the team or partnership
  - — Understand and practise compromise as needed
  - — Trust and respect others in the workplace and communicate effectively with them (includes listening to and respecting their ideas and beliefs)
  - — Time and resource management – able to set goals, complete tasks / projects in given time frame
  - — Self-awareness
- Affective, cognitive and social attributes:
  - — Can generate affective, cognitive and social questions about the work context
  - — Can question their emotional and behavioural responses to people, actions and situations
  - — Know their personal values, strengths and limitations in the context
  - — Can balance cognitive and affective elements to ensure rational decision-making in 'hot' contexts
- Civic / community engagement:
  - — Awareness of, and commitment to civic responsibility
  - — Can see the connection between what they are doing as an individual, or what their workplace is doing, and the wider community
  - — Willing to take positive action to enhance aspects of living in particular communities
  - — Respect people in different communities – engage with them in learning about them, their perspectives and how they see themselves in local and global contexts.

Cultural

Value differences:

- Awareness, knowledge and understanding of, and respect for, diverse others' perceptions, values and needs:
  - — Practise non-judgemental interaction with others
  - — Able to suspend personal attachment to particular views, values and beliefs

— Able to see benefits from diverse cultural input – different ways of knowing and doing; suggest adoption of different ways where they think these might benefit the workplace
• Share their culture:
    — Able to rationally discuss cultural similarities and differences with others; engage in cultural learning exchange
    — Able to talk objectively about 'hard issues' such as racism, sexism, religion.

Sources: Cooper and Bowden (2008); Cooper *et al.* (2003: 6–7), with permission from Flinders University Staff Development and Training Unit.

Specific Risks and Difficulties Encountered in the Workplace

Detail of specific risks and difficulties from Chapter 7, with reference to literature discussing these issues.

General concerns	Specific issues and references
Safety of student	• Harassment or bullying of a student by workers, other students, clients, consumers or learning guides (Daugherty et al. 1998; Elnicki et al. 2002; Frank et al. 2006; Moreno et al. 2001; Nagata-Kobayashi et al. 2006; Shinsako et al. 2001)
	• Sexual harassment by workers and learning guides – comments, behaviours and intimidation (Brulle and Mantarakis 1993/4; Chuang and Lin 2006; Daugherty et al. 1998; DeMayo 1997; Nicholson 2002; Rademakers et al. 2008; Wear et al. 2007; Williams et al. 1999; Yueh-Hsiu 2006)
	• Physical violence (Dunkel et al. 2000; Grenade and Macdonald 1995; Waddell et al. 2005)
	• Verbal abuse from clients (Ferns and Meerabeau 2008; Maidment 2003; Tully et al. 1993)
	• Threats of violence (Beech 2007; DiGuilio 2002)
Personal injuries and work-related stress	• Musculoskeletal injuries (Glover et al. 2005; Thornton et al. 2008)
	• Low back pain (Glover et al. 2005; Masoud 2004)
	• Infections, especially blood-borne pathogens from needle stick and other communicable diseases (Derrick et al. 1982; Leung et al. 2007; Murphy and Younai 1996; Shiao et al. 2002; Wang et al. 2003)
	• Lack of sleep (Ralph et al. 2008)
	• Emotional, physiological and psychological turmoil as a result of vicarious traumatization (witnessing death, hearing stories of torture, violence) (DiGuilio 2002; Huber 2002; Maidment 2003; Timmins and Kaliszer 2002)
	• Dormant personal issues awakened by situations in workplace (e.g. alcoholism) (Nagata-Kobayashi et al. 2006; Wear et al. 2007)

General concerns	Specific issues and references
Discrimination	• Experiences of racism by workers, clients or consumers, or learning guides in the placement process and in the workplace (Collins *et al.* 2000; DiGuilio 2002; Martin and Kipling 2006) • Discrimination of students with disabilities by workers or learning guides preventing students from maximizing learning experiences (Huckabee 2008) • Discrimination based on gender, religious beliefs, cultural orientation, sexual orientation or age (Huang and Kleiner 2001; Nicholson 2002)
Other student concerns	• Lack of financial support for students with a lengthy work integrated learning experience (Maidment 2003; Ralph *et al.* 2008) • Distance from student's home to workplaces and associated costs (Maidment 2003; Ralph *et al.* 2008) • Disclosure of personal information to the agency and learning guides (dyslexia) (Morris and Turnbull 2007)
Standards of care to clients and consumers	• Failure to disclose student status or provide name (Mason *et al.* 2002; Vivekananda and Corfield 2008) • Students breach client confidentiality or privacy or fail to seek informed consent (Kapp 1984) • Failure of mandated notifier to report (Gelman *et al.* 1996) • Student errors (falsification of records, wrongful advice, medication errors) (Beemsterboer *et al.* 2000; Daugherty *et al.* 1998; Harding and Petrick 2008) • Students under the influence of drugs when working with clients (Fiesta 1998) • Students who do not work with the level of competence determined by the profession or workplace (Fiesta 1998)
Learning in the workplace	• Lack of clear expectations by learning guide and workplace (Reams 2003) • Conflict between academic and workplace priorities (Rogers *et al.* 2003) • Student's competence or behaviour poses an unacceptable level of risk to clients or agency (Hicks *et al.* 2005; Resnick *et al.* 2006) • Inadequate information on safety policy and procedures provided to students (Kane 2002; Maidment 2003) • Heavy workloads with little time for reflection (Ralph *et al.* 2008) • Conflict between students and others in the workplace (Maidment 2003; Rogers *et al.* 2003) • General conflict and politics in workplace (Rogers *et al.* 2003) • Unfriendly and unsupportive atmosphere in workplace (Rogers *et al.* 2003) • Driving agency vehicles with clients (DiGuilio 2002) • Fear of making mistakes (Wusthoff 2001)

General concerns	Specific issues and references
Learning guides	• Learning guide is not available for assisting with learning (Curtis *et al.* 1998) • Lack of feedback on student work (Curtis *et al.* 1998) • Lack of integration of theory and practice (Curtis *et al.* 1998) • Learning guide's work performance and skills perceived as weak by any or all stakeholders (Hayes *et al.* 1999) • Inappropriate relationships between student and learning guide that compromise learning (Recupero *et al.* 2005) • Interpersonal difficulties between learning guide and student (Ralph *et al.* 2008; Timmins and Kaliszer 2002) • Conflict between the learning guide and student (Rogers *et al.* 2003)
Preparation for learning in the workplace	• Students are not orientated and are ill prepared for learning in workplace (Kane 2002; Maidment 2003) • Expectations, policies and procedures are not adequate (Maidment 2003)
University policies and procedures	• Inequities in programme policies that cause risk to students (Fiesta 1998; Osinski 2003) • University policies and procedures are not followed (Huckabee 2008; Ralph *et al.* 2008; Smith *et al.* 2001)

References

Alstete, J. W. (1997) *Benchmarking in Higher Education: Adapting Best Practices to Improve Quality*, ERIC Digest. Available online at: <http://www.ericdigests. org/1997–3/bench.html> (accessed 18 August 2009).

Anderson, J. R. (1983) *The Architecture of Cognition*, Cambridge, MA: Harvard University Press.

André, K. (1999) 'The assessment of undergraduate clinical nursing practice: The importance of negotiating the definition of nursing', colloquium in field-based education, Flinders University Adelaide, November.

Association of American Colleges and Universities (2009) *Integrative Learning: Addressing the Complexities*, Washington DC: AACU. Available online at: <http://www.aacu.org/meetings/integrative_learning/2009/CallforProposals. cfm#themes> (accessed 8 August 2009).

Bachor, D., Anderson, J. O., Walsh, J. and Muir, W. (1994) 'Classroom assessment and the relationship to representativeness, accuracy and consistency', *Alberta Journal of Educational Research*, 40(2): 247–62.

Bandura, A. (1986) *Social Foundations of Thought and Action: A Social Cognitive Theory*, Englewood Cliffs, NJ: Prentice-Hall.

Battiste, M. and Henderson, J. Y. (2000) *Protecting Indigenous Knowledge: A Global Challenge*, Saskatoon, SK: Purich Press.

Beard, C. and Wilson, J. P. (2006) *Experiential Learning: A Best Practice Handbook for Educators and Trainers*, Philadelphia: Kogan Page.

Beech, B. (2007) 'Aggression prevention training for student nurses: Differential responses to training and the interaction between theory and practice', *Nurse Education in Practice*, 8: 94–102.

Beemsterboer, P., Odom, J., Pate, T. and Haden, N. (2000) 'Issues of academic integrity in U.S. dental schools', *Journal of Dental Education*, 64(12): 833–8.

Belenky, M. F., Clinchy, B. M., Goldberger, N. R. and Tarule, J. M. (1986) *Women's Ways of Knowing: The Development of Self, Voice, and Mind*, New York: Basic Books.

Benner, P. (1984) *From Novice to Expert: Excellence and Power in Clinical Nursing Practice*, Menlo Park, CA: Addison-Wesley Nursing Division.

Bernard, J. M. and Goodyear, R. K. (1992) *Fundamentals of Clinical Supervision*, Boston MA: Allyn & Bacon.

Biggs, J. B. (1992) 'A qualitative approach to grading students', *HERDSA News*, 14(3): 3–6.

—— (1999) *Teaching for Quality Learning at University*, Buckingham: Society for Research into Higher Education and Open University Press.

—— (2003) *Teaching for Quality Learning at University*, 2nd edn, Buckingham: Society for Research into Higher Education and Open University Press.

—— (n.d.) *Aligning Teaching for Constructing Learning*, The Higher Education Academy. Available online at: <http://www.heacademy.ac.uk/assets/York/documents/resources/resourcedatabase/id477_aligning_teaching_for_constructing_learning.pdf> (accessed 17 April 2009).

Billett, S. (2001) *Learning in the Workplace: Strategies for Effective Practice*, Sydney: Allen & Unwin.

—— (2002) 'Critiquing workplace learning discourses: Participation and continuity at work', *Studies in the Education of Adults*, 34(1): 56–67.

—— (2004) 'Workplace participatory practices – Conceptualising workplaces as learning environments', *Journal of Workplace Learning*, 16(5/6): 312–24.

—— (2006) 'Constituting the workplace curriculum', *Journal of Curriculum Studies*, 38(1): 31–48.

—— (2009) 'Conceptualizing learning experiences: Contributions and mediations of the social, personal and brute', *Mind, Culture and Activity*, 16(1): 32–47.

Bogo, M. and Vayda, E. (1998) *The Practice of Field Instruction in Social Work: Theory and Process*, 2nd edn, Toronto, Canada: University of Toronto Press.

Bond, M. and Holland, S. (1998) *Skills of Clinical Supervision for Nurses*, Buckingham: Open University Press.

Bordage, G. (1994) 'Elaborated knowledge: A key to successful diagnostic thinking', *Academic Medicine*, 69: 883–5.

—— (1999) 'Why did I miss the diagnosis? Some cognitive explanations and educational implications', *Academic Medicine*, 74(10 Suppl): S138–43.

Boud, D. (2001) 'Using journal writing to enhance reflective practice', in L. M. English and M. A. Gillen (eds) *Promoting Journal Writing in Adult Education. New Directions in Adult and Continuing Education No. 90*, San Francisco, CA: Jossey-Bass, 9–18.

Boud, D. and Walker, D. (1990) 'Making the most of experience', *Studies in Continuing Education*, 12(2): 61–80.

Boud, D. and Miller, N. (eds) (1996) *Working with Experience: Animating Learning*, New York: Routledge.

Boud, D. and Solomon, S. (2001) *Work-based Learning: A New Higher Education*, London: Society for Research into Higher Education and Open University Press.

Boud, D., Keogh, R. and Walker, D. (eds) (1985) *Reflection: Turning Experience into Learning*, London: Kogan Page.

Boyer, E. (1990) *Scholarship Reconsidered: Priorities of the Professoriate*, Princeton, NJ: The Carnegie Foundation for the Advancement of Teaching.

—— (1996) 'The scholarship of engagement', *Journal of Public Service and Outreach*, 1(1): 11–20.

Brandenburg, R. and Ryan, J. (2001) 'From "Too little too late" to "This is the best part": Students' perception of changes to the practicum placement in teaching', paper presented at Australian Association for Research in Education Conference, Fremantle, December 2001. Available online at: <http://www.aare.edu.au/01pap/bra01557.htm> (accessed 7 July 2009).

Brandt, B. L., Farmer, J. A. and Buckmaster A. (1993) 'Cognitive apprenticeship approach to helping adults learn', in D. D. Flannery (ed.) *Applying Cognitive Learning Theory for Adult and Continuing Education, No. 59*, San Francisco, CA: Jossey Bass.

Bransford, J. D. (2000) *How People Learn: Brain, Mind, Experience and School*, Washington DC: National Academy Press.

Brill, N. (1985) *Working with People: The Helping Process*, New York: Longman.

Brookfield, S. D. (1986) *Understanding and Facilitating Adult Learning*, Milton Keynes: Open University Press.

Brown, A. and Bourne, I. (1996) *The Social Work Supervisor*, Buckingham: Open University Press.

Brulle, A. and Mantarakis, N. (1993/4) 'Sexual harassment in teacher preparation clinical experiences', *Action in Teacher Education*, 15(4): 5–13.

Brundage, D. H. (1980) *Adult Learning Principles and their Application to Program Planning*, Queens Park Toronto: Minister of Education Ontario.

Business Industry and Higher Education Collaboration Council (2007) *Graduate Employability Skills*, commissioned report, Canberra: BIHECC.

Butin, D. (2005) *Service Learning in Higher Education*, New York: Palgrave Macmillan.

Butterworth, T. and Faugier, J. (eds) (1992) *Clinical Supervision and Mentorships in Nursing*, London: Chapman & Hall.

Caffarella, R. (2002) *Planning Programs for Adult Learners: A Practical Guide for Educators, Trainers and Staff Developers*, New York: Jossey Bass.

Calway, B. A. (2006) *What has Work-Integrated Learning Learned? – A WIL Philosophy*, Lilydale, Victoria: Swinburne University of Technology.

Canadian Association for Co-operative Education (2005) *Co-operative Education Manual: A Guide to Planning and Implementing Co-operative Education Programs in Post-Secondary Institutions*, Toronto, Canada. Available online at: <www.cafce.ca/download.php?id=56> (accessed 12 May 2009).

Cast, J. (1995) 'Recent cognitive perspectives on learning: Implications for nurse education', *Nurse Education Today*, 15: 280–90.

Chartered Society of Physiotherapy (2005) *A Guide to Implementing Clinical Supervision*, CPD 37, London: Chartered Society of Physiotherapy.

Chuang, S. C. and Lin, H. M. (2006) 'Nurses confronting sexual harassment in the medical environment', *Studies in Health Technology and Informatics*, 122: 349–52.

Coll, R., Eames, C., Paku, L., Lay, M., Hodges, D., Bhat, R., Ram, S., Ayling, D., Fleming, J., Ferkins, L., Wiersma, C. and Martin, A. (2009) 'An exploration of the pedagogies employed to integrate knowledge in work-integrated learning', *Journal of Cooperative Education and Partnerships*, 43: 14–35.

College of Occupational Therapy (1997) *Statement on Supervision in Occupational Therapy*, SPP 150(A), London: College of Occupational Therapy.

Collins, S., Gutridge, P., James, A., Lynn, E. and Williams, C. (2000) 'Racism and anti-racism in placement reports', *Social Work Education*, 19(1): 29–43.

Community-Campus Partnerships for Health (2006) *Principles of Good Community-Campus Partnerships*, Seattle: Community-Campus Partnerships for Health. Available online at: <http://www.ccph.info/> (accessed 27 July 2009).

Cooper, L. and Orrell, J. (1999) 'The practicum: The domestic work of university teaching', *HERDSA News*, 21(2): 6–9.

Cooper, L. and Anglem, J. (2003) *Clinical Supervision in Mental Health*, Adelaide: Australian Centre for Community Services Research, Flinders University.

Cooper, L. and Bowden, M. (2008) 'Work Integrated Learning Issues for University Coordinators, Workplace Supervisors and Students', unpublished research interview data, Adelaide: Flinders University.

Cooper, L., Orrell, J. and Bowden, M. (2003) *Workplace Learning Management Manual – A Guide for Establishing and Managing University Work Integrated Learning Courses, Practica, Field Education and Clinical Education*, Adelaide: Staff Development and Training Unit, Flinders University.

Cullen, J. and Mills, R. (2006) *Widening Participation to Higher Education in the East of England: A Review of Recent Regional and National Research*, Cambridge: Association of Universities in the East of England.

Curtis, N., Helion, J. and Domsohn, M. (1998) 'Student athletic trainer perceptions of clinical supervisor behaviours: A critical incident study', *Journal of Athletic Training*, 33(3): 249–53.

Daugherty, S., Baldwin, D. and Rowley, B. (1998) 'Learning, satisfaction, and mistreatment during medical internship: A national survey of working conditions', *Journal of the American Medical Association*, 279(15): 1194–9.

DeMayo, R. (1997) 'Patient sexual behaviours and sexual harassment: A national survey of physical therapists', *Physical Therapy*, 77(7): 739–44.

Dennen, V.P. (2004) 'Cognitive apprenticeship in educational practice: Research on scaffolding, modeling, mentoring, and coaching as instructional strategies', in D. H. Jonassen (ed.) *Handbook of Research on Educational Communications and Technology*, New York: Lawrence Erlbaum: 813–28.

Department of Education, Science and Training (DEST)(2005) *Australian Blueprint for Career Development, Commonwealth of Australia*, Canberra. Available online at: <http://www.dest.gov.au/sectors/career_development/policy_issues_reviews/key_issues/australian_blueprint_for_career_dev/ http://www.milesmorgan.com.au/the-australian-blueprint-for-career-development/> (accessed 7 March 2009).

Derrick, J., Buchner, B., Bouchard, S., Larke, R., McSheffrey, J. and Vas, S. (1982) 'Response to hepatitis B vaccine in Canadian dental students', *Lancet*, 1(8265): 223.

Dewey, J. (1927) *The Public and its Problems*, Athens Ohio: Swallow Press.

—— (1933) *How we Think: A Restatement of the Relation of Reflective Thinking on the Educative Practice*, Lexington, MA: Heath.

—— (1938) *Experience and Education*, New York: Simon & Schuster.

DiGuilio, J. F. (2002) 'Concerns in the field placement', in L. M. Grobman (ed.) *The Field Placement Survival Guide: What You Need to Know to Get the Most from Your Social Work Practicum*, Harrisburg PA: White Hat Communications, 89–93.

Doel, M., Shardlow, S., Sawdon, C. and Sawdon, D. (1996) *Teaching Social Work Practice*, Aldershot: Arena.

Dunkel, J., Ageson, A-T. and Ralph, C. J. (2000) 'Encountering violence in field work: A risk reduction model', *Journal of Teaching in Social Work*, 20(3/4): 5–18.

Eames, C. and Cates, C. (2004) 'Theories of learning in cooperative education', in R. K. Coll and C. Eames (eds) *International Handbook for Cooperative Education: An International Perspective of the Theory, Research and Practice of Work-integrated Learning*, Boston, MA: World Association for Cooperative Education, 37–47.

Edgecombe, K. (2005) 'Nursing students' perceptions of the Dedicated Education Unit as an effective clinical environment', unpublished Masters Thesis, Adelaide: Flinders University.

Edgecombe, K. and Bowden, M. (2009) 'The ongoing search for best practice in clinical teaching and learning: A model of nursing students' evolution to proficient novice registered nurses', *Nurse Education in Practice*, 9: 91–101.

Elnicki, M., Curry, R., Fagan, M., Friedman, E., Jacobson, E., Loftus, T., Ogden, P., Pangaro, L., Papadakis, M., Szauter, K., Wallach, P. and Linger, B. (2002) 'Medical students' perspective on and responses to abuse during the internal medicine clerkship', *Teaching and Learning in Medicine*, 14(2): 92–7.

Eraut, M. (2004) 'Informal learning in the workplace', *Studies in Continuing Education*, 26(2): 247–73.

Evans, D. (1990) *Improving Social Work Education and Training Three: Assessing Students' Competence to Practise in College and Practice Host Organisation*, London: Central Council for Education and Training in Social Work.

Eyler, J. and Giles, D. E. Jr. (1999) *Where's the Learning in Service-Learning?*, San Francisco, CA: Jossey-Bass.

Feltham, C. and Dryden, W. (1994) *Developing Counsellor Supervision*, London: Sage Publications.

Fernandez, E. (1998) 'Student perceptions of satisfaction with practicum learning', *Social Work Education*, 17(2): 173–201.

Ferns, T. and Meerabeau, L. (2008) 'Verbal abuse experienced by nursing students', *Journal of Advanced Nursing*, 61(4): 436–44.

Fiesta, J. (1998) 'Lessons in student liability', *Nurse Management*, 29(10): 14–17.

Frank, E., Carrera, J., Stratton, T., Bickel, J. and Nora, L. (2006) 'Experiences of belittlement and harassment and their correlates among medical students in the United States: A longitudinal survey', *British Medical Journal*, 333(7570): 682.

Gardiner, D. (1989) *The Anatomy of Supervision*, Milton Keynes: Society for Research in Higher Education and Open University Press.

Gelman, S., Pollack, D. and Auerbach, C. (1996) 'Liability issues in social work education', *Journal of Social Work Education*, 32(3): 351–61.

Givens Fisher, C. and Grant, G. E. (1983) 'Intellectual levels in college classrooms', in C. L. Ellner and C. P. Barnes (eds) *Studies of College Teaching*, Lexington: Lexington Books.

Glass, A., Higgins, K. and McGregor, A. (2002) *Delivering Work Based Learning*, Scottish Executive Central Research Unit, Edinburgh: Stationary Office.

Glover, W., McGregor, A., Sullivan, C. and Hague, J. (2005) 'Work-related musculo-skeletal disorders affecting members of the Chartered Society of Physiotherapy', *Physiotherapy*, 91:138–47.

Grealish, L. and Trevitt, C. (2005) 'Developing a professional identity: Student nurses in the workplace', *Contemporary Nurse*, 19(1–2): 137–50. Available online at: <http://www.contemporarynurse.com>

Grenade, G. and Macdonald, E. (1995) 'Risk of physical assaults among student nurses', *Occupational Medicine*, 45: 256–8.

Groenewald, T. (2004) 'Towards a definition of cooperative education', in R. K. Coll and C. Eames (eds) *International Handbook for Cooperative Education: An International Perspective of the Theory, Research and Practice of Work-integrated Learning*, Boston, MA: World Association for Cooperative Education: 17–25.

Gutheil, T. and Gabbard, G. O. (2008) 'The concept of boundaries in clinical practice: Theoretical and risk-management dimensions', in D. N. Bersoff (ed.) *Ethical Conflicts in Psychology*, Washington DC: American Psychological Association.

Hager, P. (2001) 'Workplace judgement and conceptions of learning', *Journal of Workplace Learning*, 13(7/8): 352–9.

Harding, L. and Petrick, T. (2008) 'Nursing student medication errors: A retrospective review', *Journal of Nursing Education*, 47(1): 43–7.

Harkavy, I. (2003) 'Foreword', in B. Jacoby and Associates (eds) *Building Partnerships for Service-Learning*, San Francisco, CA: Jossey-Bass, xiii.

Harré, R. (1983) *Personal Being: A Theory for Individual Psychology*, Oxford: Blackwell.

Hart, P. D. and Associates Inc. (2008) *'How should colleges assess and improve student learning? Employers' views on the accountability challenge, survey of employers conducted on behalf of the Association of American Colleges and Universities*, Washington DC: P. D. Hart and Associates Inc. Available online at: <http://www.aacu.org/LEAP/employer_poll.cfm> (accessed 3 August 2009).

Harvey, L., Moon, S. and Geall, V. (1997) *Graduates' Work: Organisational Change and Students' Attributes*, Birmingham: Centre for Research into Quality, UCE.

Harvey, L., Geall, V. and Moon, S. (1998) *Work Experience: Expanding Opportunities for Undergraduates*, Birmingham: Centre for Research into Quality, UCE. Available online at: <www.uce.ac.uk/crq/publications/we/wech1.html> (accessed 12 November 2008).

Hawkins, P. and Shohet, R. (1989) *Supervision in the Helping Professions: An Individual, Group and Organisational Approach*, Milton Keynes: Open University Press.

Hawkins, P. and Smith, N. (2006) *Coaching, Mentoring and Organizational Consultancy: Supervision and Development*, Berkshire: Open University Press.

Hayes, K., Huber, G., Rogers, J. and Sanders, B. (1999) 'Behaviours that cause clinical instructors to question the clinical competence of physical therapist students', *Physical Therapy*, 79(7): 653–67.

Hesketh, A. J. (2000) 'Recruiting an elite? Employers' perceptions of graduate education and training', *Journal of Education and Work*, 13(3): 245–71.

Hicks, P., Cox., S., Espey, E., Goepfert, A., Bienstock, J., Erickson, S., Hammoud, M., Katz, N., Krueger, P., Neutens, J., Peskin, E. and Puscheck, E. (2005) 'To the point: Medical education reviews – Dealing with student difficulties in the clinical settings', *American Journal of Obstetrics & Gynecology*, 193: 1915–22.

Ho, D. W. L. and Whitehill, T. (2009) 'Clinical supervision of speech-language pathology students: Comparison of two models of feedback', *International Journal of Speech Pathology*, 11(3): 244–55.

Hodges, B., Smith, D. W. and Jones, P. D. (2005) 'The assessment of cooperative education', in R. K. Coll and C. Eames (eds) *International Handbook for Cooperative Education: An International Perspective of the Theory, Research and Practice of Work-integrated Learning*, Boston, MA: World Association for Cooperative Education: 49–65.

Holden, R. and Hamblett, T. (2007) 'The transition from higher education into work: Tales of cohesion and fragmentation', *Education and Training*, 49(7): 516–87.

Holloway, E. (1995) *Clinical Supervision: A Systems Approach*, London: Sage.

Huang, C-C. and Kleiner, B. H. (2001) 'New developments concerning religious discrimination in the workplace', *International Journal of Sociology and Social Policy*, 21(8/9/10): 128–36.

Huber, R. (2002) 'Vicarious traumatisation in field placements', in L. M. Grobman *The Field Placement Survival Guide: What You Need to Know to Get the Most from Your Social Work Practicum*, Harrisburg PA: White Hat Communications: 101–10.

Huckabee, C. (2008) 'Student who was dismissed from Michigan dental school wins $1.72-million verdict', *The Chronicle of Higher Education*, 2 December. Available online at: <http://chronicle.com/news/article/5593/student-who-was-dismissed-from-michigan-dental-school-wins-172-million-verdict> (accessed 13 April 2009).

Huitt, W. and Hummel, J. (2003) 'Piaget's theory of cognitive development', *Educational Psychology Interactive*, Valdosta, GA: Valdosta State University. Available online at: <http://chiron.valdosta.edu/whuitt/col/cogsys/piaget.html> (accessed 12 May 2009).

Ingvarson, L., Beavis, A., Danielson, C., Ellis, L. and Elliott, A. (2005) *An Evaluation of Learning Management at Central Queensland University*, Melbourne: Australian Council for Educational Research. Available online at: <http://research.acer.edu.au/cgi/viewcontent.cgi?article=1005&context=teacher_education> (accessed 2 August 2009).

Jacoby, B. (1996) 'Service-learning in today's higher education', in B. Jacoby and Associates (eds) *Service-learning in Higher Education: Concepts and Practices*, San Francisco, CA: Jossey-Bass, 3–25.

Jacoby, B. and Associates (eds) (2003) *Building Partnerships for Service Learning*, San Francisco, CA: Jossey-Bass.

Johnson, D. W., Johnson, R. T. and Smith, K. (1991) *Active Learning: Cooperation in the Classroom*, Edina, MN: Interaction Book Company.

Jones, S. R. (2003) 'Principles and profiles of exemplary partnerships with community agencies', in B. Jacoby and Associates, *Building Partnerships for Service-Learning*, San Francisco, CA: Jossey-Bass, 151–73.

Kadushin, A. (1992) *Supervision in Social Work*, 3rd edn, New York: Columbia University Press.

Kagan, N. I. (1977) *Interpersonal Process Recall: A Method for Influencing Human Interaction*, East Lansing, MI: Michigan State University.

Kane, M. (2002) 'Correlates of MSW students' perceptions of preparedness to manage risk and personal liability', *Advances in Social Work*, 3(2): 134–45.

Kapp, M. B. (1984) 'Supervising professional trainees: Legal implications for mental health institutions and practitioners', *Hospital and Community Psychiatry*, 35(Feb):143–7.

Kay, J. and Russell, L. (2008) 'Learning in the workplace and community: A discussion paper to inform review of policy', internal discussion paper, Victoria: Victoria University.

Keating, S. (2006) *'Learning in the Workplace': A Literature Review*, Victoria: Post-compulsory Education Centre, Victoria University. Available online at: <http://tls.vu.edu.au/PEC/reports.htm> (accessed 15 March 2007).

Kelton, M. (2009) 'Management of WIL', presentation to Queensland University of Technology Work Integrated Learning workshop, Queensland, September 2009.

Kerwin, A. (1993) 'None too solid: Medical ignorance', *Knowledge: Creation, Diffusion, Utilisation*, 15(2): 166–85.

Kolb, D. A. (1984) *Experiential Learning: Experience as the Source of Learning and Development*, Englewood Cliffs NJ: Prentice Hall.

Kotter, J. P. (1990) *A Force for Change: How Leadership Differs from Management*, New York: Free Press.

Lave, J. and Wenger, E. (1991) *Situated Learning: Legitimate Peripheral Participation*, New York: Cambridge University Press.

Leithwood, K., Chapman, J., Corson, P., Hallinger, P. and Hart, A. (eds) (1996) *International Handbook of Educational Leadership and Administration*, Dordrecht: Kluwer.

Leung, T., Lam, C. M. and Wong, H. (2007) 'Repositioning risk in social work education: Reflections arising from the threat of SARS to social work students in Hong Kong during field practicum', *Social Work Education*, 26(4): 389–98.

McInerney, D. M. and McInerney, V. (1998) *Educational Psychology: Constructing Learning*, 2nd edn, Sydney: Prentice Hall.

Madden, S. J. (ed.) (2000) *Service Learning Across the Curriculum: Case Applications in Higher Education*, Lanham, MD: University Press of America.

Maidment, J. (2003) 'Problems experienced by students on field placement: Using research findings to inform curriculum design and content', *Australian Social Work*, 56(1): 50–60.

Marshall, I. and Mill, M. (1993) 'Using learning contracts to enhance the quality of work-based learning', in M. Shaw and E. Roper (eds) *Aspects of Educational and Training Technology Volume XXVI: Quality in Education and Training*, London: Kogan Page, 144–8.

Marshall, S., Orrell, J., Thomas, S., Cameron, A. and Bosanquet, A. (2009) 'Academic Leadership and Management: Developing Strategies for Support, Enhancement and Succession Planning', unpublished final report of a DEST Higher Education Innovation Program Project, Sydney.

Martin, D. E. and Kipling, A. (2006) 'Factors shaping Aboriginal nursing students' experiences', *Nurse Education Today*, 26(8): 688–96.

Marton, F. and Säljö, R. (1976) 'On qualitative differences in learning 1: Outcome and processes', *British Journal of Educational Psychology*, 46: 4–11.

Mason, S. E., Beckerman, N. and Auerbach, C. (2002) 'Disclosure of student status to clients: Where do MSW programs stand?', *Journal of Social Work Education*, 38(2): 305–16.

Masoud, F. (2004) 'Prevalence and risk factors of low back pain among physical therapy professionals in Gaza Strip', unpublished thesis, Master in Community Mental Health: Rehabilitation Sciences, Islamic University of Gaza.

Merriam, S. B. and Caffarella, R. S. (1999) *Learning in Adulthood: A Comprehensive Guide*, 2nd edn, San Francisco, CA: Jossey Bass.

Mezirow, J. (1994) *Transformative Dimensions of Adult Learning*, San Francisco, CA: Jossey-Bass.

—— (1996) 'Contemporary paradigms of learning', *Adult Education Quarterly*, 46(3): 158–73.

Miller, G. E. (1990) 'The assessment of clinical skills/competence/performance', *Academic Medicine*, 65(Suppl): S 63–7.

Mills, C. W. (1959) *The Sociological Imagination*, New York: Oxford University Press.

Moody, K. (1997) *Workers in a Lean World*, London: Verso.

Moon, J. (2005) *Guide for Busy Academics No.4: Learning Through Reflection*. The Higher Education Academy. Available online at: <http://www.heacademy.ac.uk/resources/detail/id69_guide_for_busy_academics_no4_moon> (accessed 12 July 2009).

Moore, D. T. (2004) 'Curriculum at work: An educational perspective on the workplace as a learning environment', *Journal of Workplace Learning*, 16(6): 325–40.

Moreno, M., White, E., Flores, E. and Riethmayer, J. (2001) 'Student perceptions of clinical mistreatment', *Radiologic Technology*, 73(1): 18–24.

Morris, K. and Turnbull, P. A. (2007) 'The disclosure of dyslexia in clinical practice: Experiences of student nurses in the United Kingdom', *Nurse Education Today*, 27(1): 35–42.

Munson, C. (2002) *Handbook of Clinical Social Work Supervision*, 3rd edn, Binghamton, NY: Haworth Press.

Murphy, D. and Younai, F. (1996) 'Challenges associated with assessment of risk for tuberculosis in a dental school setting', *American Journal of Infection Control*, 24(4): 254–61.

Nagata-Kobayashi, S., Sekimoto, M., Koyama, H., Yamamoto, W., Goto, E., Fukushima, O., Ino, T., Shimada, T., Shimbo, T., Asai, A., Koizumi, S. and Fukui, T. (2006) 'Medical student abuse during clinical clerkships in Japan', *Journal of General Internal Medicine*, 21(3): 212–18.

National Commission for Cooperative Education (2002) *About co-op*. Available online at: <http://www.co-op.edu/aboutcoop.htm> (accessed 12 May 2009).

National Service-Learning Clearinghouse (n.d.) Available online at: <http://www.servicelearning.org/what_is_service-learning/index.php> (accessed 17 November 2008).

Newble, D. I. (1992) 'Assessing clinical competence at the undergraduate level', *Medical Education*, 26(6): 504–11.

Nicholson, S. (2002) '"So you row, do you? You don't look like a rower." An account of medical students' experience with sexism', *Medical Education*, 36: 1057–63.

Nixon, I., Smith, K., Stafford, R., Camm, S. (2006) *Work-based Learning: Illuminating the Higher Education Landscape*, York: Higher Education Academy.

Organisation for Economic Co-operation and Development (OECD) (1996) *The Knowledge-based Economy*, Paris: Organisation for Economic Co-operation and Development.

Orrell, J. (1997) 'Assessment in higher education: An examination of academics' thinking-in-assessment, beliefs-about-assessment and a comparison of assessment behaviours and beliefs', unpublished PhD thesis, Flinders University, Adelaide.

—— (2005a) 'Management and Educational Quality of Work-Integrated Learning Programmes', opening address at Work-Integrated Learning Symposium, Griffith University, Australia, November. Available online at: <http://www3.griffith.edu.au/01/ocp/getfile.php?id=821> (accessed 7 July 2009).

—— (2005b) 'Assessment literacy: A precursor to improving the quality of assessment', keynote address at *Making a Difference: Annual Evaluation and Assessment* conference, Sydney, November/December.

—— (2006) 'Feedback on learning achievement: Rhetoric and reality', *Teaching in Higher Education*, 11(4): 441–56.

—— (2008) 'Assessment beyond belief: The cognitive process of grading', in A. Havnes and L. McDowell (eds) *Balancing Dilemmas in Assessment and Learning in Contemporary Education*, London: Routledge: 251–63.

—— (2009) 'Generic Work Integrated Learning Assessment Rubric', unpublished assessment resource, Adelaide, August.

Orrell, J. and Bowden, M. (2004) *The Science and Technology Enterprise Partnerships Project Report No. 3: Final Evaluation. Education and Careers in Science and Technology Enterprise: Student Perceptions of Work Readiness, and Academics' Perceptions of the Value of Education and Research Linkages with Related Industries*, Adelaide: Staff Development and Training Unit, Flinders University.

Orrell, J. and Parry, S. (2007) 'An assessment policy framework: A Carrick Institute study', presentation to Macquarie University Assessment Working Party, Sydney, August.

Orrell, J., Cooper, L. and Jones, R. (1999) 'Making the Practicum Visible', paper presented at *Cornerstones*, HERDSA Annual International conference, Melbourne, July. Available online at: <http://www.herdsa.org.au/?page_id=182> (accessed 12 May 2009).

Orrell, J., Cooper, L., Bridge, K. and Bowden, M. (2003) *Working to Learn: Practicum Online*, Adelaide: Staff Development and Training Unit, Flinders University. Available online at: <http://www.flinders.edu.au/teach/workingtolearn/index. htm> (accessed 14 August 2009).

Osinski, K. (2003) 'Due process rights of nursing students in cases of misconduct', *Journal of Nurse Education*, 42(2): 55–8.

Page, G. (2000) 'Clinical competence and its assessment', Waterman Oration, Flinders University, Adelaide. Available online at: <www.health-sciences.ubc.ca/desd/ presentations/> (accessed 1 August 2009).

Paletta, A. (2008) 'The internship racket', *Inside Highered*, Views, 19 February. Available online at: <http://www.insidehighered.com/views/2008/02/19/ paletta> (accessed 30 July 2009).

Pallett, W. (2006) 'Uses and abuses of student ratings', in P. Seldin (ed.) *Evaluating Faculty Performance: A Practical Guide to Assessing Teaching, Research, and Service*, Bolton, MA: Anker Publishing Company: 50–65.

Perkins, K. (n.d.) *Community Service Learning in the California State University: Best Practices for Managing Risk in Service Learning.* Available online at: <http://www. calstate.edu/csl/resource_center/servlearn_risk.shtml> (accessed 5 July 2009).

Perry, W. Jr (1981) *Cognitive and Ethical Growth: The Making of Meaning*, San Francisco, CA: Jossey-Bass.

—— (1999) *Forms of Ethical and Intellectual Development in the College Years: A Scheme*, San Francisco, CA: John Wiley & Sons.

Piaget, J. (1972) 'Intellectual evolution from adolescence to adulthood', *Human Development*, 15(1): 1–12.

Polyacskó, O. (2009) *Employers' Expectations Regarding Recent Graduates*, European Working Conditions Observatory. Available online at: <http://www.eurofound. europa.eu/ewco/2008/11/HU0811019I.htm> (accessed 12 July 2009).

Pont, B. and Werquin, P. (2001) 'Competencies for the knowledge economy', in Organisation for Economic Co-operation and Development, *Education Policy Analysis*, Paris: Organisation for Economic Co-operation and Development, 99–118.

Proctor, B. (1986) 'Supervision: A co-operative exercise in accountability', in M. Marken and M. Payne (eds) *Enabling and Ensuring – Supervision in Practice*, Leicester: National Youth Bureau, Council for Training in Youth and Community Work, 21–34.

Rademakers, J. J., van den Muijsenbergh, M. E, Slappendel, G., Lagro-Janssen, A. L. and Borleffs, J. C. (2008) 'Sexual harassment during clinical clerkships in Dutch medical schools', *Medical Education*, 42(5): 452–8.

Ralph, E. G., Walker, K. and Wimmer, R. (2008) 'The clinical/practicum experience in professional preparation: Preliminary findings', *McGill Journal of Education*, 43(2): 157–72.

Ramsden, P. (2003 [1992]) *Learning to Teach in Higher Education*, 2nd edn, London: Routledge.

Ranzijn, R., McConnochie, K., Nolan, W., Day, A. and Severino, G. (2006) *Report on the Proceedings of a Workshop on Developing Curriculum Guidelines*, Adelaide: University of South Australia. Available online at: <http://www.unisanet.unisa.edu.au/staffpages/robranzijn/workshop%20report%202005.pdf> (accessed 13 June 2009).

Reams, P. (2003) 'Service learning in health care higher education: Risk or not to risk', *Education for Health: Change in Learning and Practice*, 16(2): 145–54.

Recupero, P., Cooney, M., Rayner, C., Heru, A. and Price, M. (2005) 'Supervisor-trainee relationship boundaries in medical education', *Medical Teacher*, 27(6): 484–8.

Resnick, A., Mullen, J., Kaiser, L. and Morris, J. (2006) 'Patterns and predictions of resident misbehaviour: A 10 year retrospective look', *Current Surgery*, 63(Nov/Dec): 418–25.

Rittel, H. W. J. (1984) 'Second generation design methods', in N. Cross (ed.) *Developments in Design Methodology*, Chichester: John Wiley & Sons, 317–27.

Rogan, F., San Miguel, C., Brown, D. and Kilstoff, K. (2006) '"You find yourself." Perceptions of nursing students from non-English speaking backgrounds (NESB) of the effect of an intensive language support program on their oral clinical communication skills', *Contemporary Nurse*, 23: 72–86.

Rogers, C. R. (1995) *On Becoming a Person: A Therapist's View of Psychotherapy*, New York: Houghton Mifflin.

Rogers, C. R. with Freiberg, H. J. (1994) *Freedom to Learn*, 3rd edn, New Jersey: Prentice Hall.

Rogers, G., Benson, G., Bouey, E., Clark, B., Langevin, P., Mamchur, C. and Sawa, R. (2003) 'An exploration of conflict in the practicum in four professions', *Women in Welfare Education*, 6: 26–50.

Rowntree, D. (1977) *Assessing Students: How Shall We Know Them?* London: Harper and Row.

Sadler, D. R. (1989) 'Formative assessment and the design of instructional systems', *Instructional Science*, 18: 119–44.

Scaife, J. and Walsh, S. (2001) 'The emotional climate of work and the development of self', in J. Scaife, *Supervision in the Mental Health Professions: A Practitioner's Guide*, Hove: Brunner-Routledge, 122–44.

Schofield, A. (1998) *Benchmarking in Higher Education: An International Review*, London: Commonwealth Higher Education Management Service.

Schön, D. A. (1983) *The Reflective Practitioner: How Professionals Think in Action*, New York: Basic Books.

—— (1987) *Educating the Reflective Practitioner*, San Francisco, CA: Jossey-Bass.

Scriven, M. (1967) *The Methodology of Evaluation*, Washington DC: American Educational Research Association.

Senge, P. M. (1990) *The Fifth Discipline: The Art and Practice of the Learning Organization*, London: Random House.

Shaddock, A. (n.d.) *Academics' Responses to the Behaviour of Students with Mental Illness*. Available online at: <http://www.adcet.edu.au/StoredFile.aspx?id=2006&fn=shaddock.doc> (accessed 4 July 2009).

Shiao, J. S. C., McLaws, M. L., Huang, K. Y. and Guo, Y. L. (2002) 'Student nurses in Taiwan at high risk of needlestick injuries', *Annals of Epidemiology*, 12:197–201.

Shinsako, S., Richman, J. and Rospenda, K. (2001) 'Training-related harassment and drinking outcomes in medical residents versus graduate students', *Substance Use and Misuse*, 36(14): 2043–63.

Smith, A. and Blake, D. (2005) 'Facilitating learning through effective teaching: At a glance', Adelaide: Department of Education, Science and Training, NCVER, Australian Government.

Smith, M. H., McKoy, Y. D. and Richardson, J. (2001) 'Legal issues related to dismissing students for clinical deficiencies', *Nurse Educator*, 26(1): 33–8.

Smith, P. (2005) 'Enhancing student employability: Higher education and workforce development', Ninth Quality in Higher Education International Seminar in collaboration with the Enhancing Student Employability Co-ordination Team (ESECT) and *The Independent*, Birmingham, January.

Smyth, J. (1996) 'Developing socially critical educators', in D. Boud and N. Miller (eds) *Working with Experience: Animating Learning*, London: Routledge, 41–57.

Sovilla, S. E. and Varty, J. W. (2004) 'Cooperative education in the USA, past and present: Some lessons learned', in R. K. Coll and C. Eames (eds) *International Handbook for Cooperative Education: An International Perspective of the Theory, Research and Practice of Work-integrated Learning*, Boston, MA: World Association for Cooperative Education, 3–16.

Stace, D. and Dunphy, D. C. (2001) *Beyond the Boundaries: Leading and Re-creating the Successful Enterprise*, 2nd edn, Sydney: McGraw Hill.

Stenström, M. J. and Tynjälä, P. (2008) 'Changing work life as a challenge to education', in M. J. Stenström and P. Tynjälä (eds) *Towards Integration of Work and Learning: Strategies for Connectivity and Transformation*, Netherlands: Springer Science and Business Media.

Stiggins, R. (2002) 'Assessment crisis: The absence of assessment FOR learning', *Phi Delta Kappan*, 83(10): 758–65.

Stoltenberg, C. (1981) 'Approaching supervision from a development perspective: The counsellor complexity model', *Journal of Counselling Psychology*, 28: 59–65.

Sweedler-Brown, C. O. (1992) 'The effect of training on appearance bias of holistic essay graders', *Journal of Research and Development in Education*, 26(1): 24–9.

Thompson, N. (2003) *Promoting Equality: Challenging Discrimination and Oppression in the Human Services*, 2nd edn, Basingstoke: Palgrave Macmillan.

—— (2006) *Promoting Workplace Learning*, Bristol: The Policy Press.

Thornton, L., Barr, A., Stuart-Buttle, C., Gaughan, J., Wilson, E., Jackson, A., Wyszynski, T. and Smarkola, C. (2008) 'Perceived musculoskeletal symptoms among dental students in the clinic work environment', *Ergonomics*, 51(4): 573–86.

Timmins, F. and Kaliszer, M. (2002) 'Aspects of nurse education programmes that frequently cause stress to nursing students – fact-finding sample survey', *Nurse Education Today*, 22(3): 203–11.

Todd, T. C. and Storm, C. L. (2002) *The Complete Systemic Supervisor: Context, Philosophy, and Pragmatics*, Lincoln, UK: Allyn & Bacon.

Torres, J. (2000) *Benchmarks for Campus/Community Partnerships*, Providence, RI: Campus Compact.

Tully, C., Kropf, N. and Price, J. (1993) 'Is field a hard hat area? A study of violence in field placements', *Journal of Social Work Education*, 29(2): 191–9.

Victoria University (2008) *Victoria University LiWC Policy – Learning in the Workplace and Community: Operational Guidelines*, Victoria: Victoria University.

Available online at: <http://tls.vu.edu.au/vucollege/LiWC/resources/LiWCguidelines20090109FinalV3.pdf> and <http://tls.vu.edu.au/vucollege/LiWC/managinglearning.html> (accessed 27 July 2009).

Vivekananda, U. and Corfield, L. (2008) 'Medical students and consent: Does supervision help?', *Medical Education*, 42: 322–6.

Vygotsky, L. S. (1978) *Mind in Society: The Development of Higher Psychological Processes*, Cambridge, MA: Harvard University Press.

Waddell, A., Katz, M., Lofchy, J. and Bradley, J. (2005) 'A pilot survey of patient-initiated assaults on medical students during clinical clerkship', *Academic Psychiatry*, 29(4): 350–3.

Wang, H., Fennie, K., He, G., Burgess, J. and Williams, A. B. (2003) 'A training programme for prevention of occupational exposure to bloodborne pathogens: Impact on knowledge, behaviour and incidence of needle stick injuries among student nurses in Changsha, People's Republic of China', *Journal of Advanced Nursing*, 41(2): 187–94.

Wang, V. and Farmer, L. (2008) 'Adult teaching methods in China and Bloom's taxonomy', *International Journal for the Scholarship of Teaching and Learning*, 2(2). Available online at: <http://www.georgiasouthern.edu/ijsotl> (accessed 4 April 2009).

Wang, V. C. X. (2007) 'Chinese knowledge transmitters' or western learning facilitators' adult teaching methods compared', in K. P. King and V. C. X. Wang (eds) *Comparative Adult Education Around the Globe*, Hangzhou, China: Zhejiang University Press: 113–37.

Wear, D., Aultman, J. and Borges, N. (2007) 'Retheorizing sexual harassment in medical education: Women students' perceptions at five U.S. medical schools', *Teaching and Learning in Medicine*, 19(1): 20–9.

Webber, R. (1998) 'Models of best practice in field education: Student initiatives and innovative projects', Seminar 2, Flinders University, Adelaide, September.

Wenger, E. (1998) *Communities of Practice: Learning, Meaning, and Identity*, London: Cambridge University Press.

—— (2000) 'Communities of practice and social learning systems', *Organization*, 7(2): 225–46.

William, D. (2006) 'Formative assessment: Getting the focus right', *Educational Assessment*, 11(3/4): 283–9.

Williams, T., de Seriere, J. and Boddington, L. (1999) 'Inappropriate sexual behaviour experienced by speech-language therapists', *International Journal of Language and Communication Disorders*, 34(1): 99–111.

Worth-Butler, M., Murphy, R. and Fraser, D. (1994) 'Towards an integrated model of competence in midwifery', *Midwifery*, 10(4): 225–31.

Wusthoff, C. J. (2001) 'Medical mistakes and disclosure: The role of the medical student', *Journal of the American Medical Association*, 286:1080–81.

Yueh-Hsiu, L. (2006) 'The incidence of sexual harassment of students while undergoing practicum training experience in the Taiwanese hospitality industry: Individuals' reactions and relationships to perpetrators', *Tourism Management*, 27: 51–68.

Zachary, L. (2000) *The Mentor's Guide: Facilitating Effective Learning Relationships*, San Francisco, CA: Jossey-Bass.

Zlotkowski, E. (ed.) (1998) *Successful Service-Learning Programs: New Models of Excellence in Higher Education*, Bolton, MA: Anker Publishing Company.

Index

Note: page numbers in **bold** refer to figures and tables